EARLY CHILDHOOD EDUCATION SERIES

ADVISORY BOARD: *Celia ... ullo,
Amita Gupta, Beatrice ... Honig,
B...*

FirstSchool: Transforming P...
American, Latino, and Low-... ...ers
SHARON RITCHIE & LAURA GUT...

The States of Child Care: Building a Better System
SARA GABLE

Early Childhood Education for a New Era:
Leading for Our Profession
STACIE G. GOFFIN

Everyday Artists: Inquiry and Creativity in the
Early Childhood Classroom
DANA FRANTZ BENTLEY

Multicultural Teaching in the Early Childhood
Classroom: Approaches, Strategies, and Tools,
Preschool–2nd Grade
MARIANA SOUTO-MANNING

Inclusion in the Early Childhood Classroom:
What Makes a Difference?
SUSAN L. RECCHIA & YOON-JOO LEE

Language Building Blocks:
Essential Linguistics for Early Childhood Educators
ANITA PANDEY

Understanding the Language Development and Early
Education of Hispanic Children.
EUGENE E. GARCÍA & ERMINDA H. GARCÍA

Moral Classrooms, Moral Children: Creating a
Constructivist Atmosphere in Early Education, 2nd Ed.
RHETA DEVRIES & BETTY ZAN

Defending Childhood:
Keeping the Promise of Early Education
BEVERLY FALK, ED.

Don't Leave the Story in the Book: Using Literature to
Guide Inquiry in Early Childhood Classrooms
MARY HYNES-BERRY

Starting with Their Strengths: Using the Project
Approach in Early Childhood Special Education
DEBORAH C. LICKEY & DENISE J. POWERS

The Play's the Thing:
Teachers' Roles in Children's Play, 2nd Ed.
ELIZABETH JONES & GRETCHEN REYNOLDS

Twelve Best Practices for Early Childhood Education:
Integrating Reggio and Other Inspired Approaches
ANN LEWIN-BENHAM

What If All the Kids Are White? Anti-Bias Multicultural
Education with Young Children and Families, 2nd Ed.
LOUISE DERMAN-SPARKS & PATRICIA G. RAMSEY

Seen and Heard:
Children's Rights in Early Childhood Education
ELLEN LYNN HALL & JENNIFER KOFKIN RUDKIN

Young Investigators: The Project Approach in the
Early Years, 2nd Ed.
JUDY HARRIS HELM & LILIAN G. KATZ

Supporting Boys' Learning: Strategies for Teacher
Practice, PreK–Grade 3
BARBARA SPRUNG, MERLE FROSCHL, & NANCY GROPPER

Young English Language Learners: Current Research
and Emerging Directions for Practice and Policy
EUGENE E. GARCÍA & ELLEN C. FREDE, EDS.

Connecting Emergent Curriculum and Standards
in the Early Childhood Classroom: Strengthening
Content and Teacher Practice
SYDNEY L. SCHWARTZ & SHERRY M. COPELAND

Infants and Toddlers at Work: Using Reggio-Inspired
Materials to Support Brain Development
ANN LEWIN-BENHAM

The View from the Little Chair in the Corner:
Improving Teacher Practice and Early Childhood
Learning (Wisdom from an Experienced Classroom
Observer)
CINDY RZASA BESS

Culture and Child Development in Early Childhood
Programs: Practices for Quality Education and Care
CAROLLEE HOWES

The Early Intervention Guidebook for Families and
Professionals: Partnering for Success
BONNIE KEILTY

The Story in the Picture:
Inquiry and Artmaking with Young Children
CHRISTINE MULCAHEY

Educating and Caring for Very Young Children:
The Infant/Toddler Curriculum, 2nd Ed.
DORIS BERGEN, REBECCA REID, & LOUIS TORELLI

For a list of other titles in this series, visit www.tcpress.com

(continued)

Early Childhood Education Series, *continued*

Beginning School:
U.S. Policies in International Perspective
RICHARD M. CLIFFORD & GISELE M. CRAWFORD, EDS.

Emergent Curriculum in the Primary Classroom:
Interpreting the Reggio Emilia Approach in Schools
CAROL ANNE WIEN, ED.

Enthusiastic and Engaged Learners: Approaches to
Learning in the Early Childhood Classroom
MARILOU HYSON

Powerful Children: Understanding How to Teach and
Learn Using the Reggio Approach
ANN LEWIN-BENHAM

The Early Care and Education Teaching Workforce at
the Fulcrum: An Agenda for Reform
SHARON LYNN KAGAN, KRISTIE KAUERZ, & KATE TARRANT

Windows on Learning:
Documenting Young Children's Work, 2nd Ed.
JUDY HARRIS HELM, SALLEE BENEKE, & KATHY STEINHEIMER

Ready or Not:
Leadership Choices in Early Care and Education
STACIE G. GOFFIN & VALORA WASHINGTON

Supervision in Early Childhood Education:
A Developmental Perspective, 3rd Ed.
JOSEPH J. CARUSO WITH M. TEMPLE FAWCETT

Guiding Children's Behavior:
Developmental Discipline in the Classroom
EILEEN S. FLICKER & JANET ANDRON HOFFMAN

The War Play Dilemma: What Every Parent and
Teacher Needs to Know, 2nd Ed.
DIANE E. LEVIN & NANCY CARLSSON-PAIGE

Possible Schools:
The Reggio Approach to Urban Education
ANN LEWIN-BENHAM

Everyday Goodbyes
NANCY BALABAN

Playing to Get Smart
ELIZABETH JONES & RENATTA M. COOPER

How to Work with Standards in the Early
Childhood Classroom
CAROL SEEFELDT

In the Spirit of the Studio
LELLA GANDINI ET AL., EDS.

Understanding Assessment and Evaluation in Early
Childhood Education, 2nd Ed.
DOMINIC F. GULLO

Teaching and Learning in a Diverse World, 3rd Ed.
PATRICIA G. RAMSEY

The Emotional Development of Young Children, 2nd Ed.
MARILOU HYSON

Effective Partnering for School Change
JIE-QI CHEN ET AL.

Let's Be Friends
KRISTEN MARY KEMPLE

Young Children Continue to Reinvent Arithmetic—
2nd Grade, 2nd Ed.
CONSTANCE KAMII

Major Trends and Issues in Early Childhood
Education, 2nd Ed.
JOAN PACKER ISENBERG & MARY RENCK JALONGO, EDS.

The Power of Projects
JUDY HARRIS HELM & SALLEE BENEKE, EDS.

Bringing Learning to Life
LOUISE BOYD CADWELL

The Colors of Learning
ROSEMARY ALTHOUSE, MARGARET H. JOHNSON, &
SHARON T. MITCHELL

A Matter of Trust
CAROLLEE HOWES & SHARON RITCHIE

Widening the Circle
SAMUEL L. ODOM, ED.

Children with Special Needs
MARJORIE J. KOSTELNIK ET AL.

Developing Constructivist Early Childhood Curriculum
RHETA DEVRIES ET AL.

Outdoor Play
JANE PERRY

Embracing Identities in Early Childhood Education
SUSAN GRIESHABER & GAILE S. CANNELLA, EDS.

Bambini: The Italian Approach to Infant/Toddler Care
LELLA GANDINI & CAROLYN POPE EDWARDS, EDS.

Serious Players in the Primary Classroom, 2nd Ed.
SELMA WASSERMANN

Telling a Different Story
CATHERINE WILSON

Young Children Reinvent Arithmetic, 2nd Ed.
CONSTANCE KAMII

Managing Quality in Young Children's Programs
MARY L. CULKIN, ED.

The Early Childhood Curriculum, 3rd Ed.
CAROL SEEFELDT, ED.

Inside a Head Start Center
DEBORAH CEGLOWSKI

Bringing Reggio Emilia Home
LOUISE BOYD CADWELL

Master Players
GRETCHEN REYNOLDS & ELIZABETH JONES

FirstSchool

TRANSFORMING PREK–3RD GRADE FOR AFRICAN AMERICAN, LATINO, AND LOW-INCOME CHILDREN

EDITED BY

Sharon Ritchie
Laura Gutmann

Foreword by Aisha Ray

Teachers College
Columbia University
New York and London

Published by Teachers College Press, 1234 Amsterdam Avenue, New York, NY 10027

Library of Congress Cataloging-in-Publication Data can be obtained at www.loc.gov

ISBN 978-0-8077-5481-8 (paper)
eISBN 978-0-8077-7242-3

Printed on acid-free paper
Manufactured in the United States of America

20   19   18   17   16   15   14   8   7   6   5   4   3   2

Contents

Foreword *by Aisha Ray*   vii

Acknowledgments   ix

Introduction   1
Richard M. Clifford, Gisele M. Crawford,
Sandra C. García, and Carolyn T. Cobb

PART I: FIRSTSCHOOL REFORM

1. **The Groundswell for Transforming Prekindergarten**
   Through 3rd Grade   9
   Gisele M. Crawford, Carolyn T. Cobb, Richard M. Clifford,
   and Sharon Ritchie

2. **Reinvigorating Professionalism: Involving Teachers**
   in Establishing a Culture for Reform   29
   Laura Gutmann and Sam Oertwig

PART II: CHANGE THAT MATTERS

3. **A Culture of Collaborative Inquiry**   57
   Adam L. Holland, Gisele M. Crawford, Sharon Ritchie,
   and Diane M. Early

4. **The Promise of Curricula**   81
   Sam Oertwig, Cristina Gillanders, and Sharon Ritchie

5. **Improving Instruction**   102
   Sam Oertwig and Adam L. Holland

6. **Home and School Partnerships:
    Raising Children Together**   **125**

    *Cristina Gillanders, Iheoma Iruka, Cindy Bagwell,
    Jenille Morgan, and Sandra C. García*

        **PART III: THE FUTURE FOR AFRICAN AMERICAN,
        LATINO, AND LOW-INCOME CHILDREN**

7. **Looking Forward: Program and Policy Considerations**   **151**

    Carolyn T. Cobb and Richard M. Clifford

8. **Directions for the Future**   **170**

    Sharon Ritchie

References   **187**

About the Contributors   **209**

Index   **213**

Foreword

Recently I visited a public elementary school full of eager, competent, and confident young children, dedicated teachers, exemplary administrators, and engaged families. This highly effective school serves a chronically poor African American community characterized by conditions associated with poor developmental and educational outcomes—chronic poverty, high unemployment, violence, and poorly resourced institutions, including schools. This is a neighborhood school that does not have selective enrollment, it is not a charter school, and does not have an array of special resources. How did this school become a vibrant institution capable of supporting children's learning, effective family engagement, and teaching excellence? And, can ineffective schools, those that reinforce inequality and miseducate students, be transformed into agents of educational achievement for poor children? The answers to these questions are not simple, nor are the processes that yield success accidental. Highly successful schools for young children, especially those in poverty, children of color, and children of immigrants, require deliberate, consistent and evidence-based strategies that begin with committed educators and high-quality early education. They generally possess many of the characteristics described in this thoughtful, relevant, and timely volume on the FirstSchool approach to educational reform, including well-designed professional development; meaningful partnerships between families and educators; proven research-based instructional practices; data-informed instruction; and cultures of collaboration within schools that build the capacity of educators to benefit from a community of practice. Most importantly, the designers of FirstSchool recognize that the quality and continuity of children's early school experiences (PreK–3rd grade education) will lay the groundwork for complex cognitive thinking that supports early literacy, early math, social learning and other critical developmental capacities that support educational achievement. It is during early childhood that we as a nation have the opportunity to lay the foundation for optimal development for every child regardless of circumstance—and FirstSchool provides us with a workable approach that can be employed by school districts, principals, families, and professional educators. If we fail to lay this educational foundation—despite the robust evidence from early childhood science that high-quality early childhood education, represented by FirstSchool, especially benefits poor children—we will risk failing another generation of American children. We can greatly benefit from applying the knowledge, experience, and wisdom of the authors of this important book to reforming early schooling, teaching, and learning for our most vulnerable children and thereby keep the promise of American democracy—namely, a level playing field and a chance to succeed fully on one's merits. As a nation we cannot continue to tolerate failure or make excuses when examples such as FirstSchool suggest a proven way forward.

—Aisha Ray, PhD
FirstSchool Advisory Board Chair
Senior Vice President for Academic Affairs, Dean of Faculty
Erikson Institute
Chicago, Illinois

Acknowledgments

FirstSchool is a project that has evolved over the past decade, due to the hard work, knowledge, and expertise of numerous dedicated colleagues, partners, and supporters. We thank each and every one of them for their contributions to our vision.

First, Don Bailey and Tony Waldrop of the University of North Carolina (UNC) at Chapel Hill were early champions of our work. Past team members Angella Bellota, Yvonne Caamal-Canul, Jana Fleming, Syndee Kraus, William Malloy, Erin Mason, Kelly Maxwell, Marvin McKinney, and Will Okun also made substantial contributions to FirstSchool's development.

Our partners and supporters in Michigan include Ricardo and Patricia Briones, Pat Farrell, Karlin Tichenor, and Betty Underwood.

In addition, leadership and staff at our initial partner schools in both North Carolina and Michigan remain at the heart of our efforts. In North Carolina, we partnered with Bogue Sound Elementary (Carteret Co.), Rankin Elementary (Guilford Co.), South Graham Elementary (Alamance-Burlington Co.), and Stocks Elementary (Edgecombe Co.). In Michigan, we partnered with Birch Street Elementary (Kalkaska Co.), Gier Park Elementary (Lansing Schools), and El Shabazz Academy (CMU's Center for Charter Schools).

Planning grant steering committee members included Harriet Able, Lynette Aytch, Donna Bryant, Virginia Buysse, Pam Cardoza, Maggie Connolly, Jill Kerr, Sharon Palsha, Ellen Peisner-Feinberg, Joe Sparling, and Pam Winton. We owe thanks to all those who served on the following planning committees: School Health and Wellness, Curriculum and Instruction, Diversity, Evaluation, Facilities, Family and Community Partnerships, Finance, and Professional Development.

Administrative staff who assisted with this project include Jane Foust, Toni Glatz, Barbara Lowery, and Donna Redford. Many FPG colleagues contributed to FirstSchool's efforts, including Dave Gardner and Jim Peak. We are also grateful to our many data collectors.

We give immense thanks to our funders, including the W.K. Kellogg Foundation, Foundation for Child Development, UNC-Chapel Hill, and private donors.

Other partners in North Carolina included South Lexington Elementary, Chapel Hill-Carrboro City Schools, and the North Carolina Department of Public Instruction, especially Cindy Bagwell, Eva Phillips, John Pruette, and Amy Scrinzi.

FirstSchool is a project of the Frank Porter Graham (FPG) Child Development Institute. We have also partnered with Michigan State University, North Carolina Department of Public Instruction's Office of Early Learning, the North Carolina Partnership for Children, and the School of Education at UNC-Chapel Hill.

Last but certainly not least, we are indebted to FirstSchool's National Advisory Board Members, who include Aisha Ray (chair), Betsy Ayankoya, Lindy Buch, Robert Glenn, Kristie Kauerz, Jonathan Koch, Eloise Lopez Metcalf (UCLA Graduate School of Education), Jana Martella, James Overman, Robert Pianta, Karen Ponder, and Barbara Willer.

FirstSchool

Introduction

Richard M. Clifford, Gisele M. Crawford,
Sandra C. García, and Carolyn T. Cobb

FirstSchool is a response to one of the most stubborn challenges in U.S. society: how to provide all children in our schools with a world-class education. The push for major change in our education system really began 30 years ago with the publication of *A Nation at Risk* (National Commission on Excellence in Education, 1983). Since then, as a nation we have begun to acknowledge the failure of our education system to adequately serve African American, Latino, and low-income children in particular. To be sure, writers and education advocates have held up shining examples of schools where children of all backgrounds succeed brilliantly. We can all name highly accomplished people from very disadvantaged backgrounds, and often we hear those individuals credit the dedicated teachers who set them on a journey of lifelong learning and achievement. Yet despite the evidence that at least some educators do know how to eliminate the risk of school failure presented by poverty and social inequities, here we are still trying to accomplish on a large scale the changes called for in the report. Let's examine how some of the larger forces at work in our education system present barriers to widespread adoption of successful practices, and how this book, with its focus on the PreK through 3rd-grade years, helps overcome those barriers.

HISTORICAL TRENDS

There is one overriding fact of life that governs any effort to transform early education in schools: Public education is a behemoth. With total spending on public education exceeding half a trillion dollars per year—almost all of which is geared to keeping the ship of education moving forward as it has in the past—any change is a huge challenge (F. Johnson, Zhou & Nakamoto, 2011).

Even with the recent significant new investments in the Race to the Top grants to selected states, investments in change have been miniscule in comparison to the total expenditures. As with all bureaucracies, public schools have developed mechanisms to protect themselves from frequent radical changes that would render them totally ineffective. But these same mechanisms also make even modest changes extremely difficult.

The framers of the U.S. Constitution felt that education was too important to trust to a central national government and thus reserved education as a state responsibility (Madison, 1788; Theobald & Malen, 2000; U.S. Const. amend. X). In turn, states have delegated much authority to local school districts and even to individual schools. This arrangement keeps schools tuned to the desires of local citizens, but makes systemic change in education particularly difficult. So the possibilities for change are strongly tilted toward incremental change at the local school and district level. However, financial support for the changes lies largely with state government.

A generation of research on school success and failure has shown the potential of high-quality early childhood programs to help children of all backgrounds succeed in school and life. In Chapter 1 of this volume the authors summarize the evidence for the contention that coherent, high-quality educational and instructional approaches across the PreK–3rd grade span will yield the best results for ongoing school success. The challenge is how to unite early childhood, elementary, and special education in PreK–3rd grade classrooms so their power to transform young lives is fully realized.

Issues specific to the early school years are largely related to decisions about whether to extend elementary school to serve 3- and 4-year-olds. There has been great movement to provide PreK to 4-year-olds in recent decades (Barnett, Carolan, Fitzgerald, & Squires, 2011; Clifford, Early, & Hills, 1999). Roughly half of these publicly funded PreK programs are located in public schools, while the rest are in private sector PreK settings (Clifford et al., 2005). However, at the same time we have seen a substantial increase in children actually beginning school later than allowed by law, largely from middle-class parents deciding to "red shirt" their children. Between 1986 and 2008, the percentage of 6-year-old children enrolled in 1st grade dropped from 96% to 84%. About a third of this change is the result of state laws changing the legal entry age to school. However, the remainder is due to both parents' and schools' decisions (Deming & Dynarski, 2008). Clearly, some parents hesitate to send their children to school as soon as they are eligible. In some cases this reflects a desire to gain an advantage for their specific children in relation to slightly younger peers as the term "red shirting" implies; in other cases parents may not be comfortable with the school experiences being offered to their young children. It is also possible that both state and local school officials may be encouraging this trend to make it appear that, over time, children's performance on standardized tests at the end of 3rd grade is improving.

Also, the fact that only half the publicly funded PreK programs are in public schools may have to do with the source and inflexibility of funding streams, but this may also reflect some barriers perceived by schools or districts in meeting the requirements of serving 4-year-olds. Existing private programs that serve preschool-age children may more readily adapt to providing PreK, given that they already serve 4-year-olds, while many elementary schools never have. Even at the state and federal levels, we have seen a reluctance to fully embrace programs for these younger children in schools. Few states fully fund prekindergarten programs. States have been slow to adequately staff their departments of education to serve younger children, and at the federal level, it was only in 2011 that the U.S. Department of Education created an office specifically for these young children. (One significant exception is that both states and the federal government have worked diligently to improve services to very young children with special needs and most states voluntarily chose to house such program offices in their state education agencies.)

CONTEMPORARY STRUCTURAL ISSUES

Underlying these changes in how and when young children start school are several structural issues. Schools grew out of a desire to provide skills for children to help them become successful in life, with a strong emphasis on academic skills (Crawford, Clifford, Early, & Reszka, 2009a). Programs for children prior to kindergarten such as nursery schools and child care have traditionally had a more social-development and family-support flavor. Teacher preparation programs for professionals entering these fields reflect those different emphases. The result is that many children have been forced to leap a pedagogical gulf at a critical period in their development when seamless transitions between environments can be the key to early school success. "Better coordination and integration of educational programs and practices between ages 3 and 9 will enhance learning above and beyond the impact of typically organized school experiences" (Reynolds, Magnuson, & Ou, 2006, p. 6). It is only in the very recent past that institutions of higher education have begun to bring together faculty preparing primary school teachers and faculty preparing teachers of preschoolers.

Ironically, an argument can be made that the widespread acknowledgment of the transformative power of the early years of school has resulted in new pressures on young children and their teachers. Schools and early education programs are meeting new demands for accountability, from the government agencies that oversee them as well as from the media and the general public. As

Crawford et al. (2009a) point out, "There is an increasing emphasis on academic achievement in primary grades, accompanied by, at times, controversial shifts in how achievement is measured" (p. 7). A central challenge for our society in the 21st century is how to appropriately define and measure success for diverse populations of children and the educators and programs that serve them.

As the demographics of the United States change, so do the demographics of the student populations in our schools. In the 1950s, educators were overwhelmed when baby boomers began to attend school; schools were unprepared for so many students. Now educators find themselves unprepared for the diversity they are seeing in their classrooms, at a time when it is no longer accepted that schooling will "work" mainly for middle-class and White students (Camburn & Han, 2011; Wildhagen, 2012). Immigration trends and birth rates indicate that soon in the United States no one racial or ethnic group will be the majority. According to data from the National Center for Education Statistics, between school year 1989–1990 and school year 2009–2010, the percentage of students of color and Native students in school increased from 29% to 45% (DeBaun, 2012). In 2010, 21.6% of children under the age of 18 lived in poverty (Crouch, 2012). As we watch the United States change, we are also witnessing vast and persistent educational disparities between racial and economic groups. Hispanics and African Americans continue to graduate at lower rates than their White peers, although recent data show some movement in the right direction: In 2010 non-Hispanic Whites had an 83.0% graduation rate; African Americans had a 66.1% graduation rate, up from 59.2% in 2006; and Hispanics had a 71.4% graduation rate, up from 61.0% in 2006 (Balfanz, Bridgeland, Bruce, & Fox, 2013). (Please note that, while the U.S. Census Bureau uses the term *Hispanic*, elsewhere in this book we use the term *Latino*.) Meanwhile, the achievement gap between low-income and high-income students is growing (Reardon, 2011). While such achievement gaps are clearly morally troubling, they also have serious economic and social implications.

Demographic changes have created major shifts in population characteristics, particularly in the southern and western parts of the United States. The Census Bureau projects that by 2060 the Hispanic and Asian populations will more than double, the African American population will remain fairly constant (rising to about 15% of the population), and the non-Hispanic White population will decrease from 63% to less than 43% of the population (U.S. Census Bureau, 2012b). The projections are estimates based on the information gathered by the census, so it is important to keep in mind that the census undercounts some groups; low-income African Americans and immigrant Hispanics may not be counted for a variety of reasons (U.S. Census Bureau, 2012a). Therefore, projections may be actually underestimating the changes we will see in the racial and ethnic composition of schools. Increasing rates of home schooling may also influence the composition of public schools (Bielick, 2008). These anticipated changes in school demographics are important to consider as educators prepare for a very diverse student population.

These systemic and demographic issues would be challenging enough in an ideal political and fiscal environment. The current financial situation faced by state governments is creating a great deal of uncertainty for schools. One administrator reported:

> We've been told that any state funds not spent—not just not encumbered, but anything unspent—has to be returned to the state. We have had to give non-renewal letters to many of our untenured teachers, in case the proposed class size increases are passed and we have to reduce our number of faculty. How can I select a prekindergarten teacher to participate in a school improvement project if I might have to let half my PreK teachers go? With so much at stake, how do I even know which fight to get out there and fight? (personal communication, 2010)

However, amid all these challenges, there is reason for great hope. As we've seen time and again, schools abound with teachers and leaders who are committed to improving the school experiences and outcomes of underserved children, and who have the capacity to transform the way they work when they are offered the right supports. Nationally, we see a growing recognition of developmental science in making instructional decisions in elementary school and a movement away from an acceptance of poor outcomes for African American, Latino, and low-income children. The nation is capable of enacting a comprehensive reframing of PreK–3rd grade education.

THE PURPOSE OF THIS BOOK

This book is a guide for educational leaders who are engaging in school transformation efforts focused on improving the early years of schooling. It is intended to be used for courses in education leadership programs, and by state and local school administrators who provide professional learning opportunities for school staff in the PreK–3rd grades and beyond. We believe that educators need to fully understand what the rationale and research base for change in PreK–3 are, how to promote professional learning that is genuinely collaborative and respectful, how children learn and why that is important in the instructional process, and what specific strategies address the components of FirstSchool's view of PreK–3rd grade.

The first chapter in Part I of this volume chronicles the compelling need for change in PreK–3rd grade and our journey from research to school transformation. We outline our discovery of specific ways African American, Latino, and low-income children are underserved by schools, and how we identified the cornerstones of the FirstSchool change process. The second chapter in Part I argues for reinvigorating the professionalism of teachers in order to create the conditions that make school transformation possible. Part II offers lessons learned from our collaborative work with schools, providing concrete guidance in choosing and using relevant data, enriching the curriculum, improving instruction, and developing reciprocal home–school partnerships. Part III outlines the program and policy considerations that are needed to support the widespread adoption of FirstSchool values, processes, and content in classrooms, schools, districts, and communities; and while it acknowledges the challenges we face, it presents a vision for a promising future. While lessons and strategies offered in this book apply to all groups of learners, we purposely focus on African American, Latino, and low-income (AALLI) students. In our experience, when the focus is on the needs of "all children," the needs of those three subgroups of students are often overlooked. However, the converse is not true. When the needs of these least represented groups are met, all children in school benefit, so we choose to focus on them explicitly. Throughout the book we use the acronym AALLI to refer to these important populations.

The process of collaborative inquiry that we promote is designed to help school leaders, including administrators and teachers, work from the top down and from the bottom up to improve the educational experiences of children in the early years. This book provides a conceptual framework, strategies, and case examples that can be applied across varied contexts for teaching and learning, allowing leaders to support the application of these concepts in schools and classrooms to better serve African American, Latino, and low-income children from the very start.

Part I

FIRSTSCHOOL REFORM

CHAPTER 1

The Groundswell for Transforming Prekindergarten Through 3rd Grade

Gisele M. Crawford, Carolyn T. Cobb,
Richard M. Clifford, and Sharon Ritchie

Struck by the potential of the early elementary years and at the same time by the realities of far less than optimal practices and outcomes, a group of us at the University of North Carolina at Chapel Hill decided to shift our focus from conducting research to facilitating change in schools. As researchers with professional experience as teachers, teacher educators, school administrators, and state leaders, we had long confronted the paradox of the persistent inability of educators to adequately develop and teach some groups of students (especially African American, Latino, and low-income children) despite a genuine commitment to serving them well. We wondered why the successful approaches practiced by some teachers and schools were not universally adopted. With support from the W.K. Kellogg Foundation, the Foundation for Child Development, the University of North Carolina at Chapel Hill, and private donors, we were able to think, plan, pilot, and implement a contextual approach aimed at disrupting the normalization of failure. The result was FirstSchool, a public school and university partnership dedicated to improving PreK–3rd grade experiences and outcomes for African American, Latino and low-income (AALLI) children. (While there is a multitude of cultures and languages represented in schools and our work is relevant to effectively serving many populations of students, as researchers and practitioners we feel best equipped to effect change for these underserved populations.)

FROM DATA TO PRACTICE

Early in our efforts to help educators transform the way they serve children at the very beginning of their schooling, teams of PreK–3rd grade teachers from three schools spent a year with us exploring how they could improve the early elementary experiences of those children who too often drop out of high school in great numbers: African American and Latino males. Teachers were intrigued with the idea of using data to reconsider their work with children across this age span. Together we examined data that went beyond the state assessments and same old statistics.

Using a time sampling measure called the *FirstSchool Snapshot* (Ritchie, Weiser, Kraft-Sayre, & Howes, 2007; Ritchie, Weiser, Mason, Holland, & Howes, 2010; for a more detailed description of the FirstSchool Snapshot, see Chapter 3) we were able to look at the minute-by-minute experiences of specific boys and used the information to explore a number of ways teachers could positively impact the boys' daily experiences. For example, they saw that the boys were only engaged in physical activity on average about 20 minutes a day and that most of that was during a concentrated period of outside play. Building on information from brain research (Castelli, Hillman, Buck, & Erwin, 2007; Jensen, 2000), they realized that more movement would benefit these boys by increasing their ability to pay attention and reducing times they were in trouble for being wiggly or distracted, and they found ways they could include more physical activity within the classroom setting.

They also looked at rules that demanded that children rigidly conform to one way of sitting, standing, or moving through the school and saw that African American and Latino boys were the ones most often in trouble for breaking those rules. By shifting their mindset toward ways of improving the boys' school experiences, they could see that being in trouble, singled out, and losing privileges was not motivational or positive. The teachers became more flexible and allowed the boys to find comfortable ways to sit on the carpet, work at their desks, and walk down the hallways. These changes of course applied to the whole class and teachers expressed relief at relinquishing control and discovering how capable their children were of monitoring their behavior within less stringent parameters.

Teachers also became more conscious of boys', particularly African American boys', sensitivity to disappointment. They watched them shut down from learning for long periods of time if they did not get a turn or if they experienced a perceived injustice. Teachers did not try to solve all of these problems for the boys, but rather recognized the behavior as a sign of a need for a closer relationship and validation of feelings.

Figure 1.1 is just one of the graphs we used to document African American and Latino boys' experience in these classrooms. The data helped teachers see how much time the boys were inattentive during whole-group time and seatwork (i.e., assigned individual work). Teachers immediately began to work together to find ways to engage these young boys more fully in the classroom experience. Here are just three of the comments we heard from teachers involved in this work:

> "I got rid of my behavior system. I was afraid to do it and all of the teachers told me I would be sorry. But I found out that I really did not need it. My relationships with the kids are far more important than anything I give or take away from them." (3rd-grade teacher)

> "We are really expanding the kinds of books we offer to the boys. We have a lot more books based on science and sports and are making sure that African American kids and Latino kids are in the stories and in the pictures." (Kindergarten teacher)

> "I reflect a lot more on what I am doing. I have become so much more patient and willing to listen." (PreK teacher)

Figure 1.1. Child Inattention in Activity Settings

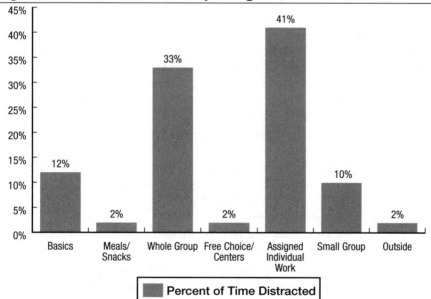

These teachers were willing and eager to look at comprehensive data on what was happening in their classrooms and to work to improve their own practices. They made a commitment to work as teams to sustain the work after our involvement ended.

These experiences illuminated potential avenues for transforming the educational trajectory of children who are too often failed by schools. As we discussed in the introduction to the book, when the focus is on the needs of "all children" the needs of African American, Latino, and low-income (AALLI) children can be overlooked, so we chose to focus on them explicitly. By working with schools that serve high proportions of AALLI children, we made sure our work was grounded in the reality that confronts children, families, and educators each day. Our vision for change included schools that challenge themselves through ongoing inquiry and use collaborative structures like grade-level meetings to focus on children's learning. Children and families would experience seamless transitions from home to school and across care and education experiences, prior to school entry and into 4th grade, and instruction would be grounded in developmental science. We wanted to see children who were engaged with their teachers, peers, and the learning environment and teachers who were well prepared, supported, and respected. Families would be partners in determining how they engage in the life of schools; leaders would be advocates for underserved children and establish a culture of caring, competence, and excellence.

Attaining this ideal is challenging. Ideological and attitudinal changes must occur in concert with concrete shifts in school structure, instructional approaches, cultural and family connections, and the use of data to drive and monitor progress. Our partners in schools are willing to work with us to reconceptualize their view of early childhood experiences within their building and create a more cohesive learning trajectory for their most underserved populations. All too often, school systems wait until children are already close to dropping out or are performing far behind standards before investing in them. Children form academic trajectories early in their school careers that tend to be stable and difficult to change over the course of their schooling (Alexander, Entwisle, & Dauber, 1993). By focusing on early childhood, we offer schools a chance to develop a proactive, preventative mindset, instead of simply reacting to entrenched problems.

This chapter chronicles the compelling need for change in PreK–3rd grade and our journey from research to school transformation. We outline our discovery of specific ways African American, Latino, and low-income children can be better served by schools and the development of the framework for the FirstSchool change process.

THE RATIONALE AND RESEARCH BASE

The Need for Radical Reform

For several decades, educational reform has attempted various strategies to raise achievement for all students, with varied and often only short-term success. The U.S. education system continues to struggle to increase the educational attainment of the population as a whole and reduce the opportunity inequity between advantaged children and those who are more vulnerable. In 1983 *A Nation at Risk* (National Commission on Excellence in Education) proclaimed our American way of life at risk due to declining achievement, lax standards, and poor use of time, among other things. While others have criticized their analyses and conclusions (see Rothstein, 2008), the report led some 25 years later to the No Child Left Behind Legislation and years of various educational reform efforts.

The 2009 Report Card on Reading from the National Assessment of Educational Progress (National Center for Education Statistics, 2009) shows— after some years of improving achievement and slight narrowing of the gap among ethnic groups— no significant change in reading across student groups for Grade 4 and only somewhat higher scores across most groups for Grade 8 since 2007. Cultural and ethnic minority children are left further behind, especially African American and Latino males (Chall & Snow, 1988; Council of the Great City Schools, 2010; Dupree, Spencer, & Bell, 1997; García Coll & Magnuson, 2000; Murrell, 2002). Disadvantaged children, specifically racial-, ethnic-, and language-minority children and children from low-income families, are more likely to enter kindergarten behind their middle-class European American and Asian American peers, to have lower achievement in reading and math, and to be assigned disproportionately to special education classrooms. Even when their family incomes are similar, African Americans and Latinos/as score lower on standardized tests than European Americans and Asian Americans (Bondy & Ross, 1998; Bowman, Donovan & Burns, 2001; Garcia, 2010; Knapp & Associates, 1995; National Center for Education Statistics, 2001; Ray, Aytch, & Ritchie, 2007; Riegle-Crumb, 2006). Further, in the last decade the dropout rates for Latino children failed to exhibit the same level of improvement as other ethnic minority groups, including African Americans (Aud, Fox, & KewalRamani, 2010).

A study of achievement and economic consequences in the United States found that the United States faces an education achievement gap when compared to other countries, as well as a persistent achievement gap by race and income within our own country (McKinsey & Company, 2009). In fact, "the achievement gap between children for high- and low-income families is roughly 30 to 40 percent larger among children born in 2001 than among those born 25 years earlier" (Reardon, 2011, p. 91). Achievement scores from as early as 4th grade can be linked to life outcomes. In short, McKinsey & Company (2009) assert that this loss of human capital amounts to a "permanent national recession" (p. 6).

In spite of decades of educational reform efforts to address the achievement gap, we still face persistent disparities between White and Asian American students compared to African American and Latino students, as well as between poor and non-poor students and between dual language learners and native English speakers. Our educational system is fragmented, with artificial divisions between levels of education and lack of alignment (Guernsey & Mead, 2010). Schools and states continue to focus on dropout prevention strategies at middle and high school, more focused and directed teaching on the "basics," and other strategies that offer "more of the same." Yet early childhood education research has clearly shown great promise in addressing learning needs and gains for all children, but especially for our most vulnerable populations.

The Compelling Case for Early Education

The grade and age range between prekindergarten and 3rd grade (PreK–3, or ages 3 to 8) is increasingly the focus of diverse policy groups, professional organizations, funders, and initiatives intent upon improving school experiences and achievement for all children. The premise for PreK–3 education is that coherent, high-quality instructional approaches across the PreK through 3rd grade span will result in positive outcomes for children throughout their early years and an increased likelihood that children will complete 3rd grade prepared to succeed in later years and with increasingly difficult academic curricula. While the literature on early education focuses largely on the importance of the period leading up to school entry, the often overlooked fact is that it is during the early years of elementary school that children learn to read and write and develop the concept of numbers and their use, and shift to using these tools as the foundation of learning for the rest of their school careers.

Research over the last 2 decades has shown that learning begins early, that brains develop most rapidly in the earliest years, and that early learning experiences are critical for the long-term success of children. The National Research Council Report *From Neurons to Neighborhoods* (Shonkoff & Phillips, 2000) makes the compelling case that the earliest years—birth through the primary grades—are critical to the long-term educational and life success of all children. In addition, evidence suggests that gains in cognitive and social–emotional skills may be greatest for children who are furthest behind when quality interventions are provided (Peisner-Feinberg et al., 2000; Shonkoff & Phillips, 2000).

Although numerous research studies find that high quality preschool experiences lead to better academic and life outcomes for children, prekindergarten programs or similar interventions alone cannot eliminate the achievement gap or maximize learning for our most vulnerable students. While benefits of prekindergarten do not disappear, they may begin to fade by 3rd or 4th grade without sustained quality instruction through the primary grades (Shanahan, 2009; Shore, 2009). Coherent, high-quality educational and instructional approaches across the PreK–3rd grade span will yield the best results for ongoing school success.

Several studies provide evidence of the longer-term benefits and outcomes both for the child and society with multiyear, high-quality programs. Four programs, in particular, are frequently cited as demonstrating long-term educational and socioeconomic effects for their participants:

- HighScope Perry Preschool (Schweinhart et al., 2005) provided 2 years of high-quality preschool, regular home visits with families, and focused transition to kindergarten. Long-term results show increased academic achievement, lower dropout rates, lower crime rates, and higher employment.
- The Carolina Abecedarian Project (F. A. Campbell & Ramey, 1995) provided full-time, high-quality educational intervention in a child-care setting for children from low-income families from infancy to entry into kindergarten. An additional school-age component used a family-support model for a subsample of the children in the study. Evaluations have shown that the preschool intervention produced greater intellectual and academic outcomes than the school-age intervention.
- The Chicago Child Parent Centers (CPC) initiative (Reynolds, 2003) was developed to promote academic success among low-income children. Studies over several years have shown PreK programs combined with high-quality elementary services (i.e., reduced class sizes, family support, and instructional support to classrooms in co-located elementary schools) significantly increased long-term academic achievement, lower grade retention rates, lower rates of special education placement, higher graduation rates and full-time employment, and lower rates of Medicaid receipt and arrests for violence (Reynolds & Temple, 2008).

- Dimensions of PreK–3 available in the Early Childhood Longitudinal Study–Kindergarten (ECLS-K) database were analyzed for their impact on academic success of children (Reynolds et al., 2006). PreK–3 variables included in the regression analyses included whether or not children had attended preschool, attended full-day kindergarten, experienced a stable K–2 school environment, and experienced certified teachers in K–3, as well as levels of parental involvement in school and amount of time for reading and language arts instruction in kindergarten. The authors found that children who had more of these combined dimensions of PreK–3, compared to children who had fewer or none, had higher achievement in reading and math, lower retention rates, and slightly lower special education placement rates. Of critical importance, the effects were most notable for the disadvantaged children.

Together, this evidence strongly suggests that a coherent approach to educating children in preschool through the primary grades that includes multiple, high-quality components of primary-grades instruction is most likely to lead to successful children by the end of 3rd grade. And, children successful by grade 4 are more likely to be successful throughout their school careers, reach higher-level outcomes, and experience lifelong success (Shore, 2009).

Putting the Base in Place

While the early years of schooling may be the key to long-term success for students, as well as positive and cost-effective social and economic outcomes for both students and society, evidence suggests that the quality of schooling at these ages is poor—or at best variable. The National Center for Early Development and Learning conducted a multistate study of prekindergarten and found wide variation in the quality of environments and instruction. Almost two-thirds of the time, observers saw no teacher–child interaction, and most of the interactions that were observed focused on routine, maintenance activities (Clifford et al., 2005). While other studies (e.g., see Frede, Jung, Barnett, & Figuera, 2009) have found more favorable practices in PreK, the overall picture is that the quality is, at best, mixed.

Stuhlman and Pianta (2009) analyzed profiles of over 800 first-grade classrooms across the United States in terms of the emotional and instructional dimensions of quality. Classrooms were classified as high quality, mediocre quality, low quality, or positive emotional climate/lower academic demand. The types of classrooms varied widely both within and across schools. "Children whose preschool achievement scores were lowest, whose ethnicity was non-white, and who were from poor or working-poor families were about twice as likely to be in the low overall quality classrooms than they were to be in the high overall quality classrooms" (Stuhlman & Pianta, 2009, pp. 334–335).

These findings make it clear that the foundations for success are not in place. The quality of the early grades must be consistently high in order to yield ongoing positive results—both academic and social, both short-term and over time. Elementary schools must actively engage with early care and education settings and families, and they must continue to work to establish high-quality learning environments at all grade levels. While the entire educational P–20 system needs to be reconceptualized, starting with a strong, seamless foundation of PreK (age 3) through grade 3 will provide the essential base for children's success in school. "But fortified with a solid start in the PreK–3rd years, our education system can finally fulfill its mission of providing the knowledge and skills to provide all Americans, no matter their background, with an equal opportunity to thrive" (Guernsey & Mead, 2010, p. 13).

MOVING FROM RESEARCH TO PRACTICE

The previous section makes the case for improving PreK–3rd grade education in the United States. Our own research over the past decade illuminates some of the specific ways children and families are underserved by schools (Barbarin et al., 2006; Barbarin et al., 2008; Burchinal et al., 2008; Chang et al., 2007; Crawford, Clifford, Early, & Reszka, 2009a, 2009b; Early et al., 2007; Early et al., 2010; Ritchie, Clifford, Malloy, Cobb, & Crawford, 2010). As researchers who have also worked as early childhood and elementary teachers and leaders, and as state-level administrators, we felt a particular responsibility to help educators and state and district leaders improve early education for AALLI children. We embarked on or participated in a series of projects in schools in our state to help those schools make key changes and learn what it would take to make change on a large scale.

Our Home District

Our local school district has been a key partner for us over the years and an incubator for new approaches to improving children's school experiences. This district is highly regarded nationally. It offers prekindergarten and has strong educational programs from elementary through high school. Two joint projects illustrate several of the challenges faced even by strong districts in meeting the needs of all young students and families (see Figure 1.2 and Figure 1.3).

The first joint project we conducted was a week-long summer institute for the district's prekindergarten and kindergarten teachers (see Figure 1.2). Most of the prekindergarten classes were housed at various elementary school campuses, and a few were located at a separate early childhood center. Prekindergarten slots in the district were funded by a combination of sources including Head Start. The district's PreK/Head Start office provided comprehensive services to students and families, as well as supervision of the teachers and other staff. The district's PreK/Head Start leadership and the central office leaders for elementary instruction were enthusiastic about identifying ways to promote seamless transitions for children and families.

Another opportunity for partnership emerged when an elementary school that had been implementing a Spanish–English dual-language program for K–5 for several years decided to begin a PreK dual-language classroom. In recent years there has been increasing interest in the implementation of "two-way bilingual (TWB) programs" (also known as "dual-language programs," "two-way immersion," and "bilingual developmental education"). Proponents of these programs point out the benefits of bilingualism both for English learners and English speakers and the need to address the achievement gap between children from immigrant backgrounds and Whites. As a result of the movement to include prekindergarten in the public school system, there is more interest in implementing dual-language programs with younger children (see Figure 1.3).

Dropout Prevention

Researchers at UNC collaborated with the Office of School Readiness of the North Carolina Department of Public Instruction (NCDPI) and the Ready Schools Initiative to conceptualize an elementary school dropout prevention project. UNC was awarded a Dropout Prevention Grant from the NCDPI to work with three schools serving high proportions of historically underserved children to improve the school experiences of African American and Latino boys. The project, Ready to Promote Academic Success for Boys of Color, was the only grant awarded for work in elementary schools (see Figure 1.4).

Based on participation in the dropout prevention project, teachers and administrators were eager to participate in a more in-depth change process. One elementary school was deeply committed to continuing this work with us. In fact, when they were notified that we were not awarded an implementation grant to support our work with them, the district administration responded by supplying the necessary support for teachers to be able to participate in activities (see Figure 1.5). We were thus able to conduct a needs assessment and facilitate schoolwide capacity building as part of intensive schoolwide consultation.

Figure 1.2. PreK–K Teacher Institute

Goals

We worked with district leaders to provide a summer institute for prekindergarten and kindergarten teachers. One of the goals of the institute was easy to accomplish: Let the prekindergarten teachers meet all the kindergarten teachers, an opportunity they had not had before. They were delighted to spend a week together learning about how children spend time in the others' classrooms. Provided with some tools for looking at the way children spend their day at school, they quickly took over their own professional development and worked together to find ways to ease the transition for children from one grade to the next. For example, kindergarten teachers offered to begin the year with a slightly longer rest time, and prekindergarten teachers were receptive to the idea of leading small groups of children in teacher-assigned work by the end of the year.

Results

The district prekindergarten classes had been housed at a few of the elementary schools and at a separate PreK center. After the institute, district leaders made sure every elementary school had at least one PreK class. While PreK students did not necessarily attend the same school for kindergarten, the district at least talked in terms of working toward this goal. Prior to the institute, a seamless transition from PreK to K was not even recognized as important.

Challenges

We proposed an ongoing series of joint professional days for PreK and K teachers for the following school year. District leaders were enthusiastic, but professional development days for PreK teachers were scheduled on different days from the days set aside for K–5 teachers. The separate calendars for PreK/Head Start and elementary professional development prevented the formation of a professional learning community for PreK and K teachers.

Lessons Learned

- In order to provide a seamless educational experience in prekindergarten and kindergarten, teachers need time together.
- Teachers need data and information that help them explore how children experience transitions.
- Teachers are able to build bridges from PreK to K that respect the needs of children and families and reflect the best of early childhood and elementary pedagogy and values.
- Separate leadership for prekindergarten and elementary programs limit the formation of collaborative structures.

Emerging FirstSchool Principle

- Collaborative Inquiry

Figure 1.3. PreK Dual-Language Classroom Consultation

Goals

At the district's request, a FirstSchool researcher provided consultation to support the teachers and administration in the first year of the implementation of the dual-immersion PreK program. The consultations focused on making the following decisions:

- Language distribution: How will the languages be used in the classroom? How much time will be devoted to each language? How will both languages be accorded high status and value? How will the languages be used in routines and activities during the day?
- Curriculum: What are the goals and objectives of the program? How will teachers integrate the Creative Curriculum into the dual-language program? What kinds of materials will be necessary to implement the Creative Curriculum in a dual-language program?
- Assessment: How do teachers integrate the Creative Curriculum assessment into the dual-language program? Do other assessments need to be included to address specific areas of language development? How can teachers take language samples and use them to understand where children are in their language development?

Results

Teachers had multiple discussions about how both languages should be used in routines and activities during the day and how to use sheltered English and Spanish teaching strategies. We worked with them to identify appropriate materials for prekindergartners. We also facilitated a discussion between the PreK and K teachers of the dual-language program.

Challenges

- We struggled to identify appropriate tools for assessing children in both English and Spanish.
- It took a long time for PreK and K teachers to find time to meet together. Teachers thought it would be a good idea to observe each other's classrooms, but there was no time allocated to do it.
- Having prekindergarten children change classrooms during the day to receive instruction in both languages is challenging. For the first two months they allowed each PreK group to stay with one teacher. The attempted solution was for teachers to switch classrooms instead of children. However, one teacher found this difficult because it would require her to move her materials each time. Once the children seemed to get used to having English for one part of the day and Spanish for the other part, it was decided to move the children instead of the teachers.

Lessons Learned

- Trying to push down the kindergarten dual-immersion program model to PreK without making adjustments did not work. There are issues for younger children that mean these programs must be designed with their needs in mind.
- Teachers need time together, within and across grades, to talk about student learning and observe each other's classrooms.

Emerging FirstSchool Principles

- Instructional Practices That Support the Success of AALLI Children
- Enriched Curriculum

Figure 1.4. Ready to Promote Academic Success for Boys of Color

Goals

We conducted ongoing professional development with vertical teams from each school, provided classroom observation and consultation, held a summer Institute which allowed all treatment schools to meet and learn together, and facilitated the use of data to provoke conversation and change in practice. Our partners at UNC, the Promoting Academic Success for Boys of Color (PAS) project, identified a number of aspects of the school day as having an impact on the experiences of African American and Latino boys including the use of chapter books, oral language development, flexibility instead of arbitrary rules, gross motor activities, and teacher negativity.

Results

Teachers used the *FirstSchool Snapshot* to capture children's experiences on a minute-by-minute basis. This lens for examining and adjusting instructional practices had a significant impact on teachers who were invested in improving schooling for African American and Latino boys in their classrooms. The dropout prevention frame allowed them to think about how important these children's experiences were to their later success and consider how instructional adjustments could help address racial inequities. As we have outlined, they talked about ways to spend more time working with small groups to maximize their engagement, how to provide more opportunities for children to move throughout the day, and how to reduce arbitrary rules that end up labeling African American and Latino boys as bad and disruptive.

Challenges

Early elementary teachers face increasingly prescribed curriculum that may limit their ability to adjust their instruction. For instance, the teachers who participated in this project were enthusiastic about focusing more on children's oral language development, but continued to struggle to find opportunities amid the demands of the instructional schedule. Also, while talented and motivated teachers may volunteer for learning opportunities and may be open to examining their practice, it remains challenging for them to bring their colleagues along on the journey with them.

Lessons Learned

Elementary teachers benefit from dedicated time to talk about children's progress; they are capable of addressing difficult topics like race, ethnicity, and gender; and professional learning communities, especially those built with vertical teams, can become sophisticated consumers of data about their own classrooms. In addition, they recognized that school experiences for boys could be negative and problematic, and that school is often not set up for their success. This gave them a focal point for examining data that brought awareness to this issue and allowed them to hook into our reform efforts.

Emerging FirstSchool Principles

- Collaborative Inquiry
- Data Drives Changes
- Instructional Practices That Support the Success of AALLI Children

Figure 1.5. Intensive Schoolwide Consultation

Goals

The school was in a small community in a largely rural area populated by children and families who are predominantly poor and African American or Latino. The school had struggled to meet the goals of Adequate Yearly Progress. We met with their school improvement team and began by asking how we could use our resources to build on what they were already doing. We jointly planned the following activities:

- Developing and facilitating a team that included representatives from the school, district, families, and community to closely examine the needs of the school using the HighScope Ready Schools Assessment and other assessment tools
- Gaining support at the district level and in the community, with a major focus on improving connections between the families, school, and community services
- Instituting and facilitating collaborative structures that ensure ongoing inquiry into different aspects of schooling
- Promoting a deliberate focus on restructuring the transition process to include child-care providers in order to create a meaningful integration of learning experiences across the PreK–3rd school years
- Sharing best practices related to developmentally appropriate instruction with new teaching staff and monitoring the degree of successful implementation

Results

The district recognized the central importance of serving all families. They committed to investing the necessary resources to create a full-service school, offering families access to social services and health services at the school site.

Challenges

Shortly after this schoolwide process began, the district hired a new superintendent. The new leader restructured this elementary school to be the prekindergarten and kindergarten school for the entire school district. The principal became the new principal of one of the 1st- through 5th-grade schools.

Lessons Learned

Schools and districts change leadership often; schools are reconfigured to meet the changing demands of the population served; and educators need to work with ever-changing policies and curricula. Creating lasting change is less about offering new programs or activities and more about providing a framework of values for examining those policies, programs, or materials. One teacher said, "You gave me permission to do what I know is right." We hope the framework that we provided will allow her to continue that work, regardless of other changes in her school's structure.

Emerging FirstSchool Principles

- Continuous Improvement
- Reciprocal Home-School Partnerships

The Power of K

The *North Carolina Position Statement on Kindergartens of the 21st Century* describes the crucial role of kindergarten in the establishment of children's and families' lifelong attitudes about learning, teachers, and school (North Carolina Board of Education, 2007). The statement goes on to describe the predicament of kindergarten teachers, "caught between what research supports as effective environments and experiences based on knowledge of how young children learn and develop, and the promotion of scripted programs and practices that typically do not respond to children's individual needs nor take into account the view of the whole child as a learner" (North Carolina Board of Education, 2007, p. 1). The primary team at the N.C. Department of Public Instructions launched a project called The Power of K to establish a group of kindergarten teacher leaders for North Carolina. We were natural partners because of our shared interest in kindergarten. Figure 1.6 describes our involvement in the Power of K project.

Ready Schools State Initiative

The Ready Schools Initiative was built on prior work in the state to bring greater focus on the early grades and the capacity of schools to be ready for *all* children (especially AALLI children). In June 2007, the State Board of Education adopted the following definition of a *ready school*:

> A ready elementary school provides an inviting atmosphere, values and respects all children and their families, and is a place where children succeed. It is committed to high quality in all domains of learning and teaching, and has deep connections with parents and its community. It prepares children for success in work and life in the 21st Century.

In addition to the definition, the State Board of Education approved nine pathways to ready elementary schools. The pathways were subsequently reduced to eight components: (1) Leaders and Leadership, (2) Transitions, (3) Teacher Supports, (4) Engaging Environments, (5) Effective Curricula, (6) Family, School, and Community Partnerships, (7) Respecting Diversity, and (8) Assessing Progress. Figure 1.7 describes our involvement in the Ready Schools State Initiative.

FIRSTSCHOOL PRINCIPLES

Our experiences working with committed educators to make change in their schools showed us that only a very sophisticated, comprehensive approach

Figure 1.6. The Power of K

Goal

The Power of K teachers participated in a 3-year comprehensive professional development project to increase student achievement by implementing practices that address the educational needs of all students. The group used an inquiry approach to engage in work in areas such as partnerships with families; authentic assessment that drives instruction; child-initiated and teacher-supported play; culturally relevant curricula; and integrating a variety of learning contexts into the day.

Results

The kindergarten teachers who participated solidified their existing knowledge and gained new knowledge about how to promote each child's success in a flexible, child-centered kindergarten environment. They also developed their skills as advocates, practicing their presentation skills and mastering the evidence that supports developmentally appropriate practice in kindergarten. Now they are adept at providing concrete examples of successful kindergarten practices to help show districts and teachers appropriate avenues for academic success.

In addition, the North Carolina PreK Demonstration Site project, which has been serving the state for the past 10 years, brought kindergarten into the project as a way of forging better links between PreK and kindergarten. They expanded the project to include many of the excellent kindergarten teachers who emerged as strong teacher leaders from the Power of K project. The mission of the project is to support PreK and kindergarten teachers in improving their own practices; to provide statewide opportunities for teachers, assistants, and administrators to engage in systematic observation; and to model, share, and promote effective learning environments, curriculum, and instructional practices to ensure optimal learning and development for all PreK and kindergarten children.

Challenges

This cohort of teachers was transformed by the investment of time, mutual support, and respect inherent in this project. However, in cases where principals were not fully supportive of the project, teachers found it difficult to enact the practices they learned. Also, the current funding climate in states makes it more challenging to support such investments in educators, despite the powerful results.

Lessons Learned

Kindergarten teachers are on the front lines of the battle to demand that schools must be ready for children, rather than expecting children to be ready for school. This project demonstrated the following:

- Classroom teachers can become leaders who effectively talk about their work to other professionals and advocate for instructional approaches that benefit children
- Investing in professional learning communities can bring powerful results
- Engaging principals is essential for success

This model could be adapted to teachers in other grades, to principals, or to other school professionals.

Emerging FirstSchool Principles

- Continuous Improvement
- Instructional Practices That Support the Success of AALLI Children

Figure 1.7. Ready Schools State Initiative

Goal

In the fall of 2008 the North Carolina Partnership for Children (NCPC), in collaboration with the North Carolina Department of Public Instruction, received a grant from the W.K. Kellogg Foundation, as well as awards from other sources, to create resource materials and provide technical assistance for communities interested in implementing the Ready Schools initiative. FirstSchool became a key resource for this initiative and provided two of the three technical assistance consultants.

Results

From 2008–2011 the consultants worked with nine schools on an invitational basis across North Carolina to facilitate the schools' development of a vertical PreK through 3rd grade team, use of the HighScope Ready Schools Assessment (2006), and selection of most needed improvement areas and action plans. They also led the development of the Ready Schools Tool Kit (North Carolina Ready Schools Collaboration Team, 2011) that was disseminated for statewide use by schools and districts across the state. Most schools focused on the area of Transitions (from PreK to K; from home to school; and so on), but the will to really implement action plans with purpose varied widely. It was from these schools, however, that FirstSchool found a cadre of schools for later implementation of its more in-depth values and practices for PreK–3rd and the focus on AALLI students.

Challenges

The main barriers reported by schools were the following:

- Gaining Ready Schools buy-in across the schools, district, and community.
- Recruiting community representatives, especially parents of AALLI children.
- Adequate time to conduct the assessments and recruit community stakeholders.
- Language (Spanish) skills needed to help develop home–school relations.
- Lack of ethnic diversity on the Ready Schools teams.
- District and school focus on end-of-grade testing.
- Implementing simultaneous programs that support student success.
- Little involvement by staff of the N.C. Dept. of Public Instruction in the pilot schools. While that was largely due to lack of available staff, schools indicated this would have been helpful in making the case for the initiative to their staff and central offices.

Lessons Learned

Characteristics for success were reported by schools to be the following:

- A good understanding of the Ready Schools concept throughout the school and in the larger community
- Active participation by school districts and principals
- Inclusion of all community stakeholders, especially early child-care providers and parents
- Ensuring all types of diversity to help address children's needs
- Facilitation by an outside consultant to keep the school on-track and to bring expertise

Linking the Ready Schools Initiative to other statewide initiatives underway was important to help schools see the holistic picture of PreK–3rd. For example, the Power of Kindergarten Initiative, FirstSchool, dropout prevention, and statewide PreK were key components of the overall PreK–3rd seamless education efforts.

Emerging FirstSchool Principles

- Continuous Improvement
- Collaborative Inquiry
- Reciprocal Home-School Partnerships

would provide lasting benefit. With support from the W.K. Kellogg Foundation, FirstSchool collaborated with four schools in North Carolina and four schools in Michigan on a long-term change process. Together we created a framework for transforming school for AALLI children, undergirded by the principles discussed below. The chapters in Part II show the specific ways we implement these ideas in schools.

Continuous Improvement Is Our Mindset

The teachers who volunteered for the Dropout Prevention Project exemplified a professional mindset of continuous improvement, where problems, challenges, and mistakes are viewed as an opportunity for learning and growth. Rather than being defensive about the struggles of African American and Latino boys in their classrooms, or blaming the boys, the teachers were willing to examine and change their own practices. In schools where a culture of continuous improvement prevails, both leaders and teachers embrace a variety of behaviors and attitudes that foster this mindset. Leaders view good teachers as those who look diligently for evidence of unsuccessful practices; successful leaders are those who can help school staff build on strengths and address areas for improvement. Teachers expect to improve the quality of their teaching throughout their professional lives through ongoing, focused effort. We discuss these ideas more fully in Chapters 2 and 3.

Collaborative Inquiry Is the Process

Transforming school for AALLI children cannot be a solitary endeavor. As we saw in all of our pilot projects, people need the support of others when taking the risks needed to make worthwhile changes. In our work with our home district, PreK and kindergarten teachers had their first opportunity to meet and talk in a relaxed environment away from the pressures of a school day. Given the chance to make connections and build trust with each other, they dug deeply into the task of learning about children's experiences in both settings and creating more seamless transitions. Kindergarten teachers in the Power of K project formed a supportive network of emerging leaders who did as much to support each other's development as the leaders of the project did. Dropout Prevention teachers found like-minded allies in their schools and other schools with whom to confront the hard reality of needing to change to meet the needs of AALLI students. In a schoolwide culture of collaborative inquiry, educators have the security to explore challenges. They can safely express the need to improve their practice, and together they develop the motivation and skill to use data to examine their practices and make changes that benefit students. Leaders at all levels support teachers' competence and autonomy through relationships built on genuine trust and respect, and processes and structures that facilitate the use of data are in place. Collaborative inquiry is integral to all we do at FirstSchool and elements of the process are explored in all the chapters in Part II.

Data Drives Change

From examining differences in the way PreK and kindergarten students spend their time to conducting a schoolwide Ready School assessment, schools can use a wide variety of data for the purpose of transforming practice rather than as an opening for criticism. Too often teachers' and leaders' main experience with data is to use it to "pass or fail" students or to be "passed or failed" themselves. FirstSchool promotes the use of data as the catalyst for change, not just an acknowledgment of success or failure. The opening section of this chapter offers a window into the ways educators can be guided and supported to rely on the power of data to reveal disparities and to engage in open and honest dialogue. These conversations focus on changes in practice and policy that result in improved experiences and outcomes for AALLI children. Chapter 3 offers a comprehensive approach to improving the use of data in schools.

Research Guides Practice

Enriched curriculum. At FirstSchool, we work with teachers to think deeply about curriculum because doing so matters tremendously to their abilities to ensure the success of the students they have right here, right now. We challenge teachers to examine what the curriculum *includes* and what it *excludes*. In the words of Slattery (2006), we aim to examine curriculum so "we find a way around hegemonic forces and institutional obstacles that limit our knowledge, reinforce our prejudices, and disconnect us from the global community" (p. 35). This work entails helping teachers integrate relevant aspects of children's sociocultural practices into their curriculum and instruction, and effectively respond to the challenges and opportunities that AALLI children encounter when navigating dual worlds—the school and their home culture. Further, we work with schools to ensure that their mission, policies, standards, assessment, curriculum, instructional practice, and learning environments are aligned for a coherent PreK–3 approach. We offer a detailed description of this work in Chapter 4.

Instructional practices that support the success of African American, Latino, and low-income children. Through a careful examination of the literature, we identified 10 research-based instructional practices that support learning and development for AALLI children and have deleterious effects when they are not present. We organized these practices into a framework designed to foster classroom cultures of caring, competence, and excellence. A culture of caring needs to be in place before substantive learning can occur. It is foundational to children's success, as it ensures that they feel safe, valued, and accepted by adults and classmates. A culture of competence ensures each child is a productive, successful, and contributing member of the classroom team, and a culture of excellence enables each learner to excel beyond minimal competencies. Chapter 5 expands upon these ideas.

Reciprocal home–school partnerships. FirstSchool believes that answering the following questions is essential to making a difference in the relationships between schools, communities, and families: (1) In what ways is education a societal and shared responsibility, where families and community members along with schools are accountable for the development of the children in their care? (2) What do families see as their role in schools? The answers are different for different school communities. It is important to move away from solutions imposed by schools and away from blaming or stigmatizing families for noninvolvement, using the contextual answers to these questions to design true partnerships between families, communities, and schools. FirstSchool helps schools consider their own contexts and provides the processes by which educators and families can jointly design and define family and community partnerships that work in their own environments. We explore this work in detail in Chapter 6.

CONCLUSION

Our ultimate goal is to improve the school experiences of African American, Latino, and low-income children and families. Our focus is on helping schools change to better meet the learning, cultural, and language needs of the children in their classrooms. This means preparing teachers and leaders by engaging them in long-term and committed work in which they challenge themselves and those around them to more fully understand the important role that race and culture play in teaching and learning. This means consistently promoting and supporting efforts to scrutinize and question policies and practices that interfere with the success of AALLI children, and enhancing the schoolwide capacity to develop the culturally responsive dispositions and teaching practices that enable them to better support the learning of their diverse students. We intend to help the reader grasp a sense of urgency for change, move from a deficit-based to a strength-based orientation, and make informed choices in both policy and practice that support AALLI children's academic and social success.

CHAPTER 2

Reinvigorating Professionalism: Involving Teachers in Establishing a Culture for Reform

Laura Gutmann and Sam Oertwig

Setting the Stage

Although most teachers say they are interested in continuous learning, professional development is often viewed as wasted time—time better-spent working on lesson plans or grading papers. So, what a pleasant surprise to see teachers routinely continue to engage in rich conversations about teaching and learning long after the day-and-a-half FirstSchool seminars were over. When we asked one group of teachers who still had a 2-hour drive home ahead of them why they continued to stay, one of them exclaimed, "You set our brains on fire! Our minds are just buzzing with so many ideas about how to work with our students and our colleagues."

Just as we want students to be enthusiastic, involved learners, we also want teachers to feel that same sense of invigoration and excitement about staying abreast of their profession. By valuing teacher expertise, providing relevant educational research and data, and creating opportunities for teachers to collaboratively inquire about how this information impacts teaching and learning, teachers come alive.

Throughout our endeavors, we have worked with a variety of people who play substantial roles in our partner settings. From the families who define a school's population, to the principals who help facilitate our project, to the children we ultimately impact, we quickly learned that in order to create seamless education and an aligned sense of purpose across PreK–3, we had to consider each of their needs—as well as their priorities and interests. In addition, we needed to provide opportunities for leadership that would move FirstSchool forward through each school's internal infrastructure and help achieve our goals for follow-up and implementation. In the long run, however, individual teachers are the ones who have played the most vital role in realizing our shared objectives and partnering with us to improve classroom experiences for African American, Latino, and low-income (AALLI) children.

Because of this, reinvigorating professionalism to create a better workplace culture for teachers is a core component of our vision for PreK–3 reform and a prerequisite for meaningful action. Since teachers figure heavily in determining schooling experiences, their contributions to furthering the principles of FirstSchool within their own contexts can significantly increase the potential for change. Boosting and then utilizing teachers' educational expertise and passion is especially important to AALLI children in their care. Because these groups of students have been historically disadvantaged by subpar instruction and a lack of unified planning within their schools (Saft & Pianta, 2001; Stuhlman & Pianta, 2002), we believe that they are particularly in need of coherent improvement strategies and well-functioning learning environments. While the approaches described within the FirstSchool framework could benefit all children, unless we disrupt institutionalized failures to provide AALLI children with quality educational opportunities, their progress will only continue to plateau. Therefore, as we consider the contexts that can either promote or limit teachers' involvement in school transformation, we pay close attention to how an educator's level of professional engagement may impact classrooms that serve AALLI populations.

Rivkin, Hanushek, and Kain (2005) contend that, among school-based factors that policymakers can influence, teachers and the quality of their instruction emerge as central determinants of student achievement, which "clearly reveals an important role for schools and teachers in promoting economic and social equality" (p. 449). While we do not discount the influence of associated resources like curriculum, training, leadership support, or other in-school factors that could be more difficult to quantify in research (R. Rothstein, 2010), we know that teachers make a difference in the lives of their students, for better or for worse. There is some evidence that an *effective teacher* can have a stronger influence on student achievement than poverty, language background, class size, and minority status, or at least significantly offset disadvantages in important areas like mathematics for at-risk children (Aaronson, Barrow, & Sander, 2007; Clotfelter, Ladd, & Vigdor, 2007; Darling-Hammond, 2000; Jacob, Lefgren, & Sims, 2008; Kane

& Staiger, 2008; Nye, Konstantopoulos, & Hedges, 2004; Rivkin et al., 2005; Rockoff, 2004; J. Rothstein, 2010).

To highlight the role of teachers as the primary drivers of curricular and instructional tasks, much of our data collection involved capturing the experiences that teachers provided for children during a typical day in the classroom. Subsequent chapters describe how we used data to highlight areas where teachers could come together to make concrete changes to their practice, working within and across grade-level teams to create opportunities for collaborative discussion and action. We intended for this information to serve as a tool to both increase awareness of their practice and empower them to make decisions about how they could best move toward improvement within their work settings.

Teachers in each of our partner schools were often surprised and excited to find that our presentation of data was not meant to be judgmental or evaluative. Rather, it offered them an in-depth look at what school meant for the children within their building, by showing them how the time they spent in classrooms was actually being utilized. It was important for them to know that we were willing to engage in meaningful conversations around each issue that arose, rather than simply dictating what they should do next or imposing a set list of to-dos on their practice. Their voices were fundamental to discussions of adjustments to their teaching, as well as avenues for growth and professional development.

We found, however, that our intentions could only take us so far, even when partner teachers were especially enthusiastic about embracing First-School principles and applying them to their particular situations. We were often stuck at the point of implementation within settings bombarded by a host of pressures and programmatic mandates, leaving little room for FirstSchool to take precedence. As we walked through their doors, we encountered a host of all-too-common barriers that made it hard for teachers to trust our claim that we wanted to fully partner with them to develop a more meaningful and organically conceptualized pedagogical process. While teachers *were* often appreciated for their immense commitment to their jobs by members of their local school community, the broader context that defined their professional status had left some of them feeling burned-out, disrespected, and helpless. They saw themselves as needing to lie low and tolerate mandates and programs that were visited upon them in great numbers, rather than feeling motivated to contribute their voice to key pedagogical decisions. Here, then, was a major problem: How could we create conditions for school transformation that truly valued teachers' voices and experiences when the context for their teaching and the nature of their job settings seemed to be working against us?

UNDER PRESSURE

While some teachers were interested in working collaboratively with us, others assumed that FirstSchool was just one more program being imposed upon their school, which they perhaps would not openly resist, but instead endure. We realized that changing this mindset was going to be a challenge, made more difficult by the priority on producing high, or at least adequate, test scores, even for the youngest children, which ruled the day and took over most of their school's decisionmaking. Within this environment, policies meant to help develop teachers' practice, such as efforts to create uniform expectations around baseline curriculum delivery, had the unintended consequence of becoming overly restrictive and punitive, further diminishing their professional status. To help teachers work within these policy guidelines more effectively, we needed to build their resiliency and better equip them to navigate these circumstances.

While this chapter further compares our ideals with workplace realities, we ultimately hope to offer practical steps that skilled leaders from the classroom and administrative offices can take to improve professional conditions for their colleagues. We first explore the role of leadership in helping staff effectively implement policies and then discuss how those efforts can contribute to a positive work culture. By facilitating a parallel process that aims to create the same supportive environment for professional learning that we expect teachers to provide for their students, teachers can feel safe admitting imperfections and working together to tackle challenges within a community of practice. Without the foundational goal of reinvigorating professionalism and boosting teacher engagement in the transformation process, attempts to collect data, establish home–school partnerships, and make curricular and instructional changes are more likely to crumble.

Discussion Questions

1. As a leader within your educational community, when do you encounter apathy, resistance, curiosity, enthusiasm, and so on? What could be contributing to these mindsets?
2. To what degree do you think teachers feel empowered to make instructional decisions and to customize instruction to meet the needs of their children?
3. What are professional conditions like within your local school and district environments?

Introducing FirstSchool: Walking into the Fire

As we began our work with the teachers in our partner schools, we were met with intense skepticism, especially when we first explained that the data we would be collecting and presenting were not to be used for evaluation, but rather as a springboard for collaborative inquiry and professional development. Even when we emphasized that no one except our research team and the teacher herself would see data at the individual teacher level, they expressed fear and concern that this information would be used to condemn them. In the current climate of high-stakes testing, we regularly encountered teachers who already had more data than they knew what to do with, who were accustomed to being "beaten up" by data, and who did not see how *more* data could help improve anything.

A different mindset is needed to see data as something valuable that can be effectively used by teachers to guide and tailor instruction to fit the academic and social, and emotional needs of their students. One important aspect of changing the mindset involves presenting data that actually promotes reflection on themselves as teachers, not just on the students as learners. The FirstSchool Snapshot measure produces unique data that provided teachers with an in-depth view of their actual instructional practices and the student experiences that resulted from the instructional decisions they made. It enabled them to determine if they were measuring up to their own standards of what effective teaching looked like, as well as whether or not they were being the kind of teachers their students needed them to be. Doing so empowered them to make changes because, as professionals, they wanted to initiate improvement rather than be mandated or dictated to change.

THE IMPORTANCE OF CONSIDERING POLICY
RESTRICTIONS ON TEACHER AGENCY

When teachers feel as if leaders are working *on* them to fix their instruction instead of working *with* them to determine how to improve, the rules and regulations that govern school reform start to feel dehumanizing. Throughout the past decade, when teachers discuss policy mandates that they see as limiting their ability to decide how to best serve their students, the No Child Left Behind Act (NCLB) of 2001 has typically been at the forefront of their frustration. While NCLB has played an important part in publicly emphasizing the responsibility that schools and their staff members have for student learning, its focus on accountability has come at an exacting price. For instance, the resulting emphasis on monitoring local education has narrowed the ways that teachers can demonstrate student achievement and reduced their instructional choices. Within this environment, recent waivers that relax schoolwide achievement goals have only been made possible in exchange for further linking individual teacher appraisals to student performance outcomes. So where did NCLB's intentions go astray?

NCLB Enforcement: Upsides and Downsides

On a positive note, we know that more uniform standards and regulations provide a better chance for quality educational opportunities for our AALLI children. Because NCLB highlights subgroup performance and compares it to baseline standards, it helps ensure that the needs of subgroups are recognized, instead of being hidden within schoolwide performance averages. Now that we can look at their relative success, as well as their growth from year to year, we can better commit ourselves to improving those outcomes and making this focus central to our professional responsibilities. By setting "clearer expectations for what should be learned in school" (Jennings, 2012), states can make more cohesive efforts to enforce baseline standards across all demographics. Moreover, Sloan (2006) points out that although such policies can be narrowly conceived, we cannot dismiss their impact on teachers who "actively read and appropriate facets of accountability-explicit curriculum policies to deliver instruction that not only is higher in quality and more equitable than their 'normal' classroom instruction, but also leads to a stronger sense of teacher agency" (p. 124). Furthermore, Haycock (1998) provides several examples of how enforcing higher-quality standards within the classroom and the teaching profession at large, including improving curriculum and training inputs, can relate to better outcomes for disadvantaged children.

On the downside, this legislation has led to a series of local restrictions on classroom curricula, instruction, and learning objectives that can directly affect a teacher's ability to serve children, especially in low-performing schools that are being closely monitored at the local, state, and federal level. There is little balance between the proclivity to embrace a silver bullet, one-size-fits-all solution to poor instruction and the notion that teachers themselves might be best suited to determine how to improve instruction for their students, given their knowledge of their school's population. Because NCLB mandates prioritize basic literacy and math standards, administrators are often hesitant to allow teachers to work more flexibly with children in response to their interests, balance the curriculum with science, social studies, and gross motor activities, or give attention to social development.

Furthermore, simply providing teachers with data about student progress on benchmarks and standardized tests has not inspired significant change. NCLB-driven tracking needs to be explicitly connected to suggestions for enhanced instructional and curricular practices in order to be more effective. For example, these enhancements could include increased cultural competence and awareness of student backgrounds on the part of teachers (Ladson-Billings, 1995; Ray, Bowman, & Robbins, 2006). Because of this, we would argue that legislation like NCLB has made problems visible without taking the necessary steps to support teachers in their efforts to improve practice for AALLI children and help close the ever-persistent achievement gap. Accepting that deep change takes time is crucial to our FirstSchool approach, especially when considering the enormity of the task of helping teachers better address the needs of our 21st-century racially and culturally diverse student population. The focus must be on assisting teachers to transform basic guidelines into customized, contextualized, and responsive instruction by providing them with differentiated feedback related to their specific pedagogical actions.

Finding Potential Within Teacher Evaluation

Even as the federal government has begun awarding NCLB waivers that ease whole-school accountability, new measures are being put in place to determine an individual teacher's competence. A growing expectation for teacher evaluation focuses on measuring each teacher's ability to bring students along a specific achievement trajectory and attaches high-stakes personnel decisions to proof of satisfactory progress. In many districts, principals must now collect both observation-based and test-score data about a teacher's impact on learning that are increasingly made publicly available.

More rigorous evaluation does have potential merit as a tool for improving teacher performance. Savvy districts and administrators can effectively use teacher evaluation data to foster valuable conversations about practice, plan professional development, encourage teacher leadership opportunities, and reward instructional efforts. Darling-Hammond (2012) contends that "if we really want to improve teaching, we should look to such districts for models of effective evaluation, as well as to high-performing countries that have professionalized teaching by ensuring excellent preparation, on-the-job collaboration, and ongoing professional learning" (p. 1). Indeed, there are several models of comprehensive instructional feedback that hold promise for promoting real professional development (Daley & Kim, 2010; Danielson, 2010). There is also some evidence that well-executed rating systems can reliably correlate observed instructional behaviors and student achievement results (H. A. Gallagher, 2004; Milanowski, 2004; Rockoff & Speroni, 2010).

However, the prevailing stance among policymakers that teachers are the primary driver of achievement within school buildings (Wenglinsky, 2002) can also lead to working conditions where teachers are held disproportionately responsible for these results, instead of assigning some of that credit or blame to other members of the school system or to the system of schooling. In addition, the overreliance on test scores that characterizes most evaluation systems creates concerns about their fairness and accuracy, given the nonrandom assignment of students to classrooms and schools that could affect results from one year to the next in a particular classroom or penalize teachers who serve more challenging demographics (Baker et al., 2010). Instead of becoming tools for fostering professional growth and continuous improvement, evaluations then pit teachers against unevenly applied expectations. As the pressure of trying to conform to these requirements weighs on teachers, their desire to push the envelope by engaging in nuanced planning that applies baseline standards to their particular classroom situation is diminished.

The Role of Leaders in Making Policy Functional

In FirstSchool we asked schools to tackle the challenge of empowering teachers to improve their practice while creating a shared sense of responsibility for student experiences and outcomes. Successful partner administrators supported the alignment of instruction around FirstSchool objectives by taking concrete steps to create support structures for change. They creatively navigated a path to set these changes in motion, even within district and state expectations for teaching and learning that sometimes conflicted with our collaborative mentality. While there were certainly time and implementation challenges, leaders found ways to support the range of abilities, motivation, and development levels within their staff structure. They also considered areas where they could best support growth and change and identified the resources needed to do so. They utilized evaluation metrics as a tool in the cycle of continuous improvement, rather than making their implementation seem rushed, incomplete, or overly punitive.

Discussion Questions

What do leaders need to do in order to effectively use performance management tools so they facilitate productive dialogue and worthwhile goals for improvement? How can they use these tools to build teachers' professional status?

As our efforts to sustain their progress continue, we see their job as one of nurturing resiliency in their teachers at a time when teaching seems more stressful than ever. Resilient teachers are more capable of productive interactions (Barber, 2002; Brock & Grady, 2000). To support the development of resilient teachers and a climate of continuous improvement, principals must establish a caring community, in which collegial relationships are the norm and replace competition and isolation. Noddings (1992) emphasizes that teachers bear the same responsibility for the moral growth of their colleagues as for their students and that such growth can only happen within a context of a relationship characterized by trust, mutual respect, and caring. When administrators develop a caring professional community, provide teachers with opportunities for meaningful participation in decisionmaking, and emphasize high expectations for both staff and students, they bolster individual and community resilience capabilities (N. Henderson & Milstein, 2003). Within this atmosphere, intellectual curiosity, greater competence, openness and willingness to share, and an increased capacity to contribute will thrive.

The Missing Pieces

As FirstSchool guides contextualized decisionmaking, we emphasize utilizing the child development knowledge base, integrating developmental science, and maximizing curriculum standards. Our goal is to help schools enhance current practice within an environment where increased monitoring of the connection between teaching strategies and learning goals has led to the narrowing of what it means to be successful in school for both instructor and student. Meeting grade-level benchmarks and producing adequate assessment results have come to define the tasks of teaching in ways that overshadow other valuable objectives such as incorporating students' home lives and cultural backgrounds into curriculum, developing their social and conversational abilities, making instruction more engaging and relevant, and building strong and supportive relationships. Later chapters detail how the child-centered, exploratory curriculum that characterizes early educational experiences often disappears in favor of significantly more structure by kindergarten or 1st grade. Under these circumstances, curriculum and instruction that attends to the whole child—or at the very least, incorporates subjects beyond tested areas of math and literacy—is not a priority and thus has to be gleaned, designed and/or modified from the basic standards by an especially motivated and confident teacher. (See Chapters 4 and 5.)

Ideally, according to Miller and Almon (2009), "teachers need to understand the ways in which child-initiated play when combined with playful, intentional teaching leads to lifelong benefits in ways that didactic drills, standardized tests, and scripted teaching do not" (p. 24), instead of being directed to stick to basic skills instruction. Unfortunately, while schools serving more advantaged children are more likely to have relaxed such restrictions, scripted programs are found, "primarily in schools serving large numbers of children from low-income families" (p. 43). Within those settings, despite clear evidence that efforts to address the range of academic, social, and emotional development can yield positive results (see Chapter 1 for related research), these early learning needs are often supplanted by the push down of the demands of higher grades, in favor of a concentration on acquisition of skills and content knowledge. As a result, many principles central to healthy development that should be carried through the first several years of schooling—and perhaps even beyond—are instead confined to classrooms serving children under the age of 5.

This ethos also contributes to a sense among teachers who serve young children that their work is less valued than the efforts of their peers in upper elementary grades. Potential solutions to this problem include identifying the specific characteristics of typical school culture that could benefit from utilizing the professional strengths and priorities of PreK–3 teachers. For instance, if increasing leaders' knowledge of child development was seen as central to improving instructional techniques, schools could promote approaching academic goals in appropriate ways and invite more learning and invigorated practice in this area. Strategies such as assessment in the form of portfolios that provide a full picture of a child's progress (as opposed to solely test scores and benchmark results), developing strong home–school partnerships that involve frequent collaborative discussions with families, and a strong infusion of student culture into the curriculum would become critical, rather than tangential to success. We highlight these strategies because of the role that leaders must play in reconsidering their value, as they act upon a new awareness of how early childhood goals could improve schooling for AALLI children across PreK–3rd grade.

Discussion Questions

1. Why are the acquisition of academic skills often considered to be at odds with key early childhood practices, such as the opportunity for choice and exploration?
2. What messages do the leaders within your school community send to teachers about the possibility of blending academic rigor with practice that remains sensitive to PreK–3 growth trajectories?

The widespread acceptance of the Common Core State Standards provides another example of how worthwhile and well-meaning efforts to better define learning can still present challenges for teachers, along with opportunities for talented leaders to help them realize more positive possibilities. From a FirstSchool perspective, the Common Core has the potential to improve instructional focus if utilized by PreK–3 teachers and grade-level teams to understand how to connect principles of higher-order thinking, collaboration, discussion, and oral language development with standards for instruction and content delivery. Already, planning teams of teachers across the country are working with these standards as a guideline they can customize, rather than adhere to strictly.

However, within the process of interpreting Common Core on behalf of their children, teachers must be able to articulate their knowledge of developmental science, including the role of play, self-regulation, exploration, and socialization in achieving academic objectives. Otherwise, that expertise will become undervalued and underutilized, ultimately preventing teachers from adequately instructing their students. Despite our hopes for the Common Core, we worry that these considerations will remain pushed to the side in favor of meeting baseline expectations that are too narrow to fully optimize the multifaceted nature of a child's early development.

In many classrooms serving disadvantaged children, policies that determine *what* is taught, as well as *how* to teach it, can force teachers to deliver scripted, basic skills–oriented instruction, making it difficult to synthesize the acquisition of key math and literacy objectives with other content areas. Some teachers are driven to incorporate their own vision of instruction, while others are less invested in doing that work or lack the experience to fully envision how to enhance bare-bones skills attainment. This stems from fear of reprisal, lack of knowledge and skill, and lack of peer support. At its best, prescriptive curriculum can act as a scaffold for teachers who need support to deliver effective instruction. Attention needs to be given to ensuring that teachers are supported in efforts to slowly and intentionally wean themselves from total reliance on set instructions and move toward a more responsive approach on behalf of the developmental and learning needs of their students.

Because federal and state government control mechanisms have increased over the past decade, local decisionmaking has become incumbent upon larger goals that aim to create a certain amount of "sameness" across educational experiences. On the positive side, sweeping regulation by government agencies may help ensure that all students have access to public schooling. For instance, the rights of students with disabilities are protected by federal legislation. However, in other cases, broad measures intended to enforce

---

Discussion Questions

1. How can school leaders introduce the Common Core in a way that motivates teachers to determine how to best apply these standards and principles to their classroom contexts?
2. What could happen to the Common Core effort if teachers are not given the opportunity to drive the implementation of some of its valuable tenets?

---

standards and create equity may fall short, because they fail to acknowledge the complexities inherent to each school context and the need to engage each school's staff in reform efforts.

In our work to bring a different mindset into our partner schools, we have had to acknowledge these realities and think about how to integrate our vision for early education into a typical PreK–3 educational setting that contains a host of policies that may run counter to what research defines as sound instruction and to the importance of placing teachers at the center of reshaping their own classrooms. We agree with Michael Fullan (1996):

> The overload and fragmentation of change is endemic in postmodern society. What is needed is a focus on efforts in teacher development and school development to reshape the professional culture of teaching. Knowledge of the change process is critical both for creating and for sustaining this kind of radical reform. It is only when the majority of teachers become moral change agents that we can cultivate the powerful cultures required to work with communities and other agencies in making a difference in the learning life chances of students. (p. 496)

Within the process of enhancing broad standards, "efforts to professionalize teaching should both build teacher commitment and improve curriculum and instruction" (Firestone, 1993, p. 7) so teachers can become fully invested and engaged in any changes to their practice. Under those conditions, they can feel as if the implementation of policy mandates is aligned with the range of considerations that they have identified as necessary to work effectively with their students.

THE IMPORTANCE OF CREATING A POSITIVE WORK CULTURE

Although top-down regulations and policies may seem to determine much of what we expect from teachers, there is still much that leaders can do to consider how their school's working conditions affect a teacher's ability to succeed. Policies that insufficiently define yet then insist upon the implementation of instructional, curricular, and academic goals are not the only factors that can hinder successful teaching practices and job satisfaction. Economic stress, budget cuts and continual turnover also make it challenging to move reform forward. In addition, there is often little formal mentoring or opportunity for teacher development beyond rushed observation feedback, beginning induction programs, and ineffective whole-group professional development sessions (H. C. Hill, 2009; Ingersoll & Smith, 2003). The low morale that can result from these conditions affects teachers on a personal level, which trickles down to impact their instructional capacity and relationships with students, families, and colleagues, as well as their overall sense of motivation.

Although decisions to leave the profession or teach in one school over another are in part due to personal preferences, we can see some evidence that school environment factors, such as leadership, salary, availability of resources, and empowerment opportunities, impact teachers' lives and ultimately affect outcomes for their students (Ladd, 2009; Loeb, Darling-Hammond, & Luczak, 2005). In North Carolina, the most recently compiled results of the Teacher Working Conditions survey reveal that while about half of the state's teachers feel that they are engaged in decisionmaking on the classroom level, they are less involved in decisions being made across their school (North Carolina Teacher Working Conditions Initiative, 2010). This perception feeds into a structural disconnect between individual decisions about pedagogy and a shared sense of purpose, which prevents teachers from better utilizing their colleagues and other community members as job partners. Broader evidence also indicates that teachers are more likely to become dissatisfied with the job environment in low-achieving schools that serve low-income communities, and "move on to more supportive and rewarding workplaces" (S. M. Johnson, 2006, p. 17). As a result, an array of organizational issues, such as a lack of opportunity to provide input, drive turnover and dissuade teachers from serving our nation's neediest students (Berry, Smylie, & Fuller, 2008; Ingersoll, 2001).

Challenges to Developing Appealing Professional Learning Communities

Part of the problem with trying to reform PreK-3 education lies within limited opportunities for teachers to receive meaningful support from administrators and other teachers across the PreK–3 spectrum. At some of our First-School sites, the increased popularity of Professional Learning Communities (PLCs) and grade-level planning teams was an encouraging sign that schools have begun to allot time during the week for teachers to work together, benefit from collaborative efforts, and thus reduce isolation. As we implemented our approach, we were able to piggyback on those team efforts and utilize this structure for discussion, which made many important conversations possible. However, we became concerned with how the time was being utilized. We wanted to see teachers discussing data about their students throughout the school year and making meaningful links between student performance, potential instructional measures, and curricular decisions. Furthermore, we wanted the use of data to become inclusive and nonthreatening by serving as a catalyst for further inquiry and development, rather than becoming entirely about end goals or any one particular measure of progress.

But in many cases, PLC time was spent talking about data mostly in terms of achieving testing results, narrowing the conversation by overemphasizing how to boost test performance for struggling students. While we want teachers to identify ways to assist low performers, in order to accomplish growth objectives, they must first make adjustments to the learning *process*, aiming to make specific changes to their instruction on behalf of AALLI children that will ultimately benefit all students. Reports from teachers indicate that they need and want help in this area. For instance, in North Carolina, while 56.8% of teachers reported needing professional development focused on closing the achievement gap, only 30.1% felt that schools adequately responded to those needs. Similarly, while 49.8% wanted support in working with English language learners, just 19.9% reported being provided with this type of assistance (North Carolina Teacher Working Conditions Initiative, 2010, p. 7).

Throughout the country, teachers feel disconnected from professional development sessions that fail to utilize their own knowledge about their students' culture or engage them in continuous reflection about how it relates to their practice (Harwell, 2003; Lesch, 2000). As a result, although we believe that PLCs and other modes of collaborative professional development and team planning have strong potential to address these gaps, it is evident that this promise is not always fully realized.

The Role of Leaders in Improving Communities of Practice

As we encouraged FirstSchool administrators to engage teachers in thoughtful conversation about meeting student needs, we also challenged them to create a work environment that remained open to adjustments—and feel prepared to structure their school day differently than before. This does not mean that we expected or wanted leaders to endorse a complete dismissal of policy-driven objectives like the ones that NCLB or subsequent accountability measures impose. Instead, we were focused on making changes that took a more robust, inclusive approach to designing the means of instruction that would lead to reaching those end goals for student learning and progress. Within these efforts, we also worked to define the job of teacher as meeting a broader range of student growth goals, which included both social and academic objectives.

For example, one aspect of teaching that seems to get undue attention from administrators is the degree to which teachers are able to control and manage their students. In other words, high levels of control have become synonymous with good teaching, and teachers receive praise for orderly, organized classrooms where students are quietly attending to seatwork or for straight-lined, quiet hallway walking with students displaying one hand on their hips and the index finger of the other hand on their lips. However, high levels of teacher control are actually detrimental to students on a personal level because they block the healthy development of self-regulation. They also interfere with academic progress because learning is an active, sometimes messy, process that contains the critical elements of uncertainty and failure. Teachers often opt out of incorporating highly effective hands-on, project-based learning into their instructional programs because they cannot "control" it as much as they can whole-group, didactic instruction.

This does not mean that FirstSchool advocates chaos as the appropriate atmosphere for quality teaching and learning to occur. Instead, we encourage administrators to work with teachers to find a happy medium in which teachers establish reasonable parameters for the children, share ownership of those community standards in partnership with the children, stay mindfully aware of what students are doing, and provide gentle guidance and assistance to those who need it. Doing so creates less stress on everyone and shifts the locus of control from solely the teacher's responsibility to a shared responsibility, one that promotes healthy development of both autonomy and skill. It also enhances the sense of equity in the classroom community when everyone recognizes that the best way of sitting, working, or solving a problem is not the same for everyone. Flexibility, inclusivity, and reason become the norm.

Meaningful Collaboration

In attempting to capitalize on preset grade-level meeting times, such as PLC gatherings, we had to determine how to steer the conversation in ways that got teachers excited about our shared work, rather than seeing us as yet another burden or time-waster. Hargreaves (1991) discusses the concept of contrived collegiality, which acknowledges that even well-intentioned collaboration opportunities can cause teachers to sometimes feel forced to participate and disconnected from meaningful discussion about their students. Meetings should be more than people being forced to sit around the same table, brought together by administrative policy mandates and arbitrary staffing decisions (T. Smith & Rowley, 2005). In the best-case scenario, they become places where relationships are built with one another as "critical friends," who have a shared respect for one another's expertise, and feel comfortable critiquing the status quo or questioning instructional practices, with the intent of helping foster growth within their fellow staff members (Bambino, 2002; Lord, 1994). We need schools and their leaders to weigh the following questions in order to move toward this ideal:

- Are leaders providing teachers with the right tools to make the most of their collaborative efforts?
- Are teachers truly empowered to come together as a grade level and best meet the needs of their student population?
- Do teachers understand how to use data effectively and engage in more in-depth collaborative inquiry?
- What support do we have to offer teachers who are struggling?

In Chapter 3, which outlines our use of data to capture student experiences, we recommend providing teachers with the opportunity to take a more detailed look at the relational, instructional, and pedagogical components that formulate their practice. This allows teachers to focus on *how* their students are experiencing their classrooms and discuss the aspects of teaching and learning that can lead to desirable progress for all students. For instance, one of our Michigan partner schools discussed ways to restructure their PLCs, which led to more collaborative opportunities for PreK and K teachers to discuss student data, visit each other's classrooms, and consider how to ease students' transition from one grade to the next. In contrast, if teachers are overwhelmed by a constant barrage of benchmark results and growth metrics, which remain disconnected from a deeper understanding of their instructional choices, their ability to drive concrete change for AALLI children will be limited. Similarly, when data is largely used as a tool for judgment and teachers have never been expected to engage in close analysis of classroom feedback, schools start from a place of diminished possibilities.

THE FIRSTSCHOOL APPROACH TO BUILDING AN EFFECTIVE SCHOOL CULTURE

Our partnerships with schools are marked by a strong conviction that the FirstSchool process needs to be defined by working *with* teachers, not

Changing the Conversation:
Helping FirstSchool Teachers Determine How to Improve

Although not always the case, the initial response of teachers to the FirstSchool data was often one of denial and blame: "This was not a typical day in my classroom." "I have so much didactic instruction because my principal makes me teach this way." However, they also fairly quickly got beyond that, realizing that this data did capture the experience of their children and that it was reflective of their teaching. This cognitive dissonance—the difference between how they perceived themselves as teachers and the reality of their teaching—created the window of opportunity for change. Had we belittled them or immediately encouraged the purchase of a new packaged curriculum, we would have slammed that window shut forever!

Instead, we linked the data to our 10 research-based instructional practices (see Chapter 5), shared information with them about why these approaches to instruction are critical for their students, especially their African American, Latino, and low-income children, facilitated conversation about their instructional decisions, and posed reflective questions. They began pulling in some of their own student data from assessments and observations and started reflecting on what they might do differently and with more intentionality. In some cases, the teachers had the wherewithal to make changes on their own (for example, deciding to shorten the amount of time spent in transitions); in other cases, they needed additional professional development (for example, gaining new knowledge about how to incorporate more scaffolded and reflective instruction in their teaching of math). Teachers became excited, invigorated, and empowered as they recognized their own potential to attain a higher level of quality for the students with whom they worked.

Within this framework, leaders helped facilitate the process of schools setting broad, overarching goals in keeping with schoolwide needs for improvement. For example, one school chose to develop a hands-on, center-based approach to math while another school selected working on helping boys be more successful in literacy. At the same time, while grade levels were encouraged to develop more specific objectives in keeping with the schoolwide goal, they could also work on different instructional aspects that were of particular interest to them. In some cases, individual teachers went beyond this to work on an area that they personally found compelling. The bottom line was that each school, grade level, and individual moved forward in a manner that was contextually personalized. The impetus to change was based on a combination of data, research, and personal interest.

against them. Although we highlight key aspects of our research findings and link them to the principles that we believe are most essential to ensuring that AALLI children have access to quality PreK–3 education, these beliefs would become hollow platitudes if they were disconnected from the experiences of real-life classrooms and school communities. We also acknowledge that in order to drive change, identifying key teachers, grade level leaders, and administrators who are dedicated to school improvement is essential. By allowing these integral individuals to take ownership of this process, we strive to create a shared vision for inquiry, characterized by a deep respect for what schools have already accomplished and for their ongoing dedication to improving the lives of their students. Therefore we do our best to listen to concerns rather than dictate reform, but at the same time challenge teachers to get past the stagnation of complaint and join us in transforming schools on behalf of their students.

This attention to the opinions and perspectives of an array of school community members, particularly teachers, is essential to developing a caring work culture marked by strong relationships, communication, and self-efficacy. For FirstSchool, this has meant balancing the initiation of collaborative conversations around how to achieve excellence with valuing teacher input and agency. At the core of this transformation effort, our principles are designed to unite teachers and administrators around a mindset that makes actionable next steps possible across the entirety of PreK–3. As such, they are designed to help schools jumpstart better conditions not only for students, but also for their instructional leaders, who are charged with delivering learning objectives on a daily basis. Here are a few examples of how our approach can lead to transformation:

- Focusing on seamless education across PreK–3 makes success less dependent on individual teachers or grade-level leaders and creates a shared goal of providing alignment as students move from one year to the next. We trust in their professional capability to problem-solve together and reduce structural barriers to cross-grade connection.
- Fostering a culture of collaborative inquiry asks leaders and teachers to build their data literacy skills and apply lessons learned from benchmarks, observations, and other sources of information about practice, instead of being handed sets of results with no follow-up engagement.
- Continually incorporating staff feedback helps leaders drive transformation forward while gaining buy-in from key stakeholders. As they create better channels for communication, they might ask: Are there diverse vertical teams in place, or multiple levels of

leadership that provide opportunities not just to let voices be heard, but to act upon those convictions? Are leaders relying on a few individuals to gain a sense of their school culture, or are they being more inclusive? What evidence do they have demonstrating that teachers feel respected as professionals?

Prioritizing Teacher Empowerment and Collaborative Decisionmaking

In our early implementation of FirstSchool, we realized how important it was for leadership to drive a prioritization of our principles that empowered teachers to make adjustments that they might otherwise have been wary of initiating and that provided them with structure and guidance in moving forward. Subsequently, we decided to work harder to develop relationships with leaders at the school and district level as well as with individual teachers, attacking problems from both ends to achieve better congruence and alignment of goals. This meant asking schools to share the ownership and onus of change, while asking leadership to realize that part of taking responsibility for improving student outcomes includes improving the professional lives of the teachers in their district.

Since leaders are already positioned in ways that allow them to be proactive, they are the first line of defense against policies and practices that diminish teachers and restrict opportunities for their development. We know how overwhelming even just one school day can be for teachers who are charged with responding to the diverse emotional and academic needs of the children under their care, and we cannot have teachers shouldering the burden of advancing their development without support or feedback. Ideally, teachers need help from caring administrators who can tackle problems with them and work to make their jobs easier.

However, within this call to action, we should acknowledge that administrators and district personnel are also overworked and pressured. To adequately tackle the enormity of these tasks, many more resources, including people power, are needed. In addition, leaders face barriers to controlling the hiring and staffing process. Too often, they must combat historical trends like students from low-income settings being more likely to experience inconsistency in teacher quality, resulting in the potential for multiple years in a row of poor instruction for children who keep getting assigned to ineffective classrooms (Gordon, Kane, & Staiger, 2006), or like teachers in struggling schools with high populations of AALLI children being more likely to be inexperienced (Adamson & Darling-Hammond, 2011; Lankford, Loeb, & Wyckoff, 2002). These trends only compound other limiting factors such as a lack of funding, scarce professional development opportunities, and the challenge of complying with state or federal policies while managing day-to-day tasks such as safety, student behavior, and communication with families and the community. This means that leaders cannot do it alone, which makes gaining the trust and respect of their staff, while engaging them in reform, vital to their efforts.

Because tackling whole-school reform on the scale that FirstSchool required was no small task, our administrators soon eased their own burden by providing excellent teachers with the space to share their skills and guide their colleagues within vertical teams that spanned a school's hierarchical structures. Although we saw that the PLC structure was one way for teachers to take their colleagues forward, we asked schools to consider other options: How else could they create a broader sense of teacher leadership that avoided highlighting or empowering just a few individuals or confining teachers to token representation? How could these opportunities help teachers feel empowered to run their classrooms in ways that they think make sense for their students and make meaningful contributions to school-level decisions? Teachers should feel some control over the process of reforms like FirstSchool, so that after administrators lay the groundwork by establishing frameworks for change and communicating key priorities, they have the opportunity to shape what the application of those priorities will look like and develop their own leadership capabilities (Boyd-Dimock & McGree, 1994; Task Force on Teacher Leadership, 2001; Terry, 1997; Waters, Marzano, & McNulty, 2003).

Focusing Leaders on Improving AALLI Outcomes

In addition to expecting leaders to facilitate collaborative inquiry and reflection, we also relied on them to keep conversation focused on meeting the needs of AALLI students and improving their schooling experiences. While problems with teacher assignment, distribution of human resources, legislative demands, and diminished resources affect many schools that serve disadvantaged children, we do not believe that the changes we propose are impossible, even under the difficult circumstances that have traditionally limited AALLI children's access to quality education. Furthermore, while many administrators, central office staff, and teachers are already working incredibly hard to improve the lives of poor and minority children, this energy could be channeled differently to move schools in an even more positive and purposeful direction.

Although our ability to collaborate with schools began with just a few deep, multiyear partnerships, the principles that drive FirstSchool can all be implemented by willing leaders who make AALLI populations a priority, and engage their teachers in understanding the concrete ways that their instruction affects student learning, while fostering relationships within their school community that will help make these efforts relevant to particular contexts for teaching and learning. To begin thinking about how to do so, there are two things leaders should consider first:

- What grade-level teams, administrators, and other educational leaders are already doing to systematically address patterns of lower achievement among AALLI populations
- How staff and teachers can be organized on the ground level to best target AALLI needs and work collaboratively to connect those results to their curriculum and instruction

If administrators work to develop teachers' professional potential within shared transformation missions, they can also help mitigate the tendency for teachers in struggling schools to be vilified as failures or held solely responsible for student progress. Furthermore, by spurring collective action to improve early grades experiences for AALLI children, they can offset overemphasizing end results without considering how the quality of educational experiences provided during a student's foundational years may have affected those outcomes.

Offering Teachers Better Support

Many of our leaders needed guidance in tackling the range of professional development needs within diverse school settings. Being well prepared to support teachers in improving conditions for AALLI children begins with understanding that their professional identity development is a complex and ongoing process (Beijaard, Verloop, & Vermunt, 2000; Gee, 2000). Determining how to effectively handle instruction and be responsive to students is not easily accomplished—nor should it be. As teachers refine their teaching approach, they encounter a variety of influences on their practice, such as their own personal background, culture, experiences with schooling, training programs, advice from mentors and colleagues, and workplace norms that they must sift through and consider. They may also have acquired beliefs about their teaching in response to interactions with the children and families that they serve (Haniford, 2009; Lasky, 2005; Merseth, Sommer, & Dickstein, 2008). This creates a complicated and interwoven set of perspectives for administrators and teachers to take into account as they begin to discuss possible reform and adjustments to practice.

In addition, it can be hard to enforce certain nonnegotiable standards for performance while leaving room for unique and individualized teaching styles to blossom. We recognize that, at times, administrators may need to get tough about bottom-line expectations. Some teachers will need substantial help, while others may simply need encouragement and appreciation for their talent and efforts. Others may resist suggestions or remain apathetic to reform priorities. Sometimes novice teachers will struggle with trying to reach the same objectives as masters of the craft, while at other times their early passion and sense of innovation may guide veterans toward change. FirstSchool seeks to provide leaders with a few framing principles that can help them organize their interactions with teachers and empower them to work within broad guidelines that can be differentiated in response to particular scenarios and learning contexts. The chapters in Part II of this volume provide further specifics about how to approach reform in ways that allow teachers to provide input and feel supported while still holding them responsible for maintaining excellence.

SIGNS OF PROGRESS

We hope that readers of this volume will be able to turn to this chapter both to launch their thinking about the conditions necessary for improving schooling for AALLI children and to reflect on the success of subsequent efforts in creating a positive culture for change. Perhaps you are a district leader working with principals to guide their teacher evaluation process, or a principal trying to reinvigorate your School Improvement Team. Perhaps you are providing professional development that you hope will be more engaging than the standard, sit-and-listen seminars that rarely end up having lasting effects. Regardless of your role, you probably feel the pressure caused by limited time and resources, as well as the enormity of school improvement needs. How will you know when deeply rooted, sustainable change has actually started to occur?

As FirstSchool researchers, we collected data and then shared results with principals, teachers, and other school community members who could utilize our findings to institute reform. As a result, while constant evaluation of our own process through follow-up observations, surveys, and other more summative means of assessing success helped us determine where we stood in terms of influencing instructional practice, we also began to note examples of ways that we could see change happening within school culture, even if it was incremental. For instance, staff meetings now had a different tenor; teachers were more engaged in their content, and a variety of voices were part of the conversation. Grade- and school-level goals that focused around improving instructional experiences for AALLI children were guided through collaborative reflection and decisions about further professional development.

In your own school setting, success may look very different from what we saw in each of our partner schools. Through our own series of trials and errors,

Measuring Changes in Mindset:
FirstSchool's Impact on Professional Settings

Educational change can often be difficult to see or identify. After all, children still come to a building that pretty much looks like it did before; teachers still develop and deliver lessons, give hugs, and send home newsletters; leaders still keep the big picture in mind, hold meetings, and evaluate teachers. While you can walk into a building or a classroom and feel the happiness of the teachers, the students, and the families, such evidence is difficult to quantify. While student achievement data is measurable, it is not necessarily the best or only gauge that a school is effective or that it is moving in the right direction. So how does one know that substantial, positive change in school culture has occurred or is occurring?

One of the places we were able to document change was in the conversations that were taking place throughout the schools. Schools and grade-level teams that had adopted FirstSchool principles and a culture of collaborative inquiry significantly changed what they were talking about as well as who was doing the talking and the level of enthusiasm regarding the conversation.

When we first began our work with schools, faculty meetings were generally focused on the business of school and completing logistical tasks. The principal did most of the talking and teachers were at best complacent and compliant in their attendance at these meetings. Grade-level meetings were similar in nature, with the grade-level chair doing most of the talking, and matters such as field-trip logistics, selection of worksheets for in-class work and homework, and plans for remediation were the popular topics. Each teacher bided her time until she could leave and get on with her "real" work.

However, as we got further into the partnership, we saw some dynamic shifts. Schoolwide and grade-level meetings were becoming more characterized by energized discussions that involved a number of participants. No one person or small group held all the power and/or all the wisdom for the group; expertise of many was now being more broadly recognized and appreciated. Grade-level teams were seen as productive times so they added more meeting times to their schedules and initiated meeting with other grade levels to gain a better understanding of where students were coming from and where they were going. The content of the conversation also changed to an emphasis on teaching and learning and included a focus on developmental science, AALLI children, and the research base behind quality teaching. Teachers began capably articulating the rationale for the instructional decisions they were advocating and became more forthcoming with ideas and information about what they were trying with their students and the results, as well as the challenges they were experiencing. Although there were still differences of expressed opinion and practice, there was still a unified purpose of and dedicated interest in doing what was best for the students. A "one-size-*doesn't*-fit-all" approach was becoming accepted and valued for the adults just as it was taking root for students.

Teachers and leaders offered affirmation of these shifts through their comments on FirstSchool sessions:

> *"By examining my data from the FirstSchool Snapshot it helps me be in charge of my own professional learning."*

> *"What we are doing now is not effective (not reaching all students), so it is okay to change."*

> *"We are restructuring—but not by moving chairs or bricks—we aren't going to just buy a new program—we are changing our instructional approach . . . (and) feel empowered to do it and to modify our existing programs to better meet students' needs."*

we often found ourselves adjusting our methods and customizing reform to match a particular school's needs and interests. We encourage you to strike your own balance between utilizing the goals that inspired initial reform as a touchstone to help maintain focus and remaining flexible to necessary adjustments.

Working Within the System

We know that individual leaders and teachers will not be able to completely erase the systematic norms that define early schooling in this country—and in some cases, they may not want to. Standards, policies, and regulations play a part in organizing our pedagogy and connecting the services that teachers provide to equality of opportunity. In that spirit, we have encouraged leaders to use the FirstSchool approach to supplement baseline guides to improvement, and to boost the professional status of classroom leaders by promoting excellence while respecting their expertise. For instance, at one elementary school, the principal decided to use FirstSchool data in combination with standard state evaluation metrics to discuss teacher's practice and identify areas of improvement. Our data informed the required rubric and helped her provide more meaningful, useful feedback to teachers that remained aligned with those expectations.

Of course, this is just one example of how our approach complements existing educational policy, allowing leaders to boost the support they offer teachers, while remaining aligned with broader performance expectations. Throughout our work with schools, we have seen several examples of how to enhance teachers' professional lives through adjustments to current practice. For instance, one partner told us, "What hooked me is that what FirstSchool is about is exactly what the Common Core is [higher level and deeper thinking], so I know that doing what FirstSchool talks about is taking me in the right direction." In Chapter 1 we also describe related reform efforts like the Power of K, which gave experienced kindergarten teachers from across the state of North Carolina the chance to reflect on their practice, enhance their expertise, and return to the classroom feeling re-energized, while also serving as a model for others on their grade level. We encourage you to research promising models of improvement, talk to others within in the field, and consider how to incorporate broad ideas that mesh with your goals for improvement into your specific school setting.

Moving into the Book

In Part II we demonstrate how specific approaches to data collection, curricular planning, instructional delivery, and home–school partnerships can benefit AALLI children and further the FirstSchool transformation mission. We hope that readers will be able to apply lessons we have learned within these areas to their own unique contexts. In particular, we are calling upon leaders at all levels within the educational system to provide the structural support necessary to drive change forward. It is our belief that although this process begins with establishing a certain mindset and attitude toward reform, leaders play a vital role in creating pathways for discussion and action, as well as sustaining these efforts over time. This chapter has emphasized the concrete ways in which work culture can affect teachers' professional status and sense of agency as they determine how to approach the classroom. As policies and procedures affect teachers' instructional decisions, they ultimately impact their ability to serve students and improve their schooling experiences. Therefore, groundwork to improve a working culture for teachers and examine the ways that current policies impact their practice is foundational to our cause. Leaders must make transformation that benefits AALLI children a priority, and value teachers' contributions to those efforts, while working within existing regulations and mandates. If this crucial step is overlooked, the road ahead will be filled with challenges, instead of the potential that it could hold.

Part II

CHANGE THAT MATTERS

CHAPTER 3

A Culture of Collaborative Inquiry

Adam L. Holland, Gisele M. Crawford,
Sharon Ritchie, and Diane M. Early

> The data gave me an awareness of my teaching practices from the
> students' point of view. While I am an advocate for all of my students, I
> find myself advocating the most for those who come to school each day
> in need of extra support. The data equip me with the information to prove
> that students who need more time in small-group instruction are not
> necessarily receiving it.
>
> —Erin Millspaugh, 3rd-grade teacher

Using data lies at the heart of FirstSchool's efforts to transform schools. From the beginning, we have focused heavily on providing teachers, administrators, and families with information, skills, and dispositions that will create positive changes in their practices for the benefit of all students, particularly African American, Latino, and low-income (AALLI) children. As the quote above illustrates, data can provide practitioners with a new lens through which to view everyday occurrences in a classroom. We want the effective use of data to motivate teachers to move beyond old habits in order to effect changes in their classrooms, as well as in their school cultures at large. This is particularly important for those students on the wrong side of the achievement gap who have, for so many years, not had their needs met in schools. While the approaches described within the FirstSchool framework could benefit all children, we believe that these groups of students are particularly in need of coherent improvement strategies and well-functioning learning environments. It is important that we use data to help illuminate habits and routines that hinder the success of AALLI children, and spotlight instructional practices that support their success.

In this chapter we begin by describing a measure that is key to our work with educators; then we consider the attitudes and beliefs that underlie successful use of data and explain the FirstSchool framework for using data in schools. Throughout we illustrate our points through vignettes and stories from our own work and explain how these ideas may be applied more broadly.

THE FIRSTSCHOOL SNAPSHOT

Throughout this chapter we examine multiple sources of data and suggest a variety of tools for collecting relevant information about classroom experiences and instructional patterns. However, we begin by providing a description of a key measure that guides our work with educators and that we use to illustrate many of the points we make. The data provided by the FirstSchool Snapshot (Ritchie et al., 2007; Ritchie, Weiser, et al., 2010) offer an innovative way of looking at instruction. The measure was created by a number of education researchers over several decades. The latest iteration is focused specifically on the PreK–3rd grade continuum and gives a minute-by-minute account of children's activity settings (e.g., whole group, small group, transitions), learning content (e.g., reading, science, math), and teaching approaches (e.g., didactic, scaffolded instruction). This information allows teachers not only to see objectively how much time is spent on various tasks and activities but also how they teach these subjects. By crossing the codes on the measure, teachers may see whether they are more likely to engage in didactic instruction during math or literacy, whether they are instructing science in small groups to the extent that they want, or whether children are engaged in collaborative conversations as part of their project work during a social studies unit. The ability to combine various codes allows an exceptionally nuanced view of how instruction occurs in a classroom. Therefore, information gathered using the FirstSchool Snapshot to capture a full day of teaching and learning is quite rich and provides a detailed picture of children's experiences in the classroom previously unavailable to teachers.

FirstSchool completed at least 2 days of FirstSchool Snapshot observation in each classroom involved in our research project, one toward the beginning and one toward the end of the school's participation in FirstSchool. The resulting data was provided to participants at the individual teacher, grade, and school level. Teachers and school administrators have found the FirstSchool Snapshot data informative and helpful as they seek to improve instruction. The data have been the catalyst for discussion across multiple realms. For example, we discovered that students in many PreK through 3rd-grade classrooms spent more than a third of their day (about 2 hours) in a whole-group setting wherein all students engaged in the same activity. On the other hand, students spent fairly little time (approximately 5% of the day, or about 20 min) in small groups working with an adult or working with peers on activities selected by the teacher. Furthermore, it was evident that transitions (e.g., moving through the halls or waiting for the next activity to begin) took close to 25% of the day (about 100 min), significantly detracting from the amount of time spent on instruction. Teachers also saw that children were engaged in gross motor activities for only about 4% of the day (about 16 min) and that they were engaged in meaningful dialogue with teachers for just 6% of the time (about 24 min). Seeing this information for their own classroom, their grade-level, or their school prompted reflection and group conversations about how time might be better used to support children's success.

As teachers made changes either to intentionally decrease or increase time spent on certain activities, the impact was dramatic. We saw that very small changes could make a big difference in instructional time over the course of a school year:

- 3% = 12 minutes/day, 60 minutes/week, 2700 minutes/year = 12 days/year = 2+ weeks more of instructional time
- 5% = 20 minutes/day, 100 minutes/week, 4500 minutes/year = 20 days/year = 4 weeks more of instructional time
- 10% = 40 minutes/day, 200 minutes/week, 9000 minutes/year = 40 days/year = 8 weeks more of instructional time

Figures 3.1 and 3.2 are examples of the graphs that our educators received after being observed using the FirstSchool Snapshot measure. The first graph depicts the percentage of time that children spent in different activity settings throughout the day, and the second graph shows the percentage of time children spent in the different learning activities that comprise literacy instruction.

Schools that are not engaged with FirstSchool may not have access to the detailed, minute-by-minute information provided by the FirstSchool Snapshot. However, reflection on these issues can come from other approaches. As described in Chapter 1, inquiry into practice can be sparked by teachers reviewing data from *other* schools. In our experience, simply seeing another way to think about their instructional day causes teachers to reflect on their own classroom practices and evaluate if their instructional time is being optimally spent.

Another possibility is for teachers to collect some similar information in their own class or the classes of their colleagues in a more targeted format. For instance, if a group of teachers decided they were concerned with the length of their transitions, they could start logging the start and end time of each transition during the day, using a small note pad or handheld device kept in their pocket (for teachers with an assistant in the classroom, the assistant could be given this task). Then, at the end of a week, they could calculate the number of

Figure 3.1. School-Level Activity Settings

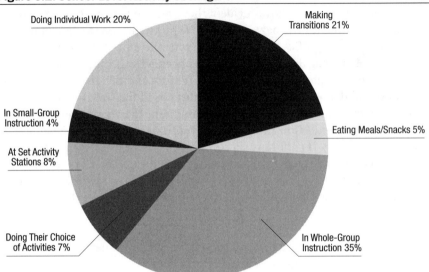

Figure 3.2. Components of Literacy

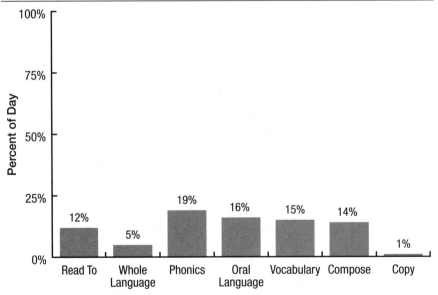

Introducing Collaborative Inquiry

Because our participants have never been asked to examine this type of detailed data before, learning how to effectively utilize information about their classroom instruction becomes part of a continual development process. We consistently observe patterns that educators move through as they become more used to using data for inquiry into their practice:

1. Blame ("It was a test prep day." "These people don't know what they are talking about.")
2. Denial ("We don't do that.")
3. Frustration ("That's terrible that we do so little X or so much Y.")
4. Acceptance and inquiry ("What can we do to make this different?")

As teachers become proficient in understanding and interpreting the data, we hear a variety of comments, especially as they observe changes made from one observation period to the next:

"I am happy to see that we are spending 13% of our time focused on vocabulary development because we noticed how little of that we were doing last time. This is true not just at our grade level, so it means this is becoming part of our school culture."

Teachers who are satisfied with changes they have made may continue to monitor their progress or seek to gain more fine-grained information, such as what teaching approaches are being used with a focus on teacher–student and peer interaction to ensure and support learning.

"That is too much whole-group time. I want there to be less."

Teachers who wish to make changes in activity settings may then think purposefully about how to reduce the time children spend in too-prevalent activity settings and what other types of activity settings might benefit children (e.g., by increasing small-group or free-choice time).

"I see that the research tells us that many of the things we want to have happen for children happen during time when children have choices and we only do that 2% of the day."

Often, teachers do not independently set up the activity settings in their classrooms. Rather, time spent in settings such as whole-group instruction or individual seatwork is dictated or influenced by school or district policies. Teachers armed with information about how children use their time, as well as the research that supports the importance of choice, are well-equipped to have frank discussions with school and district leadership about changes that could be made to improve children's experiences and increase flexibility in their instruction.

"We cut our transition time by 30 minutes per day. That translates into 12 whole school days over the course of the year."

Often, data provide the means to gauge successes. Few things are more heartening to professionals than seeing the fruits of their labors in the data and seeing how small changes led to improved instructional experiences for their students.

"We think we are so lucky to see this data. Not everyone gets to know so much about what happens in their classrooms."

Using data often begets more data use. When teachers see the power of data to provide a new lens on their practice, they often find more creative ways to use systematic information to shape and improve their pedagogy.

"If we're spending 40% of our time in didactic instruction, 15% in scaffolding, and 2% in reflection—what is happening the other 43% of the time?"

Often, teachers cannot see their own practice effectively. Here, teachers may wish to further investigate why so much of the day features children working without instruction. Some of this time may be used well as children work with one another or practice previously taught skills. Other time, however, may be ripe for additional teacher input to help scaffold students' learning. Gathering more data will allow these teachers to discriminate between the two scenarios.

"We're pleased to see that there is a connection between our kindergarten and 1st-grade classrooms in the area of whole language instruction. It looks like we are moving slowly from an emphasis on phonics to a focus on whole language skills."

Data gathered in classrooms may be most effectively acted upon when it is paired with extant research on best practices from peer-reviewed journals. Here, teachers are moving to act on research that suggests a more balanced literacy approach rather than one relying entirely on phonics. The information gathered provides the means to confirm that such changes are occurring vertically throughout the school.

minutes spent in transition and divide that by the total minutes in school to get a percentage of time spent in transitions. A similar method could be used to estimate the amount of time spent in whole group or small group, time spent in reading or math, and so on. We describe how involving teachers in collecting and discussing data contributes to developing a culture of collaborative inquiry in the section below.

Attitudes and Beliefs

Within a culture of collaborative inquiry, educators study their own teaching, identify areas for improvement, and test novel solutions. Many school transformation processes create *structural* changes within the school with the expectation that change in teaching practice, and thus better student learning outcomes, will automatically follow (Elmore, 1995). At FirstSchool, we believe that changes in beliefs and attitudes are necessary before changes in process or structure can result in significant improvements. For example, in recent years many principals have prioritized creating time for professional learning communities (PLCs) to meet during the school day by providing coverage for classes during lunch, recess, or "specials" such as art or music. However, simply providing the time does not ensure that teachers will be able to use it to focus on using data to improve instruction. Without guidance and support to focus on effective ways to use data to monitor progress and promote change and growth, many teachers simply use this time to hold grade-level meetings about upcoming school events, needs for supplies or volunteers, or personnel concerns. It is only when teachers and leaders agree to dedicate PLC time exclusively to improving instruction that they will effectively and knowledgeably utilize the time provided to them. That being said, we also often see PLCs that do center on data but end up focusing on the outcomes of instruction rather than the processes that lead to academic progress. While there is some utility in examining such things as end-of-grade test scores, we believe the major focus of PLC time should be on *using* data to guide and monitor teaching practices, rather than simply treating it as an end unto itself.

In Chapter 2 we discuss at length the need for reinvigorating professionalism. That process is dependent on the development of a culture of collaborative inquiry wherein educators display the confidence to explore challenges. They safely express the need to improve their practice and, as a group, take concrete steps toward that end. Unfortunately, school cultures and structures often conspire, albeit unintentionally and perhaps unknowingly, to promote apathy and negativity. A ceaseless round of new initiatives; top-down leadership; criticism from parents, community leaders, and the media; and the general stress of teaching all serve to demotivate teachers and create a climate of fear with regard to exposing one's weaknesses or challenges. Therefore, creation of a community of learners who feel safe and respected requires not just a shift in the mindset of teachers, but in the mindset of all those stakeholders who affect and support them. When leaders at all levels support teachers' competence and autonomy through relationships built on genuine trust and respect, then fertile ground is created for real change to occur. This then begs a pair of questions: What mindset best enables practitioners to use data for positive gains? How can school leadership facilitate the formation of such attitudes?

Teachers rarely develop a reflective mindset under conditions that fail to support recognition that their practice is not perfect without fear of reprisal. There are a number of factors that prevent practitioners from honestly and safely admitting to shortcomings. Often, this is a result of teachers' achievement goal orientations.

Much research has been conducted on students' achievement goal orientations, with studies suggesting that two major types of achievement goal

What Is Reflective Teaching?

When I was doing my student teaching, we had to teach a lesson and then write a two-page reflection about what went well and what went poorly. I never got the guidance I needed to understand why I should do this. It quickly became just one more assignment I had to complete to pass the course. Many teachers take the same attitude toward reflective practice. It's just one more assignment to complete in an already busy day; one that often seems to distract from more important day-to-day matters like setting up centers or attending IEP meetings. This is unfortunate.

Far from being an added chore, I have come to find that reflective practice is integrated into excellent teachers' professional lives, providing a mechanism for constant improvement. For me, reflective practice is the act of approaching my pedagogy with the belief that it is not perfect and could be improved. Teachers engaging in this process acknowledge this fact and actively look for the shortcomings in their own practice. They watch diligently for success when it occurs. By watching and noticing, teachers engaging in reflective practice are primed to act on these occurrences, resulting in teaching that improves daily rather than stagnating due to complacency. It is the actions teachers take to improve their practice that are the real benefit of reflective teaching.

—Adam Holland, researcher and former kindergarten teacher

orientations emerge: mastery and performance (Eccles & Wigfield, 2002; Pintrich & Schunk, 2002). Those with a mastery goal orientation focus on engaging in learning activities for the purpose of gaining understanding and improving skills and knowledge, while those possessing a performance goal orientation tend to focus on attaining favorable judgments of competence or avoiding criticisms of ability (Meece, Anderman, & Anderman, 2006). Teachers who focus on students demonstrating high ability and competing for grades or recognition play a role in building a classroom goal orientation that is focused on performance while teachers who focus on developing skills and improving understanding in their students build a classroom goal orientation that is focused on mastery (Kaplan, Middleton, Urdan, & Midgley, 2002). Students in each of these classroom types tend to adopt for themselves the goal orientation in the classroom (Urdan, 2004).

Although much of the research in this area has focused on children and adolescents, we see a parallel process when teachers are the learners. Teachers who possess a mastery orientation often engage in reflective practice by viewing data as feedback and valuable information that can be used to improve practice. Teachers who are oriented to performance, on the other hand, tend to view data as a criticism of their teaching ability, particularly when the information suggests that things are not perfect. In order to facilitate teachers' adopting a reflective mindset, they must first adopt a mastery goal orientation.

However, because teachers' goal orientations may also be influenced by their schools and districts, school leaders can play an important role in helping teachers develop a reflective mindset. When administrators focus heavily on end-of-grade test scores and performance evaluations, they remove the emphasis from the process of improving practice and place it firmly upon the outcomes themselves. Such practices lead to teachers who feel the need to justify or explain away bad scores so that they may continue to view themselves as capable educators. When administrators instead focus on the process of constant improvement, using test scores and evaluations as feedback to provoke positive changes, teachers are exposed to, and have the opportunity to develop, a mastery goal orientation. This way, they are more able to first emphasize the *process* and later the outcome. Such practices lead to practitioners who feel comfortable admitting shortcomings and building upon the information their administrators provide them rather than feeling the need to defend themselves.

As we work with teachers and help them move toward a reflective mindset, there are a number of things we do to establish a climate that allows them to move away from a performance goal orientation and toward a mastery goal orientation. First, personally identifiable FirstSchool Snapshot data is shared only with individual teachers. Administrators receive data aggregated at the grade and school level, but individual teachers are the only ones who are able to view data on exactly what happens in their classrooms. This frees them from the worry that they are being evaluated, judged, or compared to their colleagues. We avoid using evaluative statements during our meetings with teachers, instead allowing them to notice their own challenges and the successes upon which to build. As we work with teachers year after year, it is gratifying to see them move from justifying or placing blame for their data on others to accepting and using the data to explore and drive the change process. Ultimately, we aim for school cultures where teachers feel safe in sharing their data with the knowledge that it is used to guide and monitor practice and change.

Structures and Processes

When educators adopt a mastery goal orientation and begin to adapt practices that support reflective teaching, processes and structures must be in place to facilitate those practices, particularly the use of data in schools.

Lessons from the Field: Time to Adjust

Over the past few years we've learned a lot about the challenges of presenting data. We were presenting teachers with both a unique way to view their practice and an unfamiliar process. In the beginning the data bewildered them. They did not know how to read it, make sense of it, or engage with others about its meaning or implications. They needed a lot of time to digest it, and we needed to recognize and support the steps they needed to take to wade slowly into the work.

For the most part, teachers responded to areas where they thought they could make changes. Transition time was immediately identified as an area of improvement by teachers and administrators alike, as they were often startled by how much time transitions took from their instructional day. Vocabulary also caught their attention both because they were impressed by the research that strongly indicated the importance of strong vocabulary for ongoing success, and because it was a change that felt achievable. Over the course of the project, time spent on transitions went from 21% of the day to 18%; time spent building vocabulary rose from 3% of the day to 6%. Allowing time for teachers to absorb the data, make sense of it, choose attainable goals, and begin to share their ideas with others was an essential step toward deeper analysis of the data and reflection on practice.

Discussion Questions

1. How is a focus on relationships, inquiry, and reflection evident in your
    current learning situation (college class, professional development,
    and so on)?
2. Does this kind of climate support your learning? In what ways?

Although it is certainly possible for teachers to engage in reflective practice
alone, collaborating with other professionals provides some key opportunities to grow and change that are not afforded when they work by themselves.
We have found Vygotsky's (1986) work on interactive learning holds true for
teachers as they take on the role of learners. Rather than counting on teachers
to engage only in self-directed processes, collaborative inquiry enables teachers to learn in an interactive context, provide support for others' learning, and
receive support for their own inquiry processes. As professionals representing
multiple perspectives come to the table with a mutual desire to effect positive
changes for young children, they broaden the view, provide expertise, and act
as "critical friends," taking ownership of their practices while aiding one another through the provision of honest feedback (Lord, 1994; for more detail,
see Chapter 2 of this volume).

Time is a scarce resource for teachers (Ritchie & Crawford, 2009). Most
of the practitioners with whom we work espouse a sincere desire to collaborate for the purpose of improving their pedagogy but are frustrated by the
lack of time available to engage in such activities. What little time they have
away from their classes rapidly becomes occupied by necessities such as setting up centers, grading assignments, and completing necessary paperwork.
We believe that it is crucial for leaders to find creative ways to make time for
staff to meet and grow through an inquiry-based process including time out
of the classroom to plan, discuss, and work with other, similarly motivated,
staff members. Teachers need to work with leaders to identify times and spac-
es that, through the implementation of small structural changes, could allow
increased opportunities for teachers to collaborate with one another. Regardless of the nature of the changes, altering school structures is rarely easy. The
inertia of standard operation often stands in the way of enacting necessary
changes. Therefore, leaders and teachers will have to *consciously prioritize* in
order to change the things that truly matter—those areas that allow them to
better address the current challenges facing their classrooms, schools, and districts. In Part III of this book, we talk about larger state and district policies
that need to be in place to provide this important time and highlight efforts in
other countries to do so.

Lessons from the Field: Planning Time

At one of our schools common planning time was already firmly in place. These regular grade-level meetings gave teachers the time and place to more fully explore their data and to slowly make it their own. The common planning time offered the opportunity to use the data to develop goals and objectives and determine what they wanted students to know, and how they were going to find out if they learned it. It allowed them to decide ahead of time how to define desired change, and clarified necessary steps to get students where they wanted them. In the long run, using their common planning time in this way meant they came to more deeply understand children's progress and problems.

THE RELEVANT DATA CYCLE

Collecting, analyzing, and applying data are important for all educators. Many teachers will not have access to the type of minute-by-minute data provided by the FirstSchool Snapshot. In this section, we explore the FirstSchool approach to the effective use of the wide array of data that educators routinely receive or can collect. Our approach is cyclical and involves three steps: (1) *identifying an issue and choosing a data source,* (2) *collection and analysis of data,* and (3) *intentional application.* Because this process is cyclical, assessments and other types of data are *always* considered to be formative rather than summative. Student performance on an end-of-quarter reading assessment, for example, should drive reading instruction during the ensuing quarter. Excessive absences during the 1st semester in a teacher's class should drive efforts to connect with families and find strategies to ensure the students arrive at school each day ready to learn. Even state-mandated, standardized tests conducted at the end of the year provide information that should drive teachers' efforts during the next year.

Identifying an Issue and Choosing a Data Source

Other than data being used against teachers in a manner that is critical and unhelpful, the major problem many teachers have with data is not knowing how to use it. Well-meaning state and district policies often require teachers to collect reams of data on their students. However, such initiatives often serve only to further burn teachers out, as they spend hours and days collecting information that has little value to them as professionals. When teachers first identify an issue that they think is important to examine, the

---

Discussion Questions

1. What barriers or supports to finding time for collaboration and inquiry do you encounter in your setting?
2. What structural changes are possible in your setting?

---

question of what to do with the resulting data becomes more readily apparent. The issues practitioners may investigate vary widely. They may involve learning more about children and their unique needs, examining an area of classroom practice that is suboptimal, or working with others to better understand issues of school climate and policy. The impetus for the desire to learn more may arise from a number of sources. Sometimes teachers notice a classroom dynamic they wish to investigate more fully. They may wish to try something new in order to decide if it works better than current practice. Test results may highlight a deficiency or area that bears further investigation. In each of these cases, the teacher has a desire to learn more about her or his practice or ecology. Data are the means through which teachers will gain this new knowledge.

After identifying an issue, teachers must then find a source of information that will help them better understand the problem. In each case, the source of the data should match the issue. Teachers examining student achievement will need to gather information from their students using either published or self-created assessments. Those wishing to examine their own pedagogy or classroom environment may choose to have a colleague observe them using an observational protocol that focuses on the particular aspect of their practice into which they wish to gain insight. Members of a leadership team focusing on school behavior may wish to survey teachers and accumulate data on office referrals. What is important is that teachers think critically about what they wish to learn and then explore how they might go about gaining more information on the subject. The following are a list of four data sources that FirstSchool has used to some advantage in our work. In each section, we have also included an example of a measure we have found useful in our own work in deriving data from these sources.

Student

Student data includes information pertaining to individual students. This information may be demographic, like gender and ethnicity, or provide information about student progress in a variety of areas. For example, a teacher may use informal assessments to determine a student's level

Lessons from the Field: Identifying an Issue

Through participation in FirstSchool, teachers were able to look at school- and grade-level patterns in their FirstSchool Snapshot data and link them to other school data. At Bogue Sound Elementary School, the population was two-thirds boys and one-third girls, and the boys were simply not doing as well as the girls. They were having a hard time navigating school on every level, particularly in the area of literacy. Teachers wanted to learn more about boys' experiences in school and how to motivate their interest in reading and writing.

With support from FirstSchool staff and an expert in early literacy, Bogue Sound teachers made use of their interpretation of multiple sources of data as well as their day-to-day experiences with boys in the context of literacy instruction. Teachers explored boys' learning styles through brain research, and subsequently included more movement during instructional time and provided more physical space for learning experiences. They looked at the books they were using in their classrooms and made informed choices about adding both fiction and nonfiction that more fully engaged the boys. They used "wondering questions" and discovered children's ability to think critically and learned about the things that interested them. They learned how to use their analysis of reading a story to help children write better stories. They moved from basics like identification of the "front of the book" and the illustrator, to engaging children in the analysis of story construction: interesting beginnings, story resolution, and "juicy" words. These practices enabled children not only to be better readers, but better writers as well. Children wrote more frequently, used richer vocabulary and included content from areas of science and social studies.

The outcome of this work was that the teachers fell in love with the boys—they better understood them, ceased viewing their behaviors as challenges or affronts, and instead took the view of "Oh . . . they are just being boys!" to understand why these behaviors were happening. Discipline referrals went down, and teachers' stress was reduced. They had elevated expectations for the boys and marveled at the things they could achieve. Our FirstSchool data told them that they were doing more vocabulary development and more scaffolded and less didactic instruction, and that their kids were doing more writing, movement, talking, and collaboration with peers. They more fully integrated subjects like social studies and science with literacy development.

of mastery regarding an academic objective like counting or reading sight words. These data inform instructional practice. While much of the information collected by teachers and schools pertains to academic progress, educators should also collect information about student's social, physical, and language development.

With primary-grade classrooms averaging above 20 students, teachers are challenged with meeting the needs of individual students while maintaining an overall engaging classroom climate. FirstSchool has found that promoting conversations among teaching staff around data helps teachers dissect the overall classroom climate into smaller, more manageable parts that influence individual students. Conversations at one school prompted teachers and First-School staff to review research confirming that by interacting with students in a responsive, warm, individualized manner, teachers can build classroom environments in which students and teachers establish close relationships that let students feel physically and emotionally safe while exploring classroom learning opportunities (Howes & Ritchie, 2002). Teachers then discussed how to improve instructional experiences for students who needed to spend more time during the day receiving support and guidance.

One useful tool for gathering data on this is the Student–Teacher Relationship Scale (Pianta, 2001), a self-reported measure designed to help teachers reflect on their relationships with specific children. Scores help educators identify relationships that are characterized by affection, warmth, and open communication (closeness); overreliance (dependence); or negativity and conflict (conflict). This kind of knowledge, in the context of inquiry and reflection, helps teachers admit their struggles with some of their students, examine them for racial or gender bias, and ultimately focus on how to improve the relationship—on behalf of both themselves and the children.

Classroom

Classroom data describe the educational environment provided for a particular group of students. Students' learning and growth are heavily influenced by classroom factors, so measuring aspects of this environment is critical to improving school outcomes for young people. These data may then instigate changes in a teacher's instructional style through practice and professional development.

Information for teachers about how students experience a day in their classroom has the potential to improve the quality of interaction and the content and structure of teaching time. Teachers at one FirstSchool partner school made a plan for improving their practice after noting that they spent too little time engaging their students in meaningful dialogue. They collaborated with their peers to explore research related to the importance of dialogue in increasing student engagement in learning and the development of positive teacher–child relationships. The result was that teachers began to engage more often and in more meaningful ways with their students. This ultimately led to increased opportunities for students to use expressive language, build their vocabularies, and develop closer relationships with teachers and one another. We have already discussed how the FirstSchool Snapshot measure can help capture this type of data; however, there are many other means of gathering this information, including the Classroom Assessment Scoring System (CLASS).

The Classroom Assessment Scoring System (Pianta, La Paro, & Hamre, 2008) is an observational instrument designed to measure classroom quality. There is a version of the scale for use in prekindergarten and another for use in kindergarten through 3rd-grade classes. The dimensions of the CLASS are based on developmental theory and research demonstrating that the interactions between students and adults are critically important to the development of students academically and socially.

The interactions between adults and students are grouped into three domains: Emotional Support—the social and emotional functioning within the classroom; Classroom Organization—the broad array of classroom processes related to the organization and management of students' behavior, time, and attention in the classroom; and Instructional Support—the use of curriculum and materials to effectively support cognitive and language development.

A 7-point scale is used to determine the degree of holistic quality in each dimension. A low score of 1–2 indicates the presence of none or few indicators; a mid-score of 3–5 means some indicators were present; and a high score of 6–7 indicates many indicators were evident. Scores are aggregated and reported at the grade, school, and district levels and can be used to identify areas of strength and challenge and to guide practice and professional development by providing a blueprint for making changes in their classrooms.

The graph in Figure 3.3, presented to prekindergarten and kindergarten teachers taking part in FirstSchool, shows the dramatic shift in the emotional support provided for young children as they moved between prekindergarten and kindergarten in schools across the FirstSchool project. The data, coupled with knowledge about the impact of positive relationships on the success of children, helped them review their priorities and think in equal measure about both the emotional and academic experiences for which they were responsible as students transitioned from grade to grade.

Figure 3.3. PreK and K Emotional Support

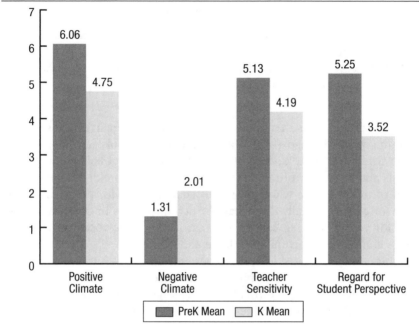

School

Information compiled on groups of students, classrooms, or grade levels can create an overall picture of the school. Figures relating to absences, suspensions, retentions, and teacher working conditions offer details about the prevailing school culture. Such data can allow teachers, administrators, and families to see how schoolwide policies differentially affect individuals or groups of individuals. This is especially important as we help educators investigate whether AALLI children in their school are overrepresented in areas of discipline, referrals, and retention. This information should be used to begin important conversations and shape practices and policies at the school and district level.

FirstSchool has found that using data from the FirstSchool Snapshot to view children's experiences across the PreK–3 continuum, rather than simply focusing on individual classrooms or grade levels, provides educators and researchers the ability to see how children's experiences change, or do not change, as they progress through school. The measure helps identify dramatic shifts in experience throughout a typical day or from grade to grade, as well as periods of static sameness that are unresponsive to children's developmental abilities and needs. For example, the data consistently reveal that the shifts in

Discussion Questions

1. How can you use observational tools to help you be a better observer in classrooms?
2. How can you use research measures to help you focus on specific aspects of classrooms and instruction?

children's experiences as they move from PreK to kindergarten are stark. As seen in the graphs in Figure 3.4, which come from schools across one of the states in which we work, kindergarten children had about half as much time for meals and snacks and time outdoors as they did in prekindergarten. The amount of time spent in whole-group instruction doubled, and their opportunities for choice virtually disappeared. Such disparities in classroom experiences for young children call for increased knowledge about settings that optimize children's opportunities to learn and thrive.

A smooth, coordinated learning experience from age 3 to 8 is important to children and families. Many children in this age range are served by multiple programs, which make it difficult to provide a continuum of learning. The experiences of children and families often vary dramatically depending on the particular program they attend. Even when children this age are served within a single setting such as a public school, continuity from grade to grade may be lacking. Many school communities are looking for ways to provide a more coordinated, systematic approach to serving young children and their families. There are a variety of published tools that schools and districts can use to learn more about various aspects of the learning environment. In many cases, the authors of these tools offer training and other forms of support in using the tools and interpreting the resulting data. A measure that is particularly relevant to improving early education is the Ready School Assessment by the HighScope Educational Research Foundation (2006).

The HighScope Ready School Assessment is a set of questionnaires that guide a schoolwide effort to gather evidence of their successes and challenges on dimensions of leadership; transitions; teacher support; engaging environments; effective curricula; family, school and community partnerships; respecting diversity; and assessing progress. (In Chapter 1 of this volume, we describe the Ready School project undertaken in North Carolina.) Teams that engage in the Ready School process should include early childhood and elementary teachers and leaders, parents, and representatives of community organizations and agencies serving children. While managing a successful collaboration is always challenging (see Chapter 1), the structure offered by an instrument like the Ready School Assessment can greatly increase the chances

Figure 3.4a. Activity Setting—PreK

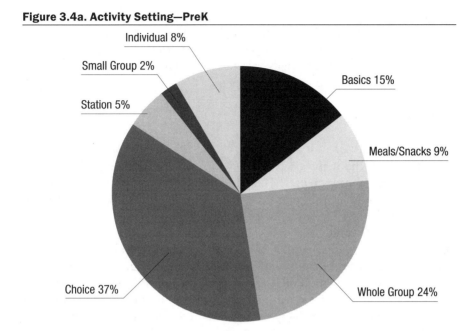

Figure 3.4b. Activity Setting—K

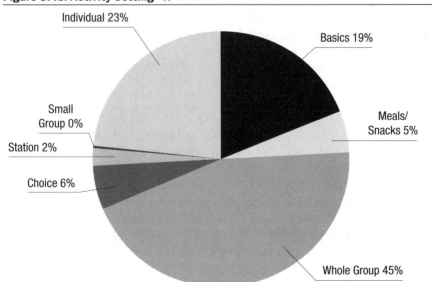

that the process will yield useful results. The HighScope foundation supports local teams by offering training on completing the questionnaires and, once teams have completed their data collection, by providing an online tool that generates a profile showing relative strengths and areas needing improvement and assistance in developing an action plan.

Families

Many parents do not participate in the life of schools in traditional ways. The FirstSchool approach gives them a voice by including them in focus groups and questionnaires. This kind of information promotes dialogue among teachers about their views regarding families and, with practice and attention, ultimately improves home–school relationships and partnerships. Families provide unique insights into children's development and their strengths, interests, and needs. Additionally, parents are uniquely positioned to provide information about family culture, strengths, and experiences. Information from a strength model, rather than the too-prevalent deficit model, is critical for school professionals in order for them to gain a complete picture of students and recognize many of the ways in which families support their children's learning. Although schools rarely include data from families, this type of information is critical if school professionals are to gain a complete picture of students' knowledge and needs.

Another area in which it is often challenging for schools to collect their own information involves gaining the perspective of parents and staff. Questionnaires and focus groups can provide rich data from diverse groups, but can be challenging or costly to create, collect, and analyze. Ensuring that everyone has an opportunity to respond and everyone understands the questions in the same way is critical. Likewise, knowing how to combine information once it has been collected so that it can be used for action requires expertise.

This is an area where partnering with a local university might be especially beneficial for schools. Often faculty and graduate students in university departments of education, sociology, psychology, and anthropology have expertise and interest in the systematic collection of information. Even if no one at a local university specializes in educational research, they can often apply their data collection and interpretation expertise as a way of helping schools. They may be willing to work with an individual school or a district to collect data of interest for school improvement, especially if they are permitted to also collect data that will be valuable to them in their own research. For instance, faculty members in an education program with an interest in educational activities in homes might help to design, distribute, and interpret a parent questionnaire about parents' perceptions of the school if they were permitted to also include some questions about books and reading at home that relate to their scholarly interests.

FirstSchool is housed at the University of North Carolina and has collected questionnaires and focus group data from parents and educators as part of the supports offered to the schools. One FirstSchool value is to foster home-school partnerships, so the questionnaires FirstSchool uses focus specifically on relationships between parents and teachers and schools.

Schools participating in FirstSchool have also each developed a home-school partnership team. Data from these parent questionnaires have been used by the teams to identify strategies for strengthening home–school partnership. For instance, upon seeing the high percentage of parents who reported not being able to help their children with homework, one school reinstated "math afternoons," a time for parents to come together to focus on how to help their children with math. During that conversation, a teacher said, "When we used to do those, every child in the class would have a relative there. Why did we stop doing them?" The evidence that we collected helped her recognize which promising practices might be most useful to reinstate.

Data Collection and Analysis

We have discussed the importance of choosing targeted areas of inquiry and determining the best means for gathering relevant information. However, once teachers have identified an issue and decided upon a data collection measure or technique, they must begin the work of gathering the data. Data collection should be focused and systematic rather than haphazard. That is, it should directly address the issue in step 1 and should provide a detailed picture of its characteristics. Teachers should think carefully about how they will collect their data to maximize efficiency, as time is such a precious commodity for educators, while ensuring the validity of the data. *Validity* is a research term that concerns a tool's ability to measure what it purports to measure. Teachers need to consider how the techniques they are using to collect data may have their validity undermined in various ways. For example, using office referrals to measure the success of school behavior plans is a good first step. However, different teachers have a different tolerance for behavior issues that may result in some teachers sending children to the office for mild violations while others staunchly refuse to send children to the office at all. Therefore, office referrals are often as much teacher-dependent as they are a measure of student behavior. Thoughtful educators will recognize that more information may need to be gathered in order to gain an accurate picture of the issue they are investigating. By front-loading effort and thinking through issues like this at the beginning of the collection process, teachers save themselves time in the long run and ensure more accurate conclusions will be drawn when all the data are collected.

In some cases, raw data provide all the information that teachers need to make decisions. In other cases, though, it is not readily apparent from the data alone what is occurring. In our example of office referrals, each month there is some variance in the number of referrals teachers send to the office. When the school attempts to implement a new classroom community initiative, how will they know if the change in office referrals is a result of the initiative or if it is just due to the variance that occurs naturally from month to month? A question like this is best answered with statistical techniques rather than simply eyeballing and guessing. Schools and teachers may wish to explore district resources that may aid them in gaining some facility with simple statistical techniques or contact university partners who may be able to facilitate more complex analyses.

Intentional Application

Data collected and analyzed are only as useful as the positive changes to which they lead. Step 3 in the process is intentional application. We have found, through our work with teachers, that this step in the cycle is often the most

---

Data Literacy

Data literacy is defined as the knowledge and skill to use various types of data to identify areas of effectiveness and target improvement efforts (Lachat, Williams, & Smith, 2006). This facet of collaborative inquiry is often overlooked in schools. Instead, it is assumed, a priori but often incorrectly, that teachers understand how to engage in a cycle of inquiry that centers on the use of information. However, when teachers engage in inquiry without possessing a high degree of data literacy, the outcomes produced will not be as strong as they would have been if the teachers better understood the various issues involved in collecting, analyzing, and using data. Leaders need to provide opportunities for teachers to gain these skills, which may not have been taught during preservice training or covered during prior professional development opportunities.

Because of its broad definition, data literacy may encompass a wide variety of skills and knowledge sets ranging from familiarity with measurement issues, research design, and basic statistics. While it is not necessary for practitioners to possess these skills at the level of university researchers, having some basic knowledge in these areas should prove useful to those involved in the inquiry process.

rewarding. Teachers and leaders who found data daunting to collect or un-nerving to analyze often find that the true rewards of engaging in this process arise from the tangible changes they make to their practices. These changes, in turn, lead to a greater sense of competence and lower stress. Other times, data confirm what teachers already know but do not have the evidence to support. Possessing data from their own classrooms and schools, teachers are armed to advocate for practices that benefit their students and families. Second-grade teacher Connie Crowe reflects on the impact of data on her teaching:

> Along with 22 years of experience come ideas that I, like most educators, have developed the best ways to reach and support the children with whom I work. However, for the first time, through FirstSchool data, I have been given much-needed support for these ideas. In particular, the importance of making better connections with families has been proven by the data gathered in the parent focus group. This data opened my eyes to the beliefs and perceptions of the mothers of students within my school. With this knowledge, I now am better equipped to connect with and provide for my students and their families. This knowledge gives me the gateway to best advocate for students. The data also allows me to know which students I must advocate for the most. Currently, advocating for students who live in the most vulnerable (crime-ridden) neighborhoods the school serves is my focus.

As this quote illustrates, data can be eye opening. Sometimes, data provide us with a new way to look at old practices, allowing us to see more clearly where success and areas for improvement lie. Other times, they help us confirm what we already know. Regardless of where data lead us, though, one of the key factors in successful data use must be dissemination. We find that teachers often operate largely in isolation, working for the most part alone in their own class-rooms. However, as they establish trusting collaborative partnerships with their colleagues, they find it easier to share the information they have gained from their efforts. It is often with some pride that teachers put forth the fruits of their efforts for consideration among grade-level teams and PLCs. Dissemination of information should not stop there, though. Part of being a leader, whether in the role of a teacher, administrator, or support staff, means being able to think critically about whom information will benefit. Therefore, those in possession of information should ensure that their data and analyses end up in the hands of those who can effect larger changes to benefit more children. Administrators and district personnel can facilitate such efforts by creating processes that allow teachers to share information without fear of judgment and collaborate with their colleagues to share ideas and make unified efforts

---

Discussion Questions

1. Who sees the outcomes of data discussions in your area of practice now? Is there anyone who could benefit who does not currently have access?
2. What are the current barriers to implementing data-based changes? How can these obstacles be overcome?

---

to improve instruction. In this way, successes may pave the way for more widespread implementation of effective techniques while struggles may garner additional support for practitioners in need.

CONCLUSION

Too often, districts rush into using data before properly laying the groundwork for teachers and schools. The first step in effectively using data to transform practice consists of changing the mindset around data and its role. Effective leaders create environments in which it is beneficial and productive for teachers to admit they are not perfect and, recognizing this, actively try to improve their practices. Additionally, leaders think critically about and implement structures and processes that support all steps in the data cycle, from choosing an issue to selecting a measure, to collecting, analyzing, and disseminating information.

Given such an environment, it is up to practitioners to find issues that bear closer scrutiny and align data collection techniques and instruments to those issues. Data collection must be systematic and followed by thoughtful analysis that reveals the underlying patterns in the information they have gleaned. Finally, all stakeholders should find ways to share with one another information that may particularly benefit AALLI children and families. In doing so, schools may move beyond stagnation and become active agents in improving the lives of young children.

CHAPTER 4

The Promise of Curricula

Sam Oertwig, Cristina Gillanders,
& Sharon Ritchie

Lessons from the Field

If there is one thing that teachers are not short of, it is curricula. Really quite the contrary! Teachers are sometimes asked to implement as many as 14 curricular packages a day, and asked to do so without questioning them, trying to integrate them, or making them responsive to the children they teach. Yet effective teachers and leaders recognize how well-developed curricular planning is an essential step in ensuring success for their students.

The word *curriculum* means different things to different people. For some, curriculum is the course of study that students experience throughout their education, but for others, it is the scope and sequence of activities that address particular content areas. FirstSchool adopts the former view of curriculum in its broadest sense. In accord with Kelly (2009), we believe that

> within a democratic society, an educational curriculum at all levels should be concerned to provide a liberating experience by focusing on such things as the promotion of freedom and independence of thought, of social and political empowerment, of respect for the freedom of others, of an acceptance of variety of opinion, and of the enrichment of life of every individual in that society, regardless of class, race or creed. (p. 8)

At FirstSchool we work with teachers to think deeply about curriculum, because doing so matters tremendously to their abilities to ensure the success of the students they have right here, right now. We challenge teachers to examine what the curriculum *includes* and what it *excludes*. In the words of Slattery

(2006), we examine curriculum so "we find a way around hegemonic forces and institutional obstacles that limit our knowledge, reinforce our prejudices, and disconnect us from the global community" (p. 35).

Frequently curriculum is conceived as encompassing both the content and pedagogy of teaching. Although curriculum and instruction are usually discussed as one entity, FirstSchool has found it beneficial to separate them and give careful consideration to each (see Chapter 5 for an in-depth look at effective instruction). To create high levels of learning for students, teachers need to recognize the important role each plays in the education of children. However, what often happens is that curriculum is given little thought as teachers dive directly into decisions about instruction (or how to deliver content), since they feel they do not have much power to impact choices that their states, schools, or districts make about the type of content to be delivered or the selection of programs and materials for doing so. Even teacher education programs tend to emphasize instruction without providing support and guidance to their novice teachers as to how national, state, and district standards need to be translated into meaningful learning opportunities before instructional approaches are even considered. Good teachers devote time to thinking about *how* the teaching will occur; great teachers also pay attention to *what* the children will be taught. The goal of this chapter is to provide a framework for critically reflecting on the curricula used in schools and how they respond to the needs of African American, Latino and low-income (AALLI) children. While the approaches described within this chapter could benefit all children, we believe that these groups of students are particularly in need of attention. Unless we disrupt institutionalized failures to provide AALLI children with quality educational opportunities, their progress will only continue to suffer. Therefore, this chapter concentrates on the impact of curriculum on their success.

FRAMEWORK: LEVELS OF CURRICULUM

FirstSchool's orientation to curriculum is mindful that a wide range of curricula successfully support children's learning in prekindergarten and elementary classrooms. Rather than develop a new curriculum of our own or advocate for specific curricula, FirstSchool offers a framework to assist schools and teachers as they work within their own set of circumstances to study, question, and improve lesson content and coherence across children's early educational experiences. As such, this broad framework for curriculum examination can be applied within unique contexts. We first describe the different levels of the curriculum that can be used to promote the learning and development of young African American, Latino, and low-income children, and then present curricular principles that translate into meaningful, potent learning opportunities for students.

It is important to understand that content can be operationalized at four different levels. We view these levels as layers essential to providing an enriching experience that prepares children to succeed both in and outside the school building. As shown in Figure 4.1, each level is nested in its relationship to the others. The Common Core State Standards and State, District and School levels establish the national, state, and district expectations for essential learning. The Funds of Knowledge level emphasizes the importance of considering children's sociocultural environments as a resource in their learning, and the Generative Curriculum level provides opportunity for the students and/or the community to have input into their paths of learning, as well as the ways in which they demonstrate it. Each of these levels is explored in detail below.

Common Core State Standards and State/District/School Core Programs

The most basic level is the *core standards* to which teachers are expected to adhere. For decades, states predominantly established what children were expected to know and be able to do by the close of a given school year.

Figure 4.1. The Four Layers of Content

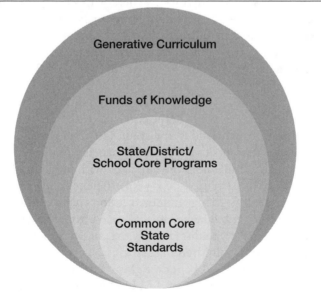

However, beginning in 2010, 45 states and the the District of Columbia adopted a nationally established set of learning goals known as the Common Core State Standards (CCSS). At their best, national standards provide the advantages of creating shared expectations of students' performance, focus and depth in curriculum content, efficiency (as states can create common materials and professional development), and finally, quality assessments that can be delivered electronically to promote baseline achievement (Porter, McMaken, Hwang, & Yang, 2011).

No matter the source for classroom content used to teach a particular skill or concept (state or district level, funds of knowledge, generative, and so on), the Common Core State Standards remain central. Regardless of how a teacher designs and delivers curriculum, a tie to the CCSS goals must be both intentional and made explicit to the learner. Instruction based on the standards can only be as good as one's understanding of them and how they appropriately translate into classroom practice designed to meet the developmental and skill level of the students. Therefore, it is imperative that teachers consistently seek opportunities to collaboratively scrutinize them with an eye toward applying them to needs of their own students. Leadership must ensure that teachers have time and support to collaboratively engage in this work.

Using the Common Core to customize lessons. The work of developing lessons that are aligned to the standards and creating a balanced scope and sequence that maximizes teaching time is clearly an *intentional* process. Working intentionally also provides teachers with *agency*, or the ability to shape what they do. This is particularly noteworthy because teachers often feel that today's educational climate is too regimented and punitive, and allows little room for personal input (see Chapter 2 for a more in-depth look at reinvigorating professionalism). Too many school reform efforts have attempted to make changes in practices through the use of prescribed or "teacher-proof" curricula. Teachers are asked to follow step-by-step instructions to ensure that they implement the curricula with fidelity and obtain the same results that were achieved in the studies in which the curriculum was tested. In practice, attempts to follow these instructions are rarely as beneficial. Teachers might implement the curricula with procedural fidelity, that is, following each of the specified steps with efficiency and accuracy, but still demonstrate low-quality, unengaging instruction (Justice, Mashburn, Hamre, & Pianta, 2008). As teachers become removed from the task of planning, they often lose their ability to discern how the curriculum can be adapted to and implemented for the children in their class. This is especially problematic when working with AALLI children. Most curricula have not been specifically designed or tested to meet AALLI children's needs or incorporate their culture (Crocco & Costigan, 2007; J. M. Gonzalez, 1993; Milosovic, 2007; Moore, 2000; Ndura, 2004; Peck & Serrano, 2002; W. E. Wright, 2002). Therefore, teachers need to be diligent in their efforts to ensure that the curricula they deliver take into account the background knowledge and experiences of all of the children in their classroom.

While some schools and districts are far too directive about what, when, and how things are taught, even the most restrictive environment leaves room for teachers to be creative and make decisions about their teaching. Curriculum is malleable, and teachers make decisions every day about what they teach that allows for customization. The difference is that the best teachers make those decisions intentionally by incorporating and adapting aspects of the content to match the specific needs and learning preferences of the children they are currently teaching (Squire, MaKinster, Barnett, Luehmann, & Barab, 2003). Being strategic and finding ways to best meet the needs of one's students also supports teacher creativity and increases one's sense of fulfillment. Therefore, it is important for teachers to ask these questions when crafting their lessons:

- Where do I have agency? What aspects of the curriculum allow me to make choices?
- What do I know about my students and how can I make curricular decisions on their behalf?
- How do I flex what I am teaching to best meet the interests and needs of my students?

As one example of how this plays out, let's consider read-aloud time, an important component of the literacy program. Perhaps the expectation is that three books are read to the children each day. One teacher may simply use three readily accessible books. However, another teacher who is intentional in examining the curriculum will consider many factors before selecting those books:

- Are the books at a higher level than the reading level of my students?
- What book topics might I select that integrate prior, current, or future units of study?
- What are some of the things my students are interested in? How is the content of the book related to the children's out-of-school experiences?
- Will the students have any opportunity to select one or more of the books? If so, what selections will I put out for them to choose from?
- What specific words can I spotlight to enhance vocabulary development?

- How can I use these books to address the Common Core Standards and district curriculum?

While some may feel that thinking about such a small matter requires too much time and energy, others will recognize that a few moments spent front-loading teaching can actually save time and energy in the long run. In the above scenario, both classrooms of children benefited from hearing books read to them. However, the intentional teacher recognized the greater benefits of investing the time in selecting the "right" books to elevate and personalize the curriculum for the students. Thereby, the read-aloud time actually served multiple purposes and learning goals, the odds of higher levels of engagement were improved, and important learning concepts were reinforced. In addition, because each book was purposefully selected and presented, it had a better chance of assisting students in reaching learning objectives and boosting their current capabilities.

Using the Common Core to effectively guide curriculum development. When FirstSchool began, the Common Core State Standards were just being developed in the hope of creating a unified approach to working collaboratively across states and pooling expertise. Over time, it has become evident that several aspects of the Common Core State Standards (CCSS) are in alignment with the FirstSchool approach. Many of the CCSS allude to the use of higher-order thinking skills for solving problems and understanding text (Porter et al., 2011) and assert that it is "essential that children have the opportunity to describe, ask, and answer questions," "participate in collaborative conversations," "express thoughts, feelings, and ideas clearly," "reason abstractly and quantitatively," and "construct viable arguments and critique reasoning" (National Governors Association Center for Best Practices, & Council of Chief State School Officers, 2010). An integrated curriculum is also emphasized. Further, the English Language Arts portion of the standards CCSS includes the goal that students become "self-directed learners who actively seek to understand other perspectives and cultures . . . and evaluate other points of view critically, and constructively"(National Governors Association Center for Best Practices, & Council of Chief State School Officers, 2010). This and other goals promote the development of higher-order thinking, executive function, written and oral language, and metacognition. A point particularly worth noting is that the Common Core State Standards include what will be required for students to know in order to have future educational and economic opportunities (Cobb & Jackson, 2011). However, as the developers of the CCSS explain, standards are not a curriculum. Therefore, CCSS do not preclude school districts and teachers from using a variety of approaches for helping children achieve the targeted goals.

In most cases, states, districts, and/or individual schools interpret the Common Core Standards and design pacing guides, adopt specific textbooks or programs, or otherwise add detailed expectations about the order, flow, and methodology for delivering the content throughout the course of the year. Teachers are expected to take these *state, district, and school core programs* into account as they plan and deliver the curriculum. However, most of these curricula do not include considerations for AALLI children. In the next section we discuss how teachers can enhance state, district, and/or individual school curricula to address these specific populations.

Funds of Knowledge

In many cases teachers do not venture beyond the Common Core State Standards or the state and district core programs when considering what to teach their students. However, limiting curriculum development to the first two levels of our nested framework does not take into account the cultural backgrounds and funds of knowledge of the students, their families, and the community. Much of the curricula developed for young children have been designed with the hidden or explicit purpose of inculcating the linguistic, literate, and cultural practices of the dominant White middle-class cultural norms. Between the 1960s and 1970s, the purpose of many educational initiatives was to eradicate the "culture of poverty" or "cultural deprivation" by replacing it with the cultural practices and norms of the dominant culture. The goal was to address the achievement gap by providing children with the learning experiences that they were allegedly deprived of in their homes (Paris, 2012). Today, we see residue of this mindset within paternalistic educational efforts that have similar aims to improve students' lives by modeling mainstream societal standards (Whitman, 2008).

However, as a reaction to these deficit views, researchers in the 1970s and 1980s began to recognize that rather than being "culturally deprived," children of minority backgrounds had experiences seen as valuable for growing up in their particular sociocultural contexts, but often left unrecognized as beneficial for academic learning. Efforts in more recent times have focused on helping educators recognize home and cultural practices as resources available for integration into curriculum and teaching. The work of N. González, Moll, and Amanti (2005) defines funds of knowledge as "the historically accumulated and culturally developed bodies of knowledge and skills essential for household or individual functioning and well-being" (p. 72). Educators use this concept to develop teaching experiences for children in a variety of content areas (A. S. Johnson, Baker, & Breuer, 2007; Marshall & Toohey, 2010; Riojas-Cortez, 2008; Sandoval-Taylor, 2005; Souto-Manning, 2010a, 2010b). These attempts are not only critical to ensure equity in students' participation and engagement in school, but also necessary to help children make explicit connections between the knowledge learned in school and that acquired outside of school.

In practice, teachers use different methods to incorporate funds of knowledge meaningfully into their classroom curriculum. As an example of how this plays out, the chart in Table 4.1 shows how teachers used four practices identified by Wager (2012) to incorporate children's out-of-school mathematical experiences into classroom mathematics.

Generative Curriculum

The most comprehensive and complex aspect of curriculum development is the *generative curriculum*. A generative curriculum provides opportunity for the students and/or the community to have input into students' paths of learning as well as the ways in which students demonstrate their learning. Lessons designed at this level encompass the other three levels while also engaging the

Table 4.1. Incorporating Funds of Knowledge into Curriculum

Practice	Classroom Example
1. Identify a specific mathematical concept to be taught and match it to children's life experiences.	A teacher learned that some of her students played soccer so she included word problems about measuring a soccer field.
2. Identify a home cultural practice that involves mathematics and a particular concept of school mathematics that can be linked to the cultural practice.	A teacher knew that a child frequently engaged in making cloth dolls with her grandmother. She took this opportunity to discuss measurement of the materials for making cloth dolls.
3. Identify how mathematics is used in a particular cultural practice and ask children to demonstrate and explain the mathematics involved in the practice.	A teacher asked some of her students what they knew about using money while shopping with their families.
4. Organize in-school activities that are related to everyday mathematics and highlight the mathematics embedded in the activity.	A teacher used a school field trip to a bowling alley as a context for mathematical problems that involved ordering food and analyzing scores.

Note. Adapted from "Incorporating Out-of-School Mathematics: From Cultural Context to Embedded Practice," by A. A. Wager, 2012, *Journal of Mathematics Teacher Education, 15*(1), 9–23.

learner as an active partner in the learning process. It is important to remember that knowledge is contextual and must begin with what is recognizable to the learner. Therefore, it is critical for the teacher to honor what is familiar and known by both incorporating it in lesson planning and including student opportunities for choice in exploring and demonstrating learning that connects to national, state, and district learning expectations.

Formulation of lessons based on the generative curriculum increase student engagement, promote learning beyond the classroom, and capitalize on the inherent curiosity children have of the world around them. Such lessons promote self-efficacy and support the development of positive racial/ethnic identity by demonstrating that both the teacher and classmates see value in what is culturally relevant and valued by the individual learners and/or the community (Agnello, 2007; Ball & Pence, 2001; Cordiero & Fisher, 1994; Kornfeld & Goodman, 1998; Wiggins & McTighe, 1998).

The chronic nature of the ongoing achievement gap underscores First-School's greatest challenge—to move teachers and leaders from a mindset of accepting underperformance as inevitable for poor and minority children to a commitment that makes *explicit* the responsibility of education professionals to broaden their repertoires and hone their skills to create schools and classrooms in which all children maximize their potential. While FirstSchool recognizes that there are children who lag behind academically and socially, the use of content at the levels of funds of knowledge and the generative curriculum enables students to more rapidly close their learning gaps. Connecting new learning to prior knowledge is a key factor in the learning process (Adams & Bertram, 1980; Garner, 2008; Rumelhart, 1980). So, the more teachers can use student knowledge, interest, values, and experiences, the more they increase the odds that students will reach the intended curricular goals. Therefore, moving into these more sophisticated and nuanced realms of curricula is a critical step to ensuring the success of AALLI children.

FRAMEWORK: PRINCIPLES OF CURRICULUM

Given the extensive challenges of the wide variety of learning needs of students, how should you approach curriculum development? How can you take the CCSS and/or the prescribed curriculum mandated by the district or school and develop lesson plans that meet student needs?

Since instruction is only as good as the curriculum upon which it is based, it is critical that a good deal of time and attention be dedicated to lesson content. To develop meaningful, potent learning opportunities for students, FirstSchool recommends that teachers use five design principles to critically examine the curriculum and to build quality into their planning right from the start. Classroom content that authentically meets the needs of the students should be aligned, balanced, integrated, relevant, and developmental. All aspects must be included to ensure high-quality learning opportunities and student success (see Figure 4.2).

Aligned

The first criterion is the explicit *alignment* of lesson content with the established standards. One of the most important jobs of a teacher is the translation of standards into classroom content. Therefore, teachers must possess a clear understanding of what the standards mean and how mastery of them plays out for the grade and age of the students they are teaching. As they develop lesson plans, teachers should be able to clearly articulate their rationale for how a particular unit is going to ensure that their students reach mastery. Teachers must be certain that what they are teaching and what the children are learning is aligned to the goals or standards of the curriculum.

All too often the translation of curricular standards into lessons becomes a series of activities that, while perhaps interesting and fun, bear little resemblance to actually teaching the children what they need to know and be able to do to succeed at the next level of learning. Frequently, this is due to the fact that dealing with standards is a time-consuming, brain-taxing

Figure 4.2. The FirstSchool A-BIRD Framework

5 Basic Criteria:

- Aligned
- Balanced
- Integrated
- Relevant
- Developmental

Wise teachers use the A-BIRD framework to develop curriculum that meets the needs of their students!

process. However, investing the time in personally knowing and understanding one's grade-level standards, rather than relying upon textbook companies or colleagues, is the foundation for quality instruction. Effective teachers are keenly aware of what each actual standard specifically states, as well as what it means for the age or grade level of the children they are teaching. They recognize that standards can be helpful when incorporated into a robust planning process.

A comprehensive understanding of the standards also helps teachers ensure that students actually spend instructional time learning what is needed for success in their day-to-day experiences and, subsequently, adequately prepares them for what is ahead. Misinterpreting or ignoring the learning goals can, for example, cost valuable instructional time when one learning target is taught beyond what is needed for future success while something else that is necessary is never covered. A blatant example of this was found within a group of 2nd-grade teachers who spent time teaching cursive writing, which was actually a district expectation for 3rd grade. When asked why they were doing this, they stated it was "because the kids enjoy learning cursive writing—it makes them feel grown up." Although that may have been true, the time spent teaching cursive writing was at the expense of teaching other important skills needed for 3rd-grade preparation. Needless to say, the 3rd-grade teachers were not a bit impressed that their rising students could already do cursive, but they were upset that students could not subtract with regrouping, which was foundational to future math instruction.

To ensure that lessons are aligned with standards, teachers should ask themselves the following questions:

- What are the standards that must be met by the children I am teaching? (Typically, as guided by the Common Core State Standards (CCSS) adapted in most states across the country, but potentially in combination with other essential subject area guidelines.)
- What do these learning targets mean for the age and grade level of the children I am teaching?
- What knowledge, skills, and behaviors does a child exhibit when the standard is met?
- What do I know about my student's readiness for the new learning?
- What are the intermediate steps in the learning process that will take the children from where they are now to mastery of the new learning target?

By taking the time to know the learning targets right from the beginning, teachers become more effective. They possess a clear understanding of where they need to take their learners, are more capable of making learning connections across content areas, and are better able to design and use formative and summative assessments in the learning process. Once the learning goal is understood, teachers can engage in what is often called "backward mapping" to develop an effective learning sequence that is needed to take the learners from where they are now to the designated target. Inherent in this process is the knowledge of children's current abilities. In addition, few grade-level standards can be mastered quickly; most take months, if not the full year, to develop. Therefore, knowing the standards well enables the teacher to consistently keep the scope and sequence of the year in mind and continuously reinforce specific goals throughout the entire learning journey.

Effective leaders provide both time and support for teachers to explore the standards, as we have discussed in our overview of the effective use of the CCSS as a baseline for further enrichment and customization. However, first and foremost, administrators themselves must be knowledgeable of the learning targets for each grade level and understand the continuum of learning. Only then can they engage in coaching conversations about important curricular issues with their staff. Principals can help teachers identify those areas in which the school as a whole is least successful. By allotting time for both horizontal and vertical discussion of specific standards, school leaders ensure teacher understanding of key learning targets and how to help students reach full mastery.

Balanced

Exposing children to a full, *balanced* curriculum is critically important to overall learning. The more experiences a child has, the more opportunity for connections and learning in the human brain (Jensen, 1998). Yet we know that time constraints or ineffective use of instructional time can easily create situations where entire strands or units of study are left out. The advent of high-stakes testing of certain core subjects has also led to a greater emphasis on the tested subjects at the expense of those not tested (Au, 2007; McMurrer, 2008; Morton & Dalton, 2007). For example, in the early grades, science is often short-changed. However, research has demonstrated that inquiry-based science instruction can improve math and reading scores as well as increasing scientific understanding (Alabama Math, Science, & Technology Initiative, 2004; Valadez & Freve, 2002). To ensure that curricula are balanced, teachers should ask themselves the following questions:

- Are the children being exposed regularly to each content area?

- Is the exposure to each content area enough to ensure mastery of important knowledge and skills? Is each strand within the content area being given adequate time and coverage?
- Is adequate time dedicated to vocabulary development and oral language development, two strong predictors of lifelong educational success?
- Is adequate time spent engaging children in learning that promotes algebraic thinking, a foundational skill necessary for tackling higher levels of math?

When teachers realize how little time is actually spent on some of these critical areas and learn the importance of high levels of exposure in these areas, they are better able to make conscious curricular decisions that improve learning outcomes for their children. The graph in Figure 4.3 shows schoolwide levels of the components of literacy (the data comes from the FirstSchool Snapshot, which is detailed in Chapter 3). Note how little of the day, not just the literacy block, is spent engaging students in oral language and vocabulary development.

The next graph (Figure 4.4) shows change that occurred when a teacher intentionally planned to incorporate oral language and vocabulary development

Figure 4.3. Time Spent on Components of Literacy Instruction

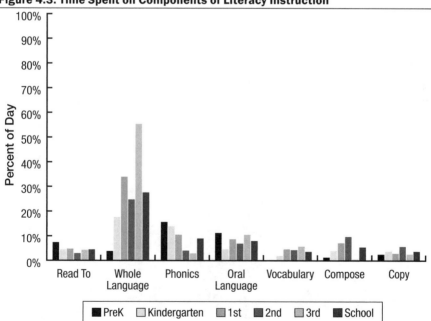

into the students' day. This was accomplished while working within the context of district expectations and with adopted curricular materials; no additional expenses or training were required. Simply by being aware of the importance of these two elements of literacy and intentionality in planning, this teacher was able to provide a far richer and more inclusive learning environment for her students.

Effective teachers who ensure a balanced curriculum reflect their recognition of the importance of the development of the whole child and their understanding that what children are exposed to early on will ultimately shape the kinds of minds they possess as adults. They recognize that teaching a rich, balanced curriculum supports closing the achievement gap, which is sometimes called the "experience gap." All the content areas, not just the ones that are formally assessed, are taught along with an inclusion of the arts in meaningful ways that support the learning of other essential content. Great teachers recognize that balance needs to be considered within each content area, not just across content areas, and that certain aspects of learning are more critical than others and should be incorporated throughout the school day into a variety of content areas. For example, teachers can promote oral language development skills no matter what subject is being taught. All of this is reflected within a balanced curricular plan.

Figure 4.4. FirstSchool Snapshot: 1st-Grade Intentional Change in Components of Literacy

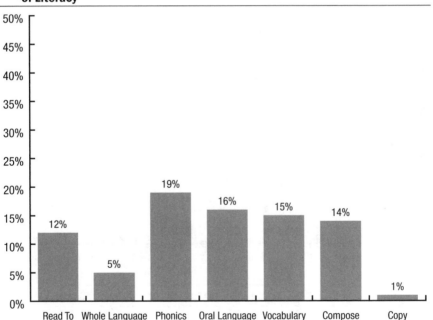

Effective leaders support a balanced curriculum by being keenly aware of what content is being taught throughout the school. While having teachers turn in daily lesson plans may not be necessary, leaders can provide time and support for grade-level teams to develop a yearly plan broken down by quarters. They can monitor the progress of these plans by routinely visiting classrooms, and at the close of each quarter hold a coaching conversation with grade-level teams to review progress and make any needed adjustments for the next quarter. Successful leaders should also pay careful attention to key content aspects that are predictors of later success such as algebraic thinking, oral language, and vocabulary development, and ensure that these aspects are being incorporated into each content area.

Integrated

One of the best ways to improve curriculum balance is through *curriculum integration*, or the purposeful planning of strategies and learning experiences to facilitate and enhance learning across key content areas. Curriculum integration does not abandon the skills and understandings that are specific to individual content areas; rather, it is a means of enhancing those areas by connecting them. In the real world, knowledge is interdependent, so it is important to help learners recognize the relationships that exist naturally across multiple fields of study. The human brain becomes "smarter" through the creation and development of neural pathways, which grow stronger and longer lasting through multiple connections (Paus et al., 1999; Sprenger, 1999).

Curriculum integration also offers support for students' ability to demonstrate knowledge, skills, values, and attitudes that transcend individual key content areas. While integrating curriculum, teachers can also enhance learning by intentionally providing opportunities for students to talk about what they are learning, reflect upon it, and write about it. Engaging students in math and science notebooking are excellent examples of ways to strengthen learning and build in higher-order thinking (analysis, synthesis, reflection). In addition, acting out a concept, drawing it, or physically building a representation of it also helps solidify new learning into long-term memory.

To ensure curriculum integration, teachers should ask themselves the following questions as they engage in lesson planning:

- How can the potency of the learning experience be increased by connecting it meaningfully to other content areas and learning goals?
- What concepts can be used to pull together various curricular areas?
- How are writing and higher-order thinking included across all content areas?

These two graphs (Figure 4.5) from the FirstSchool Snapshot depict classroom data from two different teachers in the same school and grade level. Here one can see that Teacher B is more effectively using available instructional time to provide more learning for her students through curriculum integration. (Note: 1% equals 4 minutes of instructional time.)

Rather than viewing reading, math, science, social studies, and so on as separate from one another, effective teachers know the standards so well that they can build curriculum that unites multiple learning goals. They promote the learning of knowledge and skills by helping students connect concepts and ideas, rather than viewing them in isolation. Writing and reflection are routinely incorporated into the learning of every content area.

Effective leaders encourage teachers to make curricular connections, not just within the classroom but throughout the school as well. Recognizing that all instructional specialists can promote the learning of key concepts in all content areas, these principals promote approaches for music, art, foreign language, and PE teachers to include key concepts of math, science, literacy, and social studies in their units of study. They look for opportunities to have at least one thematic unit per year that involves the entire school and engages the community as well. In one school, children, teachers, school leaders, and parents engaged in a series of activities at the beginning of the school year in a unit titled "Starting School." In this unit, older children created for the younger children maps and books about the school, and acted as tour guides for newly arrived children and parents. They also interviewed family members about their experiences starting school and wrote stories that were later read to the younger classes. The younger children read books about starting school and discussed in groups how the characters felt and their own connections to those feelings. They also participated in mathematics activities such as counting how many teachers worked in the school, how many bathrooms could be found, and so on.

Relevant

One of the primary functions of a teacher is to build connections between the students' background knowledge and new content by developing *relevant* curriculum. Whether we are adults or children, we are quintessentially sense-making, problem-solving beings, and we need to know how or why something is important in order to give it time and attention. Our brains have mechanisms that protect them from overload. With the many stimuli that come our way, we cannot possibly pay attention to everything. Those things that connect to something we already deem important or interesting stand a much better chance of capturing our attention. Relevant curriculum is flexible

Figure 4.5. FirstSchool Snapshot Data: Student Engagement Across the Curriculum

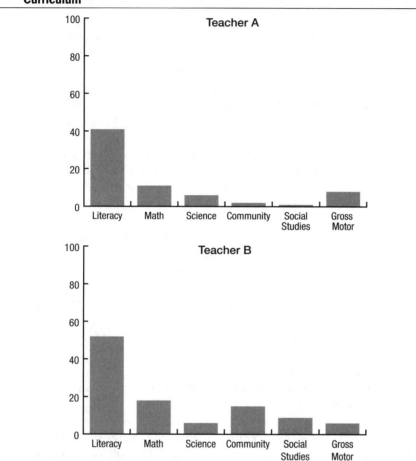

enough to allow teachers to make meaningful connections between the new knowledge and children's background, interests, and lives, thereby increasing student participation and engagement.

As we pointed out in our discussion of funds of knowledge, children learn better when teachers make explicit connections between the knowledge acquired in their homes and the new knowledge learned in school. For example, several studies on literacy development in dual-language learners indicate that using reading materials with familiar content enhances children's comprehension and motivation to read (Coleman & Goldenberg, 2012). It is also relevant to consider prior knowledge that includes content that is important for children's social–emotional and academic development.

Studies on cultural socialization, which is characterized by "messages and practices that teach children about racial-ethnic heritage and provide them with a sense of racial-ethnic pride," have indicated links for African American children between these messages and practices to an improved sense of competence, connection, and caring (Evans et al., 2012, p. 253).

Another important aspect of relevance is that learning becomes relevant not just by the situation in which it is initially presented, but also through opportunities for transferring learning to new and varied contexts. Students benefit from knowing that scientists both conduct experiments and write about them, that writers sometimes develop their work by posing hypotheses and expounding logical arguments, and that landscapers engage in problem-solving, sophisticated math, and artistic renditions. The reason for learning key concepts and skills becomes transparent and can help children understand that what is learned in school is relevant for their everyday lives in ways that they may not have anticipated.

Knowing both your content and your students is essential to developing curriculum that is relevant. The important questions to keep in mind as one considers how to connect a unit of study to the real world of the students are:

- What do my children already know, are able to do, and are interested in knowing and doing?
- How does the new learning tie to their prior knowledge?
- How does it have meaning and importance in the lives of my students while still meeting the intended learning goals?
- How am I providing time for students to explore, process, and apply their learning?

Successful teachers connect curriculum to the interests and lives of their students throughout a variety of content areas. This provides a high level of emotional support as well as cognitive support. They know and value each of their students' strengths, interests, dislikes, hopes, and dreams and respectfully include ways to help students connect school learning to the real world—the real world of the children, which is not necessarily the real world of the teacher. These effective teachers recognize that success and achievement promote self-efficacy and positive identity development, and they work diligently to ensure that all children have what they need to engage and actively participate in the school day. They begin where the children are at and strategically scaffold them to success by providing rich, meaningful opportunities to transfer and apply learning to new and different scenarios.

Effective leaders actively seek ways to engage with parents and community leaders to gain insights and knowledge about the community the school serves and to use the knowledge to enhance the school experience for children and families. By sharing learned information with teachers and promoting conversations about how it can be used to enhance teaching and learning, leaders demonstrate the value and importance of connecting students' interests and cultural knowledge to academic knowledge. This approach creates a sense of the school as the hub of the community, not just peripheral to it. Learning becomes a reciprocal process and becomes engaging and respectful for everyone.

Developmental

The final, and in some ways the most critical, aspect of designing high-quality curriculum is taking into consideration the *developmental* needs of the students across multiple domains. While it is important to pay attention to the developmental aspects of the students at any and all grade levels, it is particularly important in the education of young children, since they are developing rapidly across all domains. Research, practice, and common sense confirm that educating the whole child is the best way to prepare students for the world of today and tomorrow (Association for Supervision and Curriculum Development, 2013). To educate the whole child, the development of the social, emotional, and physical natures of children must be attended to along with their cognitive development.

Since most teachers and administrators in the K–3 continuum have received little or no training on the important aspects of developmental science, it is imperative that they seek opportunities to learn how children change and grow socially, emotionally, and physically and consider how the developmental trajectory impacts teaching and learning. Children's capabilities in any of these three domains have a major impact on their ability to advance cognitively. Therefore, the key to successfully addressing the developmental needs of the students is a combination of knowing what children are ready for in order to design and implement appropriate learning and the knowledge and ability to provide the necessary support to ensure success at that level.

At FirstSchool, we recognize that this aspect of curriculum development is the most challenging and complex dimension of teaching. In all classrooms, there are some children who possess many if not all the prerequisite skills and knowledge to meet growth targets, but there are also many who do not. Teachers have to take into account the broad continuum of student capabilities for the children presently in their classes and strategically develop units and lessons that meet individual student needs in terms of their mental, social, emotional, and physical capabilities at that age level. This is a daunting task that requires unrelenting intentionality, focus, patience, and persistence. Since young children grow and change rapidly, their learning environments and the expectations teachers have for them must change rapidly as well. However, if all the domains of developmental needs of children are not addressed within curricular design, some children are destined to failure.

Moreover, since children's development varies as a result of their sociocultural experiences and individual characteristics, teachers need to find times to carefully observe and document children's acquisition of skills and concepts. Giving children the opportunity to demonstrate their thinking in multiple ways can provide teachers with a more accurate picture of children's developmental level. This will allow teachers to provide curriculum and instruction that is more contingent to children's understandings.

To be certain that content is developmental, teachers should ask the following questions in the course of planning unit lessons:

- What developmental domains are addressed within my curriculum?
- How does this unit attend to a range of developmental abilities?
- How is brain research incorporated?

Effective teachers of children in PreK–3 are well versed in child development and understand the interrelationship of the four developmental domains. They are keenly aware of the cognitive, social, emotional, and physical needs of their students and ensure that each domain is regularly addressed by designing curriculum that is differentiated to meet the full range of abilities in their classrooms. They intentionally teach in ways that promote healthy social, emotional, and physical development, as well as cognitive development. Students in their classrooms learn how to be both independent and collaborative, routinely use manipulatives, and engage in a variety of experiences of applying their learning to novel situations. They also frequently have opportunities to talk, move, and process.

Effective leaders for PreK–3 children are themselves knowledgeable about the developmental continuum of young children and frequently engage in conversations with teachers about ways in which the needs of their students are being fully addressed. They recognize that a kindergarten classroom should look very different from a 1st-grade classroom, which should look very different from a 3rd-grade classroom. Resources that support development and creative thought, such as math manipulatives, blocks, games, and puzzles, are provided to teachers with the expectation that they will be regularly used. These leaders promote active, engaging learning and expect to see their young learners involved and enthusiastic about what they are doing, rather than merely quiet and compliant. Choice and mature play are recognized as critical aspects of strong development and promoted as important aspects of a quality learning environment.

CONCLUSION

One critical challenge that leaders and teachers face is that it takes years of implementation for teachers to fully bring life to curriculum. Elementary teachers are expected to teach a minimum of six different content areas throughout the course of the school year, and although most of these are not formally tested, learning goals in the areas of English language arts, math, science, social studies, healthful living, and technology have been established and are expected to be mastered by the children in their classrooms. To be knowledgeable about curriculum, teachers must continuously engage in an ongoing, deep, and reflective process that includes unpacking the standards for each content area, crafting the standards into lessons that take into account the learning needs, interests, and culture of their students, delivering those lessons, assessing and monitoring student learning, and reflecting upon the outcomes to see how they can improve.

This continuous cycle of inquiry, reflection, and improvement must routinely occur for teachers to become masterful. A great deal of time must be invested before one can authentically interpret content standards in terms of the children one is teaching, recognize how one content area intersects and overlaps with other content areas, and deliver it in a manner that enables children to make connections and meaning in their individual lives. Teachers accomplish this best when they work together and engage in ongoing discussions about curricular matters. Leaders play a critical role when they offer guidance and set aside time for improving the quality of the content delivered in classrooms. By taking into account the different operational levels and using the A-BIRD framework, grade-level teams can develop solid curricular plans that authentically meet the needs of all students, especially African American, Latino, and low-income children who may be otherwise overlooked within standard curricular practices.

CHAPTER 5

Improving Instruction

Sam Oertwig and Adam L. Holland

> However noble, sophisticated, or enlightened proposals for change and improvement might be, they come to nothing if teachers don't adopt them in their own classrooms and if they don't translate them into effective classroom practice.
>
> —Michael Fullan & Andy Hargreaves,
> *What's Worth Fighting for in Your School?*

Instruction is at the heart of learning and teaching, and it is the role of the educator to facilitate the acquisition process of knowledge, skills, and habits necessary for each child to grow into a fulfilled, competent, productive adult in our society. It is important to recognize and optimize the fact that the quality of teaching significantly impacts student performance. As we emphasized earlier in this volume, effective teaching has the potential to close the achievement gap for traditionally disadvantaged groups (Aaronson et al., 2007; Darling-Hammond, 2000; Jacob et al., 2008; Nye et al., 2004; Rivkin et al., 2005; Rockoff, 2004; Rothstein, J., 2010). Despite how much is known about the critical nature of instruction and the role of the teacher, we still have too many children who spend much of their educational career disengaged and unsuccessful. At FirstSchool, we have found that the best approach to ensuring the success of all children is to approach instruction with the following:

- A working understanding of research-based instructional practices applied to deliver well-designed curricula (see Chapter 4)
- A personal knowledge about students and families
- A large measure of intentionality and forethought

Throughout their formative years, children spend a great portion of their lives in classrooms; thus the decisions that teachers and administrators make in structuring the classroom environment and delivering instruction play heavily into influencing not only children's academic development, but other areas of development as well (e.g., social–emotional, motivation, gross motor). Children develop along multiple domains simultaneously; therefore, it is critical for teachers to attend to these multiple dimensions both uniquely and in interaction as children grow and mature (Bronfenbrenner, 2005). Unarmed with knowledge, proficiency, and forethought, it is far too easy to foster growth in one area (most often academic) to the detriment of others. Such practices lead to children who, for example, may be exceptionally proficient at adding two-digit numbers but cannot self-regulate, leaving them unable to control their impulses during whole-group time, center-based activities, and the world at large.

We are particularly concerned with regard to African American, Latino and low-income (AALLI) children. Teachers may feel a need to provide a narrower, more prescriptive and didactic curriculum for African American and Latino children as a means of directly addressing the achievement gap (Lee & Ginsburg, 2007). However, this strategy may be backfiring by giving African American and Latino children less time to explore materials on their own and fewer scaffolded or personalized teaching interactions, inadvertently exacerbating the achievement gap by reducing their opportunities for engagement, autonomy, and relatedness.

At FirstSchool we have organized 10 research-based instructional practices into a framework designed to foster classroom cultures of *caring, competence,* and *excellence* (see Figure 5.1). A culture of caring needs to be in place before

Figure 5.1. FirstSchool Instructional Framework: Classroom Cultures

Culture of Caring

Nurturing Positive Relationships

Strengthening Self-Efficacy & Identity

Developing the Whole Child

Culture of Competence

Encouraging Peer Interactions

Supporting Independence

Promoting Self-Regulation

Prioritizing Communication

Culture of Excellence

Balancing Teaching Approaches

Integrating & Balancing Curriculum

Building Higher Order Thinking

substantive learning can occur. It is foundational to children's success as it ensures that they feel safe, valued, and accepted by adults and classmates. A culture of competence ensures each child is a productive, successful, and contributing member of the classroom team, and a culture of excellence enables each learner to excel beyond minimal competencies. Within each of these cultures are three or four instructional strategies that have been identified as highly beneficial for African American, Latino, and low-income children in PreK–3 environments. Although these practices are ones that will benefit *all* children, their absence is particularly detrimental to minority and poor children. FirstSchool views these instructional strategies as a complete package and believes that focusing on all ten is what will ensure academic and social–emotional success for each child. While incorporating a few of these is better than none, high quality classrooms intentionally maintain all of these practices at the heart of their instruction.

CULTURE OF CARING

A culture of caring is the foundation for a successful classroom. Schools cannot possibly accomplish their academic goals without focusing on the fundamental needs of students to engage in reciprocal caring relationships with teachers and peers (Noddings, 1992). While not everyone wants to be hugged, coddled, or fussed over, we all desire to elicit a positive response from others. We need to be understood, received, respected, and known. Caring is a way of being in relationships; it is not a set of specific behaviors and cannot be achieved by formula or recipe. Good teaching begins with the establishment of trusting relationships that develop caring in our students. To build their own capacity for caring, children need to both experience care and receive guidance and support in caring for others. The emotional quality of the classroom, including the warmth of the adult–child interactions and the adults' ability to respond to children in a sensitive and individualized manner, is a consistent predictor of both reading and math skills (Pianta, Belsky, Vandergrift, Houts, & Morrison, 2008).

Nurturing Positive Relationships

Research identifies the need for relatedness as one of three basic human needs (Ryan & Deci, 2002) along with autonomy and competence, which we discuss later in this chapter. *Relatedness* refers to the need to feel connected to others and to experience a sense of belonging to a larger community. It involves sincere caring about and for others and having others reciprocate those feelings. Having a sense of relatedness helps one balance an egocentric perspective, to move beyond a natural first-person viewpoint. Relatedness enables us to interact effectively with others, to give and accept responsibility, to cooperate, to have compassion, to show respect—all abilities that enable us to function as productive members of a community.

In the classroom, it is important to dedicate time and energy to the development of relatedness, as it is a critical aspect of good socioemotional health. Supporting relatedness in the classroom begins with the notion that all members are on a journey together to grow and improve over the course of the year. Such a mission requires the members of the classroom, both children and adults, to work together toward their shared goal. The role of teachers then shifts to a focus on helping their students develop in positive ways throughout the year. Content delivery is both secondary to and served by this goal. When teachers approach student behavior from this proactive vantage point, students do not feel alienated from the teacher, as they do when teachers punish them, and they learn what *is* expected rather than simply what *is not*.

Lessons from the Field: Classroom Management Missteps

In our classroom observations we often see that teachers interpret requests to help students develop in a positive manner throughout the year with overly effusive, saccharin-sweet praise. "I like the way so-and-so is sitting" and "I like the way these kids are keeping their hands to themselves" are an almost constant counterpoint to instruction. While such praise may be an improvement over harsh punishments and yelling, it does little to help children develop positive relationships for a few reasons. First, it is inherently false and manipulative. Teachers praise those who are sitting nicely with the hope that other children, eager to receive the same praise, will begin meeting expectations. By tricking children like this, teachers actually harm the real relationships they build with their children based on respect and mutual regard. Second, it conditions children to act appropriately in order to receive praise rather than because they identify with the request and understand the reason behind it. Unfortunately, this means that even if children would have sat quietly before coming to this classroom, they will now expect praise in order to accomplish such a task. Removing the praise later will remove their motivation to act appropriately, leading to future misbehavior. Instead of attempting to shape children's behavior in a manipulative way (i.e., via verbal bribery), teachers should provide clear expectations as well as a justification for why children need to act in a certain way. By doing so, children will readily identify with teachers' requests and internalize the reasons, providing them with greater long-term incentives to self-regulate.

Unfortunately in today's educational climate, little attention is given to providing time and attention to this critical aspect of teaching and learning. Often, pressures from administrators, testing demands, and district-level policies lead teachers to believe that content delivery is their sole concern. However, students are not blank slates, ready to receive instruction regardless of other factors in the immediate environment. Factors such as their motivation and emotional state play a key role in dictating their engagement and memory (Deci & Ryan, 2000; Fredricks, Blumenfeld, & Paris, 2004). Therefore, while teachers who focus on content delivery to the detriment of establishing close, personal relationships with their students may *deliver* more content per day, their students fail to remember and adequately *understand* this information, thus defeating the purpose of such a strong content focus. The time and effort teachers put into creating a classroom community centered on caring and mutual respect pay dividends far beyond the initial investment (Hamre & Pianta, 2001; Pianta & Stuhlman, 2004).

The question remains for many teachers, "How do I create a caring, nurturing environment in my classrooms?" Although some important steps can and should be taken by teachers, developing and sustaining a culture of caring in the classroom requires less of a step-by-step process and more of a shift in teachers' and administrators' underlying perceptions of their purpose and goals. Schools are multipurposed institutions that have a responsibility to the future of our society to develop students who are capable of caring about others as well as about ideas, objects, living creatures, and the environment. Teachers must examine their beliefs since they ultimately dictate their actions. As Linton notes in the foreword to Davis's work (2012) on culturally relevant instruction, "Today's youth rely on teachers who will stretch themselves to meet the needs of the student. It begins with the teachers changing their practices, beliefs, assumptions, and biases, and ends with the student succeeding because a caring adult has provided equitable access and support to the necessary learning" (p. vii).

At a time when the need for care is perhaps the greatest, the structures of school seem to work against it, as many current policies and practices are based on outdated research. For the past sixty years, most classroom management practice has been based on behaviorism and the maximal operant principle of motivation (Boggiano, Barrett, Weiher, McClelland, & Lusk, 1987). That is, teachers believe that the correct way to motivate children is to punish behaviors they wish to eliminate and reward those behaviors they wish to foster. These forms of motivation have dominated and continue to dominate policy discussions and classroom practices, evident in movements such as Positive Behavior Interventions and Supports (PBIS) and classroom management systems such as "card charts" or "clips." Although these systems are an improvement over laissez-faire management practices, they are inherently ineffective (Deci & Ryan, 2000; Reeve, 2009; Ryan & Deci, 2002). The problem with these systems, at their most basic level, is that they place students and teachers on opposing teams with opposing goals. Teachers are encouraged to work *on* students rather than *with* students. Interruptions to the delivery of content are viewed as oppositional to the teacher's mission rather than integral to all aspects of child development, including social, emotional, physical, and self-regulatory capacities.

For example, we often see that young boys have trouble remaining still and quiet for 30 minutes during whole-group time in kindergarten. Most teachers respond by repeatedly asking the boys to stop, making them move their card or clip, and eventually sending them to time-out. Unfortunately, while all these actions communicate to the boys what they may not do, none of them teach the child what to do instead or help bolster their self-regulation. Teachers who view misbehavior as an opportunity to teach children the correct behavior respond differently. Instead of punishing the boys, they offer supports that allow them to sit still for longer (e.g., offering them a chair or a small object to hold). For boys who are overly disruptive, they send them to a designated place in the room where they may calm their bodies using pretaught exercises such as deep breathing, allowing them to return of their own accord when they decide their bodies have calmed. Along with communicating respect, this kind of response allows children to develop strategies for managing an optimal level of arousal in the classroom and helps them to be more cognizant of their own bodies and brains.

Strengthening Self-Efficacy and Positive Racial Identity

Research indicates that teachers often have low expectations and are more critical of children of color than of their White peers (Wang, Oates, Weishew, 1995). Sensitivity combined with good judgment and warm, nurturing interactions are needed to raise emotionally healthy, comfortable, and cheerful children. The place a child holds in one's heart should not be impacted by academic progress or the color of his skin. This is particularly significant in PreK–3rd grade, because research suggests children's patterns of engagement and achievement formed during the first three years of school impact their long-term academic trajectories (Hamre & Pianta, 2001). Since academic trajectories tend to be stable and difficult to change over the course of their schooling (Alexander et al., 1993), it is critical that a child experiences early success and develops a positive self-concept and a strong sense of self-efficacy.

Since 1977, when Albert Bandura published his groundbreaking work, "Self-Efficacy: Toward a Unifying Theory of Behavioral Change," this topic has become one of the most researched in the field of psychology. Self-efficacy is defined as "the belief in one's capabilities to organize and execute the

Perspectives from the Field

Like most teachers, I definitely believed that I have always loved all of my children in my classroom. But I also used to view them as "objects" in a way—something that I was supposed to teach and fix. I looked at education as something I was to do to them as opposed to with them. Now I really see my students as precious individuals who are partners with me in learning. It is a subtle shift inside me, but it makes a world of difference in how I operate my classroom and how I treat my children.

—Marsha Sirkin, 2nd-grade teacher

courses of action required to manage prospective situations" (Bandura, 1995, p. 2). A person's belief in his or her ability to succeed in a particular situation impacts every aspect of learning. Children with a strong sense of self-efficacy recover quickly from setbacks and disappointments, willingly tackle challenging problems, develop deeper interest in the undertakings in which they participate, and form a stronger sense of commitment to their interests. On the other hand, children with a weak sense of self-efficacy quickly lose confidence, avoid challenges, believe they cannot be successful when things are difficult or challenging, and focus on their failures (Bandura, 1994).

Because the development of these beliefs begins in early childhood, PreK–3rd grade teachers play a critical role in whether or not children in their classrooms engage in the experiences and situations that promote the development of strong self-efficacy. In a supportive, respectful classroom designed to strengthen self-efficacy, attention is paid to four psychological processes that directly affect learning (Bandura, 1994):

- *Mastery Experiences*—Working to perform a task successfully improves one's sense of self-efficacy. Success builds a robust sense of personal efficacy while failure can undermine it, especially if failure occurs before a sense of efficacy is firmly formed.
- *Social Modeling*—Seeing other people similar to oneself persist to success increases one's belief in one's own abilities to be successful. The greater the perceived similarity, the stronger the influence of success and failure.
- *Social Persuasion*—Receiving verbal encouragement motivates children to give their best efforts.
- *Psychological Responses*—Learning how to minimize stress and elevate mood during challenging tasks helps improve one's self-efficacy.

These four psychological processes are the foundation through which self-beliefs of efficacy are formed.

A salient point is the importance of seeing others "similar to oneself" succeed. For White children from low-income families, this is less problematic since, despite the challenges of poverty, the world is filled with examples of successful people who look just like them or their family members. But for children of color, this is not necessarily a regular occurrence, due to the constant media bombardment of negative stereotypical images in the world outside of schools and classroom environments and curriculum that are not fully representative of the school community. Teachers themselves have been primarily educated with Eurocentric curriculum that is quite devoid of the contributions made by individuals from all races and cultures. Our classroom observations reveal that teachers generally do not include examples of geologists, architects, doctors, writers, artists, astronomers, activists, and historians of color, perhaps because they are unaware of their existence and the important contributions they have made or are currently making. Yet the development of a positive racial/ethnic identity is an important factor in the development of a strong sense of self-efficacy, which ultimately plays a pivotal role in the success of the individual. Therefore, teachers need to be intentional in ensuring that their classroom environments, resources, materials, curriculum, and exemplars are representational of the students and families they serve throughout the year.

For example, an African American boy needs to see other African American boys in his class experience success in order to believe that he too can be successful. He needs to feel and believe that he is an important, contributing member of the classroom, that his ideas and interests have merit, and that he is smart and capable. He also benefits from regularly hearing about African American men who are currently making significant contributions to our society. These examples must go far beyond Hollywood stars, pop singers, and professional athletes to include scientists, writers, judges, researchers, engineers, inventors, mechanics, and so on so he has a myriad of examples of characteristics and professions to which he can aspire.

In contrast, the experience of failure in others similar to the individual has an equal and reverse impact. In the early days of working with our partner schools, it was not unusual to see African American boys sitting isolated behind filing cabinets or in a corner of the room, standing in the hallway outside the classroom, sent to the office or otherwise singled out for some infraction. For example, when Black boys make up 90% of the discipline referrals but only 18% of the school population, a clear message is sent to every adult and every child in the school that Black boys are problems. As a Black boy, even if you are not the person in trouble, this repeated situation is internalized and experienced as "School is not a good place for people who look like me, and it's only a matter of time until I am in trouble."

To prepare children to function in our modern world, *all* schools need to intentionally focus on issues of race, ethnicity, and culture. However, for schools and teachers with non-White children in PreK–3rd grades, doing so is essential to the overall healthy development of students' psyches and positive racial identity development. Unfortunately, many educators never engage in important dialogue with children regarding race for fear of "saying the wrong thing" and avoid the often taboo topic of race by retreating to the false security of "color-blindness" that ultimately devalues diverse students' contributions to the classroom environment (Delpit, 2006; R. Smith, Moallem, & Sherrill, 1997). Their avoidance actually promotes forms of discrimination and can affect attitudes and expectations that directly impact student academic outcomes (Barnes, 2006; Howard & Denning del Rosario, 2000). As Tatum (1997) expresses, "Stereotypes, omissions, and distortions all contribute to the development of prejudice. *Prejudice* is a preconceived judgment or opinion, usually based on limited information. I assume that we all have prejudices, not because we want them, but simply because we are so continually exposed to misinformation about others" (p. 5).

Much has been written about how to become a culturally proficient and culturally relevant teacher, a goal to which every teacher should aspire (Davis, 2012; Ladson-Billings, 1995). It would be impossible within the scope of this chapter to adequately do justice to this expansive and essential aspect of teaching. The point that FirstSchool makes is that race, ethnicity, and culture have an impact on teaching and learning and must be carefully considered when developing curriculum and delivering instruction. This must be done not merely for the sake of helping children meet grade-level standards but also for the larger purposes of developing a healthy self-concept that will be with an individual for one's entire life and of ensuring a future world that is inclusive and valuing of our rich diversity.

Developing the Whole Child

Since all domains of development and learning are important and interrelated, the whole child must be known and nurtured. Throughout this section, a case has been made for the importance of developing the socioemotional well-being of children as a critical aspect of developing their cognitive capabilities. However, it is also important to give consideration to how children grow and develop physically and to recognize the needs young bodies have. The cerebellum, which is the part of the brain involved in memory, spatial perception, language, attention, emotion, nonverbal cues, decision making, and complex emotional behavior, also controls movement (Tomporowski, Davis, Miller, & Naglieri, 2008; Tomporowski, Lambourne, & Okumura, 2011). From the time of our birth and throughout our entire lifetime, movement and learning are interconnected, and physical activity is one of the best ways to stimulate the brain and learning (Hannaford, 1995; Jensen, 1998; Kempermann, Kuhn, & Gage, 1997). Brain research also suggests that physical activity prior to class and during class, increases students' ability to process and retain new material (Kubesch, et al., 2009; Ratey, 2008). Movement has been shown to reduce stress, lift one's mood, fight memory loss, sharpen intellect, and improve the ability to focus and concentrate.

Furthermore, researchers (Ayres, 2005; Hannaford, 1995) have confirmed that sensory motor integration is fundamental to school success. The skills that make it possible for the sensory (nervous) system to effectively communicate with the motor (muscle) system are primarily developed through age 7, but the fine-tuning of this developmental process continues beyond the PreK–3 years. As a general rule, girls tend to develop more rapidly in this area than do boys. Children with an immature sensory motor integration system may experience difficulties with performing fine-motor activities (e.g., handwriting), knowing where their bodies are in space, maintaining balance, putting on clothes, identifying left and right, and hand–eye coordination (e.g., copying from the board). Movements, especially those involving the full body, improve sensory motor integration and thereby improve the school experience for children (Ayres, 2005).

With increasing evidence from today's brain and body research that firmly establishes the significant link between movement and learning, teachers need to intentionally integrate movement activities into every part of the day. This includes much more than hands-on learning activities. It denotes regular stretching, walks, dance, drama, brain energizers, physical education, and daily recess.

A CULTURE OF COMPETENCE

While developing a culture of caring provides children with an environment in which they feel safe and supported throughout their school days, experiencing a culture of competence establishes a setting in which children develop the skills necessary for them to experience personal success as learners and members of society. FirstSchool has identified four instructional principles that are pivotal to this process: supporting independence, promoting self-regulation, encouraging peer interactions, and prioritizing communication.

Supporting Independence

Children, just like adults, have a strong need to feel control over themselves and their lives. Although no one can be completely independent, teachers need to understand that becoming autonomous is a critical developmental process that must be supported within the classroom. Research has shown that children who do not develop autonomy are more likely to be dependent upon adults and excessively influenced by their peers (Erikson, 1950; Gartrell, 1995). Therefore, teachers, especially teachers of young children, should intentionally create opportunities for children to learn how to become self-reliant. In doing so, they are helping increase students' self-confidence along with improving their social, cognitive, and moral development (DeVries & Zan, 1995; Erikson, 1950; Fordham & Anderson, 1992; Maxim, 1997; Morrison, 1997).

In the stages of psychosocial development, Erikson (1950) defined 5–12 years of age as the "competence" period. At this time in a child's life, they are becoming more aware of themselves as individuals and are interested in being responsible, being good, and "doing it right." Schools have the potential to provide rich opportunities for children to achieve recognition for being productive—making things, solving problems, writing sentences, and so on. When children are encouraged to be productive and then are praised for their accomplishments, they begin to demonstrate industry by putting work before pleasure, persevering, and working till a task is completed. If they are ridiculed, punished, or not capable of meeting the teacher's expectations, they begin to develop feelings of inferiority and become unmotivated.

One of the best ways to encourage autonomy is by providing plenty of opportunities for students to make choices throughout the day. To do this, a teacher must recognize the importance of choice and be tolerant of a variety of activities and behaviors occurring in the classroom at the same time. Children need continuous opportunities to develop their decision-making capacity and should not be subjected to arbitrary and unexamined rules. In order for this to happen, adults must adopt a delicate balance between the guidance they provide students as they facilitate socialization and/or learning and an allowance for child preference and independence (Grusec, 2011). Teachers can begin to find this balance by critically examining their own practices with the purpose of clarifying their own need for controlling rules and practices, replacing any that could be accomplished by providing students with choices and autonomy. This child-centered approach to learning has long been recognized as a measure of the quality of a classroom (Hendrick, 1996).

Lessons from the Field: Fostering Independence

Many teachers require students to gain permission to use the restroom, even when it is located conveniently in the classroom. The basic premise behind this rule is that it restricts students from interrupting lessons or goofing off in the restroom rather than going at need. However, it also serves to place students under the jurisdiction of the teacher and denies them control over something as basic as caring for their own personal physical needs. Alternative rules could be created in which students may use the bathroom at will but may only leave the activity one at a time. When students are truly engaged in interesting lessons and see the need for participation in a classroom learning community, such a simple guideline will likely be all that is required to maintain the basic goal of maximizing student participation while allowing students choices about how they care for their own needs. Some students may need more guidance and support, but prioritizing student autonomy rather than teacher control ensures that students' needs are fulfilled rather than frustrated as they learn to take responsibility for their own actions.

Promoting Self-Regulation

Supporting children's autonomy not only provides a setting in which they are respected by adults in the classroom, but also gives them the necessary skills and practice to develop crucial self-regulation skills. Blair and Diamond (2008) define self-regulation as the volitional behavioral and cognitive processes through which people maintain levels of motivational, cognitive, and emotional arousal that facilitate positive adaptation and adjustment, as reflected in high levels of productivity and achievement as well as positive relationships and a positive sense of self. That is, it is what allows young children to remain focused and persistent as they meet the daily challenges in a rigorous classroom.

Self-regulation may be contrasted against "other-regulation," a situation in which children's behavioral and cognitive processes are tightly controlled by an external source, such as a teacher. The danger of other-regulation is that it fails to provide students with opportunities to bolster their own self-regulation skills. Without consistent opportunities to develop these skills, it is unlikely that they will be well prepared for later schooling, which requires them to maintain impulse control, motivate themselves, persist through difficult situations, and utilize effective academic strategies to independently master new information (Corno & Mandinach, 1983). Students will have understandably come to expect others to fill these roles, leaving them ill prepared for later challenges in school and life.

In order to facilitate the development of these crucial skills, teachers must once again reorient themselves toward their own practices. Rather than viewing themselves solely as content deliverers, they must understand the critical role they play in teaching children to self-regulate and then provide them with opportunities to practice these skills (Bodrova & Leong, 2007). Doing so requires an understanding that children are not perfect and have not fully developed their abilities in this domain. Breakdowns in self-regulation are rightly viewed when they are seen as an opportunity to instruct, correct, and guide children toward more adaptive and successful habits and practices.

Encourage Peer Interactions

In addition to providing children with opportunities to practice and develop self-regulation, a culture of competence also requires teachers to develop in their students the ability to work with their peers toward common goals. Like self-regulation, collaboration is becoming an increasingly important life skill for young learners and is essential for language, cognitive, social, and emotional development. According to D. W. Johnson (1981), "Experiences with peers are not a superficial luxury to be enjoyed during lunch and after school. Constructive student–student relationships are a necessity for maximal achievement, socialization, and healthy development" (p. 5). Results from over 600 research studies that have investigated learning in cooperative, competitive, and individualist goal structures have indicated students learn more, are more highly motivated to learn, enjoy learning more, feel more positive toward the subject being studied, have increased positive regard for their teachers, and are more accepting of one another when they work together with peers as opposed to working competitively or individually (R. T. Johnson & Johnson, 2013). Since teachers who promote a culture of caring already spend a great deal of time emphasizing the common goals of learning and personal growth through acceptance and support, it is a short, but intentional, step to promoting positive peer collaboration and integrating it into the daily classroom experience.

When children work with their peers on projects, center tasks, and learning activities, they must practice social skills that require empathy, perspective taking, sharing, conflict-negotiation, persuasion, and diplomacy (Bernard, 1991). Collaboration also serves an important role in the development of self-concept and self-esteem as children learn about themselves through the eyes of others, engage in self-reflection, imitate desirable characteristics and behaviors, and experience success (Slavin, 1990; Tsay & Brady, 2010). Additionally, time for collaboration provides opportunity for more capable peers to scaffold the learning of less capable peers while simultaneously reinforcing their own knowledge through the process of articulating their thinking (Fawcett & Garton, 2005). Structuring learning activities in such a way provides an efficient means for teachers to support young learners as they gain and practice new knowledge and skills in all developmental domains.

Prioritizing Communication

Children need to be actively engaged in their learning, and one of the best ways to make this happen is to provide a variety of opportunities for them to verbally express what they know, how they personally connect to the learning, and what it all means to them. No one would debate that being capable of expressing one's thoughts and ideas is a critical skill for academic and social success. Yet, even 30 years ago, major studies revealed a decline in the amount of classroom time dedicated to improving children's abilities to effectively communicate as teachers talked more and students talked less (Holbrook, 1983; Stabb, 1986). Recent FirstSchool Snapshot data show this is still the case. Typical classroom data indicate teachers generally spend 75–90% of instructional time engaged in "teacher talk" while 3–4% of the day is spent engaging students in oral language development. This holds true even in classrooms with non-English-speaking students. Besides the fact that these teacher-dominated classrooms do not support language acquisition, they also tend to produce passive learners who are less engaged and less able to reason and problem-solve (Stabb, 1986).

Common Core State Standards (National Governors Association Center for Best Practices & Council of Chief State School Officers, 2010) include the notion that students must have ample opportunities to take part in a variety of rich, structured conversations as part of a whole class, in small groups, and with a partner, and that being productive members of these conversations requires that students contribute accurate relevant information, respond to and develop what others have said, make comparisons and contrasts, and analyze and synthesize a multitude of ideas in various domains. Therefore, teachers need to be mindful that "to teach" does not mean "to talk" and that their primary role is to facilitate the process of learning. Doing this involves encouraging students to bring their ideas, thoughts, and background knowledge into classroom learning activities and connecting them to the current content, and it requires teachers to be good listeners, responsive to children's talk. Teachers need to place an emphasis on intentionally creating regular opportunities for students to ask for clarification, respond to their peers, summarize what they've learned, explain a process, and respond to someone's work rather than personally dominating the conversation.

A classroom emphasis on oral language development has been identified as one of the premier instructional strategies for ensuring the success of children, especially those in low-socioeconomic communities (Mason & Galloway, 2012). While children often come to school with strong oral language, their development is interrupted, rather than promoted, by an overabundance of teacher dominance. As Mason and Galloway (2012) point out, "When seen from a strength-based perspective, these children are competent communicators in their families and in their communities where language is a medium to form social connections and to communicate needs, wants, and hopes" (p. 30). Therefore, it is critical that teachers embrace dialect and home language, recognizing them as assets and building upon them to promote learning and development through speaking.

Another key aspect in prioritizing communication is the deliberate emphasis of expanding children's vocabulary. Studies have shown a high correlation between student vocabulary knowledge and academic success in upper elementary as well as high school (Cunningham & Stanovich, 1997; Storch & Whitehurst, 2002). Unfortunately most attempts at teaching vocabulary involve mentioning a word or synonym and/or assigning words to be looked up in a dictionary. These approaches actually have little to no effect in enhancing student vocabulary (J. A. Scott, Jamieson-Noel, & Asselin, 2003). Instead vocabulary knowledge needs to be rich and imparted to students in energetic ways that include multiple ways for children to think about words and use them. Teachers need to provide explicit explanation of the meaning of words, incorporate multiple exposures to the word's meaning and uses, and integrate a variety of opportunities for children to interact with and use the word to relate to current and previous experiences (Beck, McKeown, & Kucan, 2013). Even with our youngest learners, teachers support learning best when they regularly use sophisticated language and elaboration in their interactions with their students (Dickinson & Porche, 2011).

A CULTURE OF EXCELLENCE

In addition to creating a culture of caring and a culture of competence, teachers and leaders should be working to build a culture of excellence. Teachers do this by providing high expectations for student learners and then giving children the necessary support to meet those expectations. Although many current curricula emphasize the acquisition of discrete facts or bits of knowledge, high expectations should not be limited to this. Although the knowledge of specific curricular objectives is a necessary precursor to excellence, great teachers recognize that their students benefit from more than these isolated elements. Instead, great teachers develop in their children rich, complex schemas of knowledge in which these facts are connected in myriad ways, allowing children to manipulate them for the purposes of synthesis, analysis, and argument. In doing so, students develop their capacities to engage in higher-order thinking as well as knowing the content with which they work.

Balancing Teaching Approaches

Teaching students in this manner requires teachers to become adept at a number of pedagogical approaches, choosing the appropriate type of instruction based on student need and content. At FirstSchool, we differentiate between three main teaching approaches: didactic instruction, scaffolding, and reflection. *Didactic instruction* refers to situations in which teachers are presenting information directly to students or asking closed-ended questions. Here, teachers seek to communicate content as directly as possible. Corresponding questions merely confirm or deny that students have acquired the information. *Scaffolding*, on the other hand, may come in multiple formats. One way teachers scaffold is by asking children open-ended questions. Such questions have multiple possible answers, requiring students to consider alternate possibilities before advocating for one solution over another. Another way teachers scaffold is to build on student responses. That is, if a student answers a direct question, the teacher may then follow up with further questions. Finally, teachers may utilize a student's expressed interest to link instruction. In each of these cases, teachers are using techniques that allow students to more readily connect new information to prior knowledge, placing content into a rich schema rather than attempting to memorize isolated facts. Such strategies have been linked by researchers to greater retention of knowledge (Hedrick, San Souci, Haden, & Ornstein, 2009). The third type of instruction, *reflection*, is closely linked to scaffolding. However, reflection adds a metacognitive aspect to the process. In reflection, teachers ask students to purposefully think about and articulate their own thinking. This may come in the form of asking students to justify their responses or explain how they solved a math problem. It goes beyond merely having students answer questions and helps them think critically about their own cognitive processes.

Each of these teaching strategies should be balanced, as each has a place in great teachers' repertoires. Didactic teaching, for example, allows teachers to communicate new information to students in the most efficient manner. Scaffolding, on the other hand, permits students to connect such knowledge and deepen their understanding of both new knowledge and the facts and issues to which it connects. Finally, reflection gives students the opportunity to be critical of their own thought processes. In doing so, children learn to self-assess and more thoughtfully support the positions they take.

Unfortunately, test preparation and broad curricula lacking in depth often encourage almost exclusive use of didactic teaching strategies (Graue, 2011). Teachers feel compelled to impart as much knowledge as possible in the limited time frames they are given. Unfortunately, while the amount of information imparted is greatest when teachers lean heavily on didactic teaching, retention is not (Zull, 2002). Without the opportunity to connect new knowledge to old, children often either quickly forget new information or fail to gain an adequate understanding of how and when to use such knowledge. Because of this, we encourage teachers with whom we work to find opportunities to purposefully connect the content they deliver to other, relevant content.

Additionally, we advocate for the use of open-ended questions that allow students to consider and discard multiple possible answers before choosing a defensible response. Excellent teachers not only ask these open-ended questions but also use them as a jumping-off point to have students verbally explain their thinking, building metacognitive skills in the process. Students are not the only beneficiaries of this line of questioning because when students verbalize their answers, teachers are provided with diagnostic/formative information about students' thinking, allowing them to better assist students in correcting misconceptions.

In fact, allowing students to explain their thinking can be one of the most powerful ongoing assessment tools in teachers' repertoires. Unfortunately, it is rarely used. In math, for example, we often see teachers poll students to find the correct answer. However, when students answer incorrectly, educators move on to find another child who may provide a more adequate response. Although this is done with good intentions to spare children embarrassment, mastery-oriented classrooms focus on the process rather than the end result. Students view incorrect answers not as a termination of the problem-solving process but as feedback to keep trying. When teachers move away from students who guess incorrectly, this viewpoint is undermined. However, when teachers stick with students who guess incorrectly and ask them to explain their thinking, they receive rich information regarding where students have gone wrong in the process of solving the problem. Teachers may then assist students in identifying their mistakes and place them on the path toward the correct answer. Peers watching this process come to understand that the correct answer is not what matters but instead that the problem-solving process itself is what's important. Teachers, on the other hand, gain insight into where students are having difficulty in the process rather than simply knowing that there is an issue somewhere. This then allows them to shape their teaching more responsively to target specific misconceptions.

Lessons from Research: Student Motivation

Motivation researchers differentiate between two different types of classroom goal structures: mastery and performance. In mastery-oriented classrooms, the focus is on developing new skills and abilities and attempting new challenges. Success is evaluated in terms of self-improvement (Meece et al., 2006). Meece and colleagues contrast this approach with a performance goal orientation in which the focus is on comparisons of ability and on the end product (i.e., test grade or number correct). These orientations tend to influence students to embrace the goal structure of the environment in which they spend their days.

Although research is somewhat mixed on the relative benefits of each of these goal structures, some clear findings have emerged. Of particular importance is that students with a mastery orientation tend to view success as a matter of effort while students with a performance orientation view it as a matter of ability. Failures, then, are interpreted differently depending on which orientation children possess. For children in a mastery-oriented classroom, failure is feedback that forces them to continue striving. For children in a performance-oriented classroom, on the other hand, failure lets them know that they possess low ability, leading to lower self-efficacy and a lack of persistence in completing difficult tasks. For children who do not experience early success upon arriving to school, this difference can be critical.

Balancing and Integrating Curriculum

Teachers can also assist students in creating complicated knowledge schemas by effectively integrating curricula. Integrating across the curriculum provides two key benefits over more traditional, separate instructional practices: It allows teachers to communicate and teach more material and facilitate smoother connections between various topics. First, we acknowledge that the broad courses of study outlined by most districts require teachers to instruct students on a tremendous number of topics within a wide array of subject areas. In order to cover these myriad topics, teachers may choose to utilize lessons that touch on a number of objectives, thereby maximizing the efficiency with which they instruct their students. Second, when students utilize reading and math skills to explore science and social studies topics, they see firsthand the ways that knowledge connects rather than experiencing learning as a series of discrete exercises with no end beyond the learning of the topic. Later in this section, we discuss a few ways that teachers may thoughtfully integrate separate content areas through the use of mature play and project approaches. Readers should also refer back to Chapter 4 of this volume for much more information on related curriculum topics.

Building Higher-Order Thinking Skills

Our interest in AALLI children has also led us to note that, in many of our schools serving large populations of these kids, the persistent achievement gap has been addressed through a remediation model. In such a model, basic skills are nearly the sole focus of the curriculum for children who do not possess high achievement. We believe that although basic skills instruction is critical for AALLI children, particularly those from low-income families (Connor, Morrison, & Katch, 2004), focusing only on isolated skills will not yield excellence. Another means of approaching the achievement gap is through the provision of differentiated, enriched instruction to all children (Beecher & Sweeny, 2008). Schools using this approach rely on open-ended activities that promote critical thinking, creativity, problem solving, and metacognitive skills while providing children with the opportunity to apply, synthesize, and extend the knowledge they have gained during basic skill instruction.

With the implementation of the CCSS, we are hopeful for a concurrent shift away from instruction viewed as the presentation of isolated facts and toward instruction on not just *what* to think but *how* to think. While terms like *higher-order thinking skills* have been buzzwords in the field of education for quite a while, we rarely see a commitment to building such skills in our observations of classrooms. Teachers largely remain focused on basic skill instruction and mastery on a daily basis while providing one or two token experiences each year that build students' abilities to synthesize, analyze, and apply what they know. We feel strongly that this is not enough. Students will never become the critical thinkers they need to be when the opportunities provided for them to build these skills are so rare. Teachers must find a way to effectively integrate daily experiences that focus on higher-order thinking skills into their pedagogy.

Often, teachers can adapt current lessons to provide more fruitful opportunities for students to exercise higher-order thinking skills. The questions teachers ask can mean the difference between students merely receiving a lesson and engaging in it themselves in order to gain critical-thinking skills (Halpern, 1998; Miri, David, & Uri, 2007). For example, when involving young children in small-group or whole-group read-alouds, teachers often check for understanding by asking questions about what has happened in the story. However, teachers could take the additional time to also ask students to think about characters' motives, offer predictions, and solve problems. As opposed to asking children, "What happened to the main character," they could ask students, "What do you think would happen if . . . ?" In doing so, students must make inferences, draw on previous knowledge, synthesize information, and assemble these pieces to form a cohesive answer. Allowing students to share and critique one another's answers in pairs builds oral language, particularly among dual-language learners (J. Hill & Flynn, 2006), and helps students become comfortable taking criticism for the purposes of improving their thinking. Moreover, having students explain the thinking that led to their answers promotes metacognitive development and stronger listening skills (R. Campbell, 2011).

Integrating Approaches to Creating a Culture of Excellence

In this section we discuss two ways teachers may choose to adapt their school days to purposefully include activities that promote excellence. In each case, the structure of the activities themselves serves to promote connections between discrete facts, allowing students to think critically and engage in problem solving across multiple content areas.

One underused pedagogical tool, particularly in grades K–3, is play. We believe that play has a place in the elementary school classroom when it is used purposefully by teachers to promote student development in specific areas. Students who engage in play rather than other activities have been shown to develop superior creative-thinking and problem-solving skills (Berretta & Privette, 1990; Feitelson & Ross, 1973). Play also appears to support children's language development by providing a mechanism for scaffolding their use of oral language in multiple pretend settings (Levy, Wolfgang, & Koorland, 1992; Neuman & Roskos, 1993). Other research links play to the development of theory of mind in young children (Burns & Brainerd, 1979; Fink, 1976). Finally, there is strong evidence that dramatic play related to literature builds children's story comprehension skills (Pellegrini & Galda, 1982; Saltz & Johnson, 1974).

These studies are frequently cited by those advocating for more play in classrooms, although some suggest limitations to the benefits of play when it is not guided by adult interaction (Burns & Brainerd, 1979; Saltz & Johnson, 1974; P. K. Smith & Syddall, 1978). Additionally, studies examining the effects of play-based curricula on academic growth when compared to more traditional curricula have shown no greater academic gains at the student level in preschoolers (National Center for Education Research, 2008).

Based on this evidence, it is clear that practitioners seeking to implement play as a tool for teaching in the classroom cannot use it without some thought. Intentionality is a hallmark of effective instruction: Good teachers clearly understand their students' developmental needs and utilize teaching

Lessons from the Field: Using Centers to Enrich Learning

One approach we have seen used with success in FirstSchool classrooms to enrich student learning and integrate play is the use of structured centers. Using this approach, teachers take traditional play centers, such as home living and blocks, and provide guidance that requires children to use both curricular knowledge and critical thinking skills. Such centers also provide teachers with an opportunity to integrate across multiple content areas. For example, a teacher might turn the home living center into a camping center while the children are learning about animals in science. Children visiting the center must set up a camp and create a plan to track and learn about animals in the area. Teachers provide books and websites that children may use as resources to create their plans and learn about when and where such animals can be found. Adults routinely visit the center to scaffold children's learning, ask them questions that require them to make connections between discrete pieces of knowledge, and assist them in finding relevant information. Experiences like this harness children's natural engagement through play, instruct them in basic curricular objectives related to language arts and science, and permit children to use higher-order thinking skills on a daily basis. Such centers are changed biweekly to provide children with new experiences throughout the year.

techniques that will allow them to fulfill those needs. In the areas that play positively affects, providing and facilitating play can be highly effective. For areas in which play has not been found to be effective, other methods such as authentic experiences and direct instruction may hold more promise. Regardless of which approach teachers take, though, enrichment should have a place in the daily lives of young children.

For older children, who may be less inclined to engage in center-based play or for whom school budgets do not allow for material purchases, project-based approaches may prove fruitful for teachers working to integrate curriculum while building higher-order thinking skills. Building from units in which students are engaged or utilizing expressed student interests, teachers may create projects for students which allow them to use basic skills focused on comprehension and content knowledge to learn new information while engaging in higher-order thinking to complete more complex aspects of the project. Teachers may block off 30 minutes per day during which children engage in project activities, building on the skills and competencies developed during other parts of the day. Such projects allow teachers to differentiate instruction individually and work with students one-on-one to develop new proficiencies that students are motivated to learn through their project participation.

For example, a kindergarten teacher interested in providing students with rich opportunities to study animals created a project in which students chose animals from a single biome and studied them extensively. They used the information they gained in combination with the information gained by their classmates to create a life-sized, three-dimensional exhibit, with the backdrop depicting the biome itself, and students creating costumes that allowed them to become their animals. Students were required to use relevant information, attending to body coverings and methods of movement in creating the costumes. At the conclusion of the project, parents were able to tour the exhibit, pushing buttons on each child to receive information about that particular animal. Such a project required students to not only know the basic content but fit it together with content gained by others to form a rich knowledge schema on the flora and fauna of the biome on which they focused.

ROLE OF LEADERS

As instructional leaders, principals, along with curriculum specialists and central office personnel, must develop and nurture a school and district culture in which these important instructional practices can thrive. Creating an enriched environment for all students involves multiple tasks; FirstSchool recommends four that are essential to the process. First and foremost, leaders must develop a parallel process in which they create for the adults what they want adults to create for their students. Everyone in the school environment should be viewed as a learner for whom the cultures of caring, competence, and excellence are developed and nurtured. Second, leaders need to adopt curricula that focus on depth as well as breadth and emphasize the CCSS goals of developing the abilities of students to clearly express their thoughts, feelings, and ideas, to reason abstractly and quantitatively, and to construct viable arguments and critique reasoning. In so doing, leaders remove much of the pressure that forces teachers to deliver only didactic instruction. Third, teachers benefit from seeing effective practice in action. Leaders can support this by identifying teachers who are comfortable utilizing quality pedagogical approaches and making arrangements for other teachers to systematically visit and observe in these classrooms. Finally, leaders should put in place data systems that enable teachers to critically examine their own practices. The FirstSchool Snapshot and the CLASS (described in Chapter 3) provide rigorous data that illuminates practice, but schools without access to these measures can collect similar data more informally by allowing colleagues to observe and provide feedback to

Perspectives from the Field

It is easy to say we have "data-driven practices," but only with time spent discussing the data results, looking at classroom practices, moving past excuses, and really having personal examination of educational instructional practices will change occur. Professional conversations can take place, but relationships of teachers and administrators are key to true teacher buy-in.

—Terrie Beeson, principal

one another. By facilitating an environment in which teachers are comfortable moving away from pedagogy that relies solely on didactic instruction, providing educators with models on which to base changes in their practice, and giving them the tools with which to track their progress, leaders can have a profound impact on the prevailing culture of pedagogy in schools.

CONCLUSION

Clearly, quality instruction is crucial to student success, and we have identified and demonstrated many effective approaches for teachers to incorporate. At FirstSchool we found it important to keep teachers focused on a manageable number of quality aspects that generate positive outcomes for African American, Latino, and low-income children. This is why we organized 10 strategies that foster academic and social–emotional development into a conceptual framework, which highlights the cultures of caring, competence, and excellence. We also connected research to each of these instructional practices, so teachers could understand the significance of the instructional decisions they make and data to monitor progress. Such pedagogical changes require deep levels of change, and with intentionality, time, effort, supportive leadership, data, and collaboration, all classrooms can become places where quality instruction is the everyday experience for all learners.

CHAPTER 6

Home and School Partnerships: Raising Children Together

Cristina Gillanders, Iheoma Iruka,
Cindy Bagwell, Jenille Morgan, and Sandra C. García

Most school personnel believe that parental involvement in school is a critical aspect of children's learning and development. Extensive research supports the importance of home- and school-based parent involvement in children's learning, social competence, and achievement (Epstein, 1990; Epstein & Dauber, 1991; Fantuzzo, Davis, & Ginsburg, 1995; A.T. Henderson & Mapp, 2002; Jeynes, 2010; McWayne, Hampton, Fantuzzo, Cohen, & Sekino, 2004; Miedel & Reynolds, 1999; Parker, Boak, Griffin, Ripple, & Peay, 1999). Although previous research is valuable in highlighting the importance of connections between schools and families, in this chapter we underscore the reciprocal nature of these relationships, and begin by explaining our choice of the term *home–school partnerships* rather than *parent involvement*. The term *parent involvement* typically suggests a view wherein parents are involved in ways defined by the school and directed toward achieving goals that parents have no part in setting. In this type of relationship, power is held by the school rather than being shared between the school and the families. Since the focus in all of our work is on African American, Latino and low-income (AALLI) children and families, who have been fundamentally disenfranchised from the school culture, we use the term home–school partnerships to reflect the view that schools should "partner" with families, thus creating a balance of power and a more equitable exchange of ideas.

The goal of this chapter is to describe FirstSchool's approach for promoting positive and reciprocal home–school partnerships. We begin by highlighting the value of home–school partnerships for the well-being of children and families. We then provide a historical perspective of the changes in views with regards to home–school partnerships in the United States,

---

Assessing Your Thoughts

Before reading further, make a list of all the reasons why you think home–school partnerships are important for children's learning and development.

---

with a focus on families from minority backgrounds. We also describe the challenges of developing a school culture that promotes greater congruency between the school's ideals of home–school partnerships and their actual practices, especially with regard to AALLI children and families. We end with FirstSchool's approach to reframing home–school partnerships with the hope that as school leaders, teachers, and teacher educators read about our experiences, they will engage in a process of self-reflection that leads to reaffirming, extending, or changing perspectives on working with AALLI families and children within their classrooms.

WHY HOME–SCHOOL PARTNERSHIPS?

Effective home–school partnership practices that are positively associated with children's outcomes are characterized by a common focus on children's development, consistent communication, sharing between parents and teachers, and parents acting as advocates for their children (Epstein, Coates, Salinas, Sanders, & Simon, 1997; Hughes & Kwok, 2007; Knopf & Swick, 2007; Minke & Anderson, 2005; Robinson & Fine, 1994). Iruka, Winn, Kingsley, and Orthodoxou (2011) examined parents' and teachers' perception of their relationship (i.e., trust, clarity of communication, agreement) and found that strong parent–teacher relationships were related to kindergarten children's socioemotional development, as rated by teachers. This was specifically the case for African American children. Furthermore, research findings indicate that when kindergarten teachers perceived that their education values were different from the parents, they were more likely to rate children as low in literacy and math skills and indicated lower expectations for children's future academic success (Hauser-Cram, Sirin, & Stipek, 2003). Home–school partnerships that "include trust, two-way communication, respect, and commitment" (Minke & Anderson, 2005, p. 182) help both parents and teachers understand children in different settings, and promote more individualized instruction and support. These partnerships also improve children's attitude toward school and their relationships with teachers and school personnel (Cowan, Swearer, & Sheridan, 2004).

Home–school partnerships benefit schools in multiple ways, including improving school climate (e.g., Noblit, Malloy, & Malloy, 2001), teachers' sense of efficacy (Hoover-Dempsey, Bassler, & Brissie, 1987), safety (e.g., Phillips Smith et al., 2004), problem behaviors (e.g., Minke & Anderson, 2005), and children's learning. That is, when teachers and parents are able to discuss and understand what happens in both the home and school context, then teachers and families can better individualize activities and supports to scaffold children's learning and development (Cowan et al., 2004). Furthermore, home–school partnerships provide the opportunity for teachers and families to strengthen children's learning by making explicit connections between home and school experiences, which facilitate children's use of knowledge in these different settings. For example, teachers can find out from the families about children's shopping experiences in their communities and incorporate them into lessons in mathematics about money (Taylor, 2009).

Historical Views of Home–School Partnerships in the United States

Historically, there has been a constant interplay between parents and schools about who has the authority for the education of America's children. In early colonial settlements the vast majority of children were educated in the home by their mothers. When America's first public schools were established, they were located in small, unified communities in New England and governed by laypersons who were parents from the community (Carnes & Garraty, 2006). Parents were responsible for decisions regarding teacher selection and the curriculum taught in the schools. Teachers often taught an entire community of children in one-room settings and lived in the towns where they taught. As such, they were familiar with the beliefs and practices of families in the community. Consequently, families and schools often shared values and worked together as partners in the task of educating and raising children (Hiatt-Michael, 2008). Schools were seen as instruments of local communities that ensured literate citizens and instilled the virtues and values of the communities in their children (Carnes & Garraty, 2006).

In the years preceding the American Revolution, some of the country's most influential leaders began promoting education of the masses as critical to the survival of the emerging nation. This led to a more systematic approach to education and the creation of publically supported elementary schools designed to ensure that citizens had basic literacy and computational skills and the knowledge necessary to exercise their rights and duties as American citizens. Increasingly, schools were administered on a statewide basis and taught by teachers who had received formal training (Kliebard, 2004).

With the advent of the industrial revolution and the expansion of public education, power in schools shifted from parents to the school authorities. In an effort to minimize child labor, laws for compulsory education made it illegal for a parent to keep a child out of school (Ensign, 1921). In order to educate a growing number of children, many of whom were immigrants, schools substituted the individualized instruction used in the single-room schools with a factory model of schooling and a graded curriculum. This model of education required professional preparation for teachers and organizational structures for efficient management of the school. It was believed that parents lacked the knowledge, time, and skills to educate children and therefore that this task should be transferred to professional educators (Hiatt-Michael, 2008).

In the case of African American children, they were not afforded the educational freedoms that their White contemporaries enjoyed. However, in spite of being the only immigrant group to have been legally denied access to education, African American parents have a long standing history of being invested and involved in their children's learning (Anderson, 1988; Bullock, 1967; Salzman, Smith, & West, 1996; Williams, 2005; R. R. Wright, 1909). During slavery, African American parents defied antiliteracy laws, risked severe punishment (e.g., violent beatings, amputation of fingers and toes) and even death to create paths to learning for their children (Rawick, 1977; Stroud, 1827; United States Work Projects Administration, 1936). Because of the high risk associated with becoming literate during this time, the small percentage that managed to attain it employed surreptitious strategies (e.g., eavesdropping, late-night lessons) that required the cooperation and efforts of several participants. For enslaved youth, learning was a communal effort that often included their parents, peers, extended kinship networks, church, and community (Salzman et al., 1996; Williams, 2005).

After Emancipation, African American parents seized the opportunity to acquire education for themselves and their children. They provided land and donated money, time, labor, books, and other resources to establish schools (Anderson, 1988; Williams, 2005). In June 1863 the American Freedmen's Inquiry Commission, a federal agency, determined "one of the first acts of the Negroes when they found themselves free was to establish schools at their own expense" (p. 7). They further discovered that African American parents were "eager to obtain for themselves, but especially for their children, those privileges of education which have been jealously withheld from them" (p. 30). As religious and abolitionist organizations such as the Quaker missionaries and American Missionary Association sought to provide them with much needed physical and material resources, African American parents expressed yearnings for education (Salzman et al., 1996; Williams, 2005). While many times they partnered with these organizations to fund the boarding, payment, and protection of White Northern teachers, conflicts arose over who would do the hiring and make pedagogical decisions (Jones, 1980; Williams, 2005). Similar contentions manifested when

White planters began to provide land for schoolhouses on their property to attract and retain a Black workforce. While the planters wanted teachers who would instruct in lessons of docility and hard work for little pay, the former slaves who built the schools and paid the teachers wanted to select and employ their own teachers (Williams, 2005).

The fervor with which former enslaved people pursued education was instrumental in initiating the movement for universal public education through taxation in the American South, which benefited African American and White children alike (Anderson, 1988; Dubois, 1935; Gutman, 1987; Williams, 2005). Some African American parents advocated for their children through passionate letters to the president and Freedmen's Bureau (Berlin, Glymph, et al., 1990; Berlin, Miller, Reidy, & Rowland, 1993; Williams, 2005). Meanwhile, others organized statewide conventions where they publicly expressed arguments supporting the right to education for their children (Cromwell, 1904; Foner & Walker, 1980; Williams, 2005). Despite these attempts, progress was slow, as they lacked the economic and political status to advance their educational agendas.

During the era of segregated schooling when parents faced inadequate funding, acts of discrimination, and threats to their personal safety, African American parents persisted as advocates for their children. In a series of court cases beginning as early as 1849 with *Roberts v. City of Boston*, African American parents fought to secure public education as a civil right. Similarly, in later years Mexican American parents also engaged in legal struggles for school desegregation in a series of cases starting in 1925 in Arizona, Texas, and California. One of the most prominent of these cases that paved the way for *Brown v. Board of Education of Topeka* (1954) was *Mendez v. Westminster* (1946) (Valencia, 2005). In this case, five Mexican American fathers challenged the practice of school segregation in the U.S. District Court in Los Angeles. They claimed that their children, along with 5,000 other children of Mexican ancestry, were subject to discrimination by being forced to attend separate schools (Valencia, 2005). These parent-initiated attempts resulted in *Brown v. Board of Education of Topeka* (1954), a landmark case in which the U.S. Supreme Court declared racially segregated public schools unconstitutional.

While the intent of this historic decision was to allow African American students access to the material benefits and opportunities that integrated schooling could offer, the process by which this should be accomplished was not prescribed. As such, policymakers assumed this objective could best be reached by dismantling materially and culturally "deficient" African American governed schools and dismissing, demoting, or redistributing their students, staff, and administrators to "superior" White schools (Trent & Artiles, 1995). With this approach came the unintended consequence of disrupting the educational process of African American youth in schools that reflected the norms and customs of their communities and placed them in an educational environment with "administrators and teachers who were unprepared to deal with their cognitive styles, social values, beliefs, customs, and traditions" (Trent & Artiles, 1995, p. 229). It also upset the "unique institutional arrangements" within the African American community in which families, schools, and churches were intimately intertwined (C. S. Johnson, 1954).

Similar initiatives to advocate for equal educational opportunities for their children have been initiated by other nondominant parents groups in later years. Examples of these initiatives are *Serrano v. Priest* (1971), a suit involving a public school parent demanding statewide equalization of school funding; *Lau v. Nichols* (1974), in which the Chinese community sued the San Francisco Unified School District for not providing equal access to educational opportunities to students who did not speak English (Hiatt-Michael, 1994); and finally, *Leandro v. State of North Carolina* (1997), where parents from 11 school districts argued that the state failed to provide adequate funding to properly educate children living in rural areas and disadvantaged students from urban districts with disproportionately high numbers of poor, special education, and "Limited English Proficient" populations.

These legal battles reflect parents' commitment to provide educational opportunities for their children, and yet, through history, we have witnessed a progressive disconnection between the teachers' and the parents' roles in the education of children. This is especially true for families and children who come from low-income, minority, and immigrant backgrounds. During the 1960s and 1970s, AALLI children were viewed as coming from "deficient" or "culturally deprived" home environments that they needed to overcome. Schools had the task of providing the experiences needed for children to succeed in school (Paris, 2012; Valdés, 1996). The unspoken purpose of schools was to reproduce and perpetuate the dominant culture, and as parents were perceived as unable to accomplish this goal, communicating with them was not a priority. Schools had the mission of helping children succeed in the dominant culture *despite* the families, rather than *with* the families. When parents were included in the process, the focus was on "educating" parents in the ways of school rather than learning from them.

Present Day Views

In recent years, the pendulum has once again shifted toward including parents in schools. Researchers, policymakers, educators, and parent and community advocates have called attention to the importance of establishing closer relationships between teachers and parents. Also, schools have realized that it is not possible to educate children in isolation and that partnerships with families are integral to children's success. The early childhood field has a strong tradition of parent involvement. For example, parent policy councils in Head Start are designed as a way of soliciting parental input in the program's decision-making process. Recently, the Office of Head Start created the *Head Start Parent, Family and Community Engagement Framework* (Head Start Resource Center, 2011) as a guide for programs to support ongoing partnership between families and staff. This tradition, though, is not prevalent in early elementary schools. Frequently, the reasons for involving parents in elementary school continue to perpetuate "deficit" views. Schools include parents in order to "help" them do things at home that are in accord with school values and culture, implying they aren't doing enough or doing the "right" things at home. Some have called these practices "schoolcentric" (Lawson, 2003) since the main goal of these parent involvement activities is to fulfill the mission of the school rather than regard parents' goals and values.

A more informed view calls for home–school partnerships that support families in the task of raising children and provide opportunities for schools to become knowledgeable of family and community values and practices. Schools have the potential to serve as places for families to find social networks and supports. Social institutions that in the past provided social networking, such as extended families and churches, no longer serve that function for some families. Wilcox, Cherlin, Uecker, and Messel (2012) found that church attendance among less educated, lower-, and lower-middle-class Whites has declined dramatically over the last 4 decades, which reinforces the social marginalization of this group, although this has not been the case for African Americans and Latinos (Newport, 2010; Hartford Institute of Religious Research, 2011; Pew Forum on Religion & Public Life, 2008).

Overall, language and ethnic minority children and families are likely to live in poverty, have fewer employment opportunities, and live in racially segregated enclaves with fewer resources and networks that support families raising children. In addition, recent immigrants have fewer opportunities for social networking due to limitations of language, fear of deportation, discrimination, and so on (Lawson & Alameda-Lawson, 2012; Meyers & Jordan, 2006; National Center for Children in Poverty, 2007). In the case of recently-arrived immigrant families, for example, the school could be a hub for community resources and contacts with other immigrant families, which could minimize economic and material difficulties (Sheldon, 2002; Wanat & Zieglowsky, 2010). Schools could also be a place in which families find solace from the stressful conditions brought on by poverty and fear of deportation and develop bonding relationships with other parents in the community (Lawson & Alameda-Lawson, 2012). Additionally, schools can strengthen parents' sense of competence (i.e., self-efficacy) by providing information, support, tools, and resources that enable parents to support their children's academic and social competence (Owen, Klasli, Mata-Otero, & Caughy, 2008).

Home–school partnerships also can inform schools about children's out-of-school sociocultural experiences. Certainly, in order to succeed academically, children need to acquire school knowledge or the "culture of power" (Delpit, 1995). In school, children learn to read school materials, write for an academic audience, turn work in on time, interact with adults and peers other than family members, organize their thoughts and talk about what they know. However, educators must also recognize that children also learn within the environments of their communities and homes, and that these kinds of learnings enrich their understanding of fundamental concepts about the world and life. Educators who are unaware of the power of children's out-of-school experiences to enrich their lives, or do not see these experiences as relevant to school learning, miss the opportunity to utilize children's prior knowledge as a foundation upon which to build meaningful understanding of new ideas (for detailed thinking in this area, see Chapter 4 of this volume). As Lisa Delpit warned us in 1995, "When we teach across boundaries of race, class, or gender—indeed when we teach at all—we must recognize and overcome the power differential, the stereotypes, and the other barriers which prevent us from seeing each other. Until we can see the world as others see it, all educational reforms in the world will come to naught" (p. 134).

This perspective of home–school partnership requires that teachers view families as a resource rather than a liability. Unfortunately, few teacher education programs prepare teachers to establish positive relationships with parents, especially those from minority and low-income backgrounds. Epstein and Sanders (2006) surveyed schools, colleges, and departments of education to assess efforts in teacher preparation for promoting family engagement. While more than half of the respondents reported offering a full course on family engagement, nearly half were offered only at the graduate level. More respondents indicated that family engagement was addressed within other courses and covered in one or more class periods. Respondents noted that course content related to family engagement was most commonly covered as a component of early childhood coursework or special education. While those completing the surveys strongly agreed that teachers, administrators, and counselors should be knowledgeable about working with families, few felt that graduates from their programs were prepared to work with students from families with a minority background.

Given the lack of opportunities in preservice professional development to examine home–school partnerships, teachers rely on their own personal experiences to determine how best to work with families (Graue & Brown, 2003).

This is particularly problematic when working with minority families since the majority of the teachers come from White, middle-class backgrounds and their experiences with AALLI children and families is often limited, and potentially based on stereotypical images. In FirstSchool we encourage teachers to reflect on their own beliefs and practices regarding their relationships with families so that they can move beyond their personal experiences. For example, we asked teachers to describe their beliefs about AALLI families, and then we compared them with what parents told us in our focus groups. In this way, FirstSchool expands on the limited knowledge and opportunities provided to teachers at the preservice level through inservice experiences.

We have found that in all our partnering schools, teachers often recognized their difficulties with working with AALLI families and wanted to find ways to improve their home–school partnerships. In our questionnaire to teachers in North Carolina and Michigan, 98% of teachers agreed that parent involvement was important for a good school. We use this information as our starting point for creating more inclusive and collaborative partnerships between teachers and parents.

FIRSTSCHOOL APPROACH TO PROMOTING HOME–SCHOOL PARTNERSHIPS

FirstSchool Beliefs

In our initial work with schools we introduced our beliefs about home–school partnerships and encouraged schools to examine their own beliefs (see Figure 6.1). In our view, schools need to ensure home–school partnerships in order to incorporate children's and families' sociocultural practices into their curriculum and instruction.

In order to operationalize these beliefs, FirstSchool focuses on three core components of home–school partnerships:

- Shared vision
- Communication
- Relevant curriculum and instruction

Shared vision. *Partnership* is defined as "a contract entered into by two or more persons, in which each agrees to furnish a part of the capital and labor for a business enterprise" (Pickett, 2001). For home–school partnerships, this means that both families and schools need to contribute part of their "cultural capital" in order to achieve a genuine partnership. The definition also implies

Figure 6.1. Ensuring Home–School Partnerships

FirstSchool Beliefs about Home–School Partnerships

1. The school strives to be welcoming and to accommodate the unique needs of families in order to strengthen the home–school partnerships.
2. The school has a system in place characterized by two-way communication (mutual exchange) and frequent contacts in a variety of forms in a language(s) that is/are accessible to both partners.
3. The school provides a variety of opportunities for home–school partnerships, including the opportunity for families to network with each other.
4. Teachers and family members meet frequently to discuss shared goals and unique challenges in educating AALLI children.
5. The school informs families about community resources that assist in children's healthy development.
6. Teachers continuously examine how their cultural biases and misconceptions can affect their relationships with families and children.
7. Teachers validate nontraditional ways in which families contribute to children's learning and development.

Incorporating Children's and Families' Sociocultural Practices

1. Schools create multiple opportunities to obtain information about the families' sociocultural beliefs, attitudes, and practices.
2. Teachers continuously identify a variety of learning opportunities and sociocultural practices in children's homes that support school learning.
3. Teachers integrate relevant aspects of children's sociocultural practices into the curriculum and instruction.
4. Teachers make explicit connections between the knowledge learned in school and at home.
5. Teachers continuously examine the challenges and opportunities that AALLI children encounter when navigating dual worlds—the school and their home culture.

---

that there needs to be an agreement as to the goals of the enterprise. It is often the case that ethnic- and language-minority and low-income families have differing views on helping children learn and develop. For example, some Latino mothers in our focus groups disagreed with rewarding children with toys and certificates when they had done good work at school. They believed that children should be taught to consider it a reward to feel proud of their own work and for making their parents happy (Gillanders, McKinney, & Ritchie, 2012).

Strong home–school partnerships afford the opportunity for families and schools to work together to establish a shared vision of their roles in supporting children, as well as their goals for children. The ultimate goal is seeing that educators and families assume collective responsibility for providing support in the development and education of young children. This means that educators and families must welcome and utilize a variety of approaches that come from the school, home, and community. This openness is essential for families and acknowledges efforts that occur in the school setting (e.g., PTA, parent–teacher conferences, family nights), in the home (e.g., arranging tutoring, developing responsibility), and in the community (e.g., community service fairs).

Communication. A close and trusting relationship is crucial to creating and sustaining reciprocal home–school partnerships. Essential to this is open, mutual, and frequent communication. To sustain this partnership, the communication between the partners has to have specific characteristics:

- There has to be a system in place characterized by two-way communication (mutual exchange), frequent contacts in a variety of forms with a coherent message and in a language that is accessible to both partners.
- Communication has to promote effective relationships that are respectful, additive, meaningful, culturally aware, and responsive, which can best occur when school staff have personal knowledge of and relationships with the families of children they serve.
- The purpose of communication has to promote the shared vision of teachers and parents with the aim to improve curriculum and instruction and children's success in the classroom.

Relevant curriculum and instruction. Home–school partnerships allow educators to identify aspects of children's life outside the school that can be integrated into more meaningful curriculum and culturally responsive instruction. For ethnic- and language-minority and low-income children, whose lives and culture are often not represented positively or realistically, this is critically important. Families have a wealth of knowledge that can inform schools about how children have to navigate dual worlds—the school and dominant society (i.e., White, middle-class societal norms) and their own family background. For example, parents can share with schools that their children may respond to certain voice tones and eye contact that might be different from what is typically used or perceived as acceptable in schools.

Furthermore, families can illuminate for school staff the ways in which knowledge is used in different settings and contexts. Following the work of others (e.g., Gutiérrez, Morales, & Martinez, 2009; Moll, Amanti, Neff, & González, 1992; Souto-Manning, 2010b), we view families' activities as resources rather than liabilities. We envision that families and schools can work together to create hybrid practices in which the separating line between school and home knowledge becomes blurred and less defined (Gutiérrez et al., 2009). As described in

Chapter 4, children's experiences in their homes and communities are important elements of their learning. When teachers make explicit connections between the knowledge of the home and community, and that of the content they are teaching, children learn to use both as resources. Accessing children's prior knowledge provides them with ways to make sense of new information.

FirstSchool's work is centered on supporting schools to make the First-School principles and components a reality within their own contexts. In the following sections we describe the positive experiences as well as the challenges that we encountered in supporting their implementation in schools.

Barriers in Promoting Home–School Partnerships

We have faced a series of barriers that limit the ability of families and schools to work in partnership. These barriers have also been identified in the research literature (e.g., see Doucet, 2011; Hornby & Lafaele, 2011; Rowley, Helaire, & Banerjee, 2010) and seem to be the norm rather than the exception.

Schools perceive families from a deficit perspective and focus on "teaching" parents through unidirectional communication. As described earlier, historically schools often have the view that children and families from AALLI backgrounds are *deficient* and need to be *remediated*. For example, in our interviews with a small sample of White teachers, we found that the majority of them talked about African American families both negatively and as if they were all the same (Bagwell, 2012). In general, they described African American parents as uninvolved. One teacher stated, "Most of the time you don't see most [African American parents] and those are the kind of ones you need to see." Another stated, "They [African American students] don't have much support from home. I mean, you know, they don't help with homework." Seldom did teachers use any qualifiers that would indicate their perceptions applied to some African American parents and not others.

Many of these same teachers described their relationships with African American families as fragile and attributed these circumstances to factors such as poverty, single-parent households, having children "who are exceptional children or who've got social problems or psychological problems," and negative school experiences of African American parents. They appeared to be unaware of how their broader views of African Americans as poor, uneducated, single parents likely impacted their interactions with the African American parents of students in their classrooms, as well as the students themselves. The blame for unsatisfactory relationships rested on African American parents, and teachers seemed to assume that nothing could be done to change these circumstances (Bagwell, 2012).

In questionnaires, teachers indicated their belief in the importance of parent involvement in their children's education; yet the majority did not believe parents of AALLI children know how to help them with schoolwork. This viewpoint became even more prevalent as children moved through grade levels. As early as 2nd grade, teachers began to question the value of parents as partners and had significant questions about parents' abilities to support their children's learning.

Schools do not prioritize home–school partnership and it is only included when "there is enough time." Schools seldom establish the collaborative structures that allow time for planning future opportunities for partnerships and learning about children's families and cultures. Often, the responsibility of "parent involvement" activities lies with the social worker, family liaison, or school counselor. Communications with families are sporadic and opportunities to interact become "random acts of family involvement" (see Weiss, Lopez, & Rosenberg, 2010) rather than an integral aspect of school life.

Teachers often feel overwhelmed by the demands of accountability measures and delivering curriculum. While working to develop partnerships with parents is regarded as an important aspect of teaching, it is not considered critical. Teachers focus on ensuring children's success in the classroom, but underestimate the positive impact of relationships with children and their families on that success. We found that most teachers in our schools tended to rely on written forms of communication, such as newsletters, agendas, progress reports, and report cards as their primary method for keeping parents informed about what is happening in the school and classroom. Equating the notions of *informing* and *connecting* is a fundamental issue and illustrates the difficulty of moving from parent involvement to partnership. Personal communication, such as individual notes or phone calls, occurred infrequently and then only to address problems that had not improved through general written communication. Face-to-face meetings between teachers and parents often took place in large-group settings rather than one-on-one. For example, the first meeting between the teacher and parent is often at the Open House, which frequently is not conducive to individual conversations. Although this is often a well-attended event, parents are frequently asked to complete paperwork and have limited time to interact with the teacher.

Lack of identification of the unique needs and strengths of families (one-size-fits-all mentality). Traditionally, parent involvement activities include chaperoning field trips, participating in PTA meetings, attending parent–teacher conferences, and volunteering in the classroom. In our focus groups we explored how parents perceived schools' invitations for involvement.

Rather than providing opportunities to include parents, these traditional strategies frequently exclude AALLI families who do not find it possible to participate in those ways for a variety of reasons. Parents are less willing to participate on field trips when they cannot bring along their younger children or cannot take time off work without penalty. Immigrant parents with low levels of English proficiency cannot meaningfully participate in PTA meetings, in parent–teacher conferences and classroom volunteering when there are no interpreters, or when they cannot use their home language. Scheduling and transportation are often obstacles for families to attend school events (Gillanders et al., 2012). Therefore, traditional school involvement activities are designed for families in which a parent, usually a mother, has a flexible schedule, has educational experience in U.S. schools that bolsters her ability to volunteer in the classroom or in the school, has assumed leadership roles in the past, has the English proficiency to actively participate in discussions, and is empowered to defend the interests of her children (Doucet, 2011).

Parents' distrust of schools or meeting schools' expectations—especially historically disenfranchised or underserved parents. In our focus groups and interviews, parents often referred to their distrust of teachers and administrators. For example, the Latina mothers in our focus groups who are of undocumented status expressed a mistrust of social institutions, including the schools their children attend. These mothers do not attend school functions or parent teacher association meetings for fear of being identified as undocumented. In addition, they are often afraid to complain or express disapproval of anything that occurs within the school and classroom out of concern that their actions will have negative repercussions for their children. They refrain from asking too many questions about their children in order to avoid being seen as "problematic." This fear can create unique challenges for communication between home and school.

In focus group and individual interviews, African American parents discussed the importance of developing in their children a strong sense of self (Bagwell, 2012; Gillanders et al., 2012). From parents' perspectives, this foundation is critical in a world where racism continues. They want their children to know about their heritage and grow up "knowing that, you know, we play a part in society too." Unfortunately, schools often neglect the history, culture, and accomplishments of African American people, as expressed by one mother: "Teach them who was the first person . . . who was *really* the first man to do the open heart surgery? Who? But do you teach that to the kids? You don't hear talk of things like this . . ." Another mother described how her daughter had come from school describing the "gloomy" mood of the teachers when Barack Obama won the election in 2008.

African American parents also expressed concern about the way African American children are treated in school and described repeated instances of disrespect and neglect. When describing a classroom visit, one parent reported, "I didn't like the fact that one of the little Black boys that failed the 3rd grade before was in the back of her classroom and instead of him seeming like he had a lot of support, he was sitting there facing the wall all day." Another, in describing her son's experiences in 3rd grade, said, "There were some issues with how when he'd be at school and he would raise his hand . . . and he'd tell the teacher he needed some help, she was like, 'Well, figure it out on your own. Didn't your mama say you smart, you know what you're doing,' like that. So he would come home sad and depressed and say, 'Mama, the teacher won't help me.' So I went and spoke with her again on that and she was like, 'Well, I got so many students in the classroom and he just need to pay attention to his work.'"

A history of discrimination and racism can undermine parents' trust in schools to fulfill their goals for their children. Rowley, Helaire, and Banerjee (2010) examined whether African American mothers' perceptions of teacher racism when they were students related to their current level of involvement at their child's school, and whether the mother–teacher relationship makes a difference. In their study, they found that mothers with a perceived history of discrimination, who also had a negative relationship with their child's teacher, were highly involved in their child's school (i.e., attending open houses, talking to teacher, participating in PTO). The authors suggested that the mothers' frequent presence in school was a way of protecting their children from the same racism and discrimination they perceived when they were children. We found similar beliefs in our focus groups as described by this mother:

I believe they were, I mean they [*her children*] were treated with fairness and respect. For one, I believe because of parental involvement. Because my husband and I, we were here. They always saw our face constantly. But, at the same time, if you have a parent that may not be able to come here every day or be able to . . . I think they may be a little . . . [*from the teacher's point of view*] "I know this mom is coming if something happen to this child and I know this mother, but this child right here, I don't hardly see her mother or her father so I'm just gonna push her off to the side." So, you know, I think when I come I think it play a big role in fairness with the teachers. They need to treat every child the same, whether you see that mother's face or not. You still need to treat that child the same as if that mother came here every day like the other mother did.

***Lack of understanding of families' cultural practices and knowledge
limits teachers' ability to use children's background knowledge for learning.***
In an attempt to respond to AALLI children's inequitable school experiences,
educators often address children's diverse cultural experiences based on stereotypical characteristics of racially and ethnically diverse groups. Generalizations about group characteristics are used to define "learning styles" that are
then matched to specific teaching strategies (Gutiérrez & Rogoff, 2003). For
example, individuals from some groups are characterized as "holistic learners" whereas individuals from another group are characterized as "analytic."
Although this approach can be commendable (since it at least makes an effort to address diverse kinds of learners), it views cultural differences as static
and inherent to the individuals, rather than as a product of children's participation in the everyday practices of their homes and communities (Gutiérrez
& Rogoff, 2003). Many times teachers base their instructional approaches on
these broad generalizations without consideration for the wide diversity within groups. These generalizations limit teachers' curiosity about children's experiences outside of school. When time and resources are scarce, broad and
unexamined generalizations of children and families are the easiest ways to
address cultural differences.

A more useful approach for understanding children's sociocultural experiences is to create strategies and structures that allow teachers to become
learners or cultural anthropologists of children's lives outside of schools (we
provide examples of this approach later in the chapter). However, in order to
gain access to children's lives within their homes and communities, teachers
need to establish positive relationships with parents.

REFRAMING HOME–SCHOOL PARTNERSHIPS

As a starting place, we encourage schools to develop structures—regular
meeting times and places—in which issues related to home–school partnerships are discussed and planned. Schools are encouraged to create a team
comprised of school leadership, teacher representatives from each grade level, and family members. At times it might be challenging for parents to meet
with school personnel during school hours, so schools need to find alternative times and places convenient for parents to participate. This team should
meet regularly to discuss what kind of data or information they need to inform their efforts, how to gather it, and how to subsequently plan events and
strategies that are responsive to what they find (see Chapter 3). Moreover,
these meetings should promote regular and frequent examination of preconceived ideas about families, children, and teachers in a safe environment. We

have found that when regular meeting times are not prioritized, schools tend to view the work with families as secondary, or as the sole responsibility of the social worker or counselor.

As facilitators of the meetings of the partnership teams, FirstSchool staff helped raise the awareness of school personnel of the implicit beliefs of the *school culture* and of their impact on children's learning and development. We worked to reframe teachers' views of families from "deficient" toward a partnership view, in which families' resources are incorporated into the life of the school. We conceptualized this as a four-stage process in which we support and provoke teachers to (1) examine the school's beliefs and practices related to home–school practices, (2) change the perception of parents as unconcerned about their children's education, (3) create opportunities for teachers to build positive relationships with families so they can learn about their sociocultural practices, and (4) integrate children's knowledge acquired through their participation in the sociocultural practices in their homes and communities into the classroom.

Step One: Examining the Existing School's Beliefs and Practices Related to Home–School Practices

We begin by identifying the school's vision of home–school partnerships. In order to bolster the conversation, we share the Four Versions of Partnerships as described by A. T. Henderson, Mapp, Johnson, and Davies (2007) and facilitate a discussion in which the school personnel examine current practice and engage in the planning of next steps. Part of the conversation includes illuminating school staff views of parent participation in their children's education and ways to support children's learning. We push staff to examine their beliefs about families' resources and ability to raise their children.

Step Two: Changing the Perception of Parents as Unconcerned About Their Children's Education

As discussed earlier, it is often the case that AALLI parents do not actively and frequently engage with schools. As detailed in Chapter 3, we encourage teachers to inquire into the data we provide about AALLI parents' views about their children's learning and the school, and their own data (i.e., parent attendance at school events, children's homework completion, parent's contacts with school, and so on). Teachers are often interested and surprised when we report parents' responses to the focus groups and questionnaires. In one of our sessions one of the teachers expressed her dismay that one Latina mother reported paying a neighbor to help her child with homework. In another school

Assessing Your Thoughts

After reading the excerpts from focus groups in Figure 6.2, consider the following questions for further discussion:

1. What are these mothers' beliefs about their children's learning?
2. What is the potential for this kind of learning at home to help children learn at school?

the teachers were surprised to see how much time parents reported that they spend helping their children with homework. Through data we work to dispel myths about the parents' disinterest and provide a more accurate view of parents' beliefs about school and their role in their children's learning. In Figure 6.2, we provide an example of excerpts from focus groups with mothers held at our partner schools.

One school decided to take these ideas further and invited a group of parents who had participated in some of our focus groups to discuss in small groups with teachers the following questions: (1) What are your hopes and dreams for the children in your care? (2) What values do you think are important for children to develop in order to succeed in school? and (3) What ideas would you suggest for developing home–school partnerships at our school? Through these conversations, parents and teachers were able to identify common values and beliefs on the education of young children.

Step Three: Creating Opportunities for Teachers and Families to Build Positive Relationships

We often find that school structures unintentionally create obstacles to building positive relationships with families. Meaningful relationships take time and require opportunities for people to have one-to-one conversations through which they can learn from one another. However, we have found that schools provide few opportunities to build these relationships. For example, most children have different teachers each of the years they are in school, meaning that each year requires a new effort on the part of both teachers and parents to learn about each other. As children enter into elementary school, school buses are often used for transportation. Parents are not required to bring their children to school, limiting everyday contacts between teachers and parents.

In our focus groups some African American mothers indicated that they would like to be able to observe in their child's classroom. Although the

Figure 6.2. Mothers' Ideas About Children's Learning at Home

The following exchanges occurred in our focus groups with low-income White, Latino, and African American mothers.

Excerpt from a focus group with low-income White mothers

INTERVIEWER: What things do you have at your home that you use with your children to help them learn? What kinds of things do you do with them at home?

TRACY: Cooking and measuring and just everyday things.

MARY: Sometimes I think those things are more important than— I mean we all—at least uh we have lots of little tools and games and books, but really probably just my time whatever we're doing is the most important thing I guess, but it's—it's probably the most useful thing whether it's cooking, or I don't—it could be watching TV, but we're talking and . . .

SUSAN: Well, and like everything you do you're pretty much teaching them. If they're right there, you're teaching them. Like when I do laundry I throw all the socks in a basket, and my little one comes over and matches them up and hands me matches as I'm folding the rest of the stuff.

LAURA: Nice. I get them to do that every once in a while.

THERESA: I should have done that one. *[Laughs]*

SUSAN: Yeah. As long as they're there with you, they're learning everything that you're doing.

LAURA: But that's good because that's matching and that's finding.

SUSAN: So if the question is what tools, then I think probably . . .

MARY: Motherhood. *[Laughs]*

SUSAN: The great—the greatest tool is our knowledge, you know our awareness of what to—our awareness of what things that we can be doing and talking about to help them maybe more than a specific tool.

Excerpt from a focus group with Latino mothers

INTERVIEWER: ¿Y qué cosas tienen ustedes en la casa que creen que ayude a sus niños aprender matemáticas? (*What things do you have at home that you think help your children learn math?*)

GABRIELA: Ah, yo donde tengo las flores en el centro de la mesita, ahí tengo piedritas de estas, ¿cómo se llaman?, que son de colores. Mi hija cuando está haciendo su tarea agarra piedritas . . . para contar. Y eso le ayuda mucho. (*Ah, where I have the flowers on the center of the table, I have these small stones, how do you call them?, they have colors. My daughter when she is doing her homework takes the stones . . . for counting. And this helps her a lot.*)

VIVIANA: Pues yo a veces a la mía, a veces yo le digo, agarra una hoja aparte, y haz palitos, tacha todos los palitos, súmales palitos, quítales palitos y así. (*Well, sometimes I tell mine, take this sheet of paper, and make sticks, strikeout the sticks, add the sticks, take out the sticks, and so on.*)

LUCÍA: Yo a los míos, le enseñé con las semillitas de melón, o de sandía o jugar con palitos también. (*To mine, I taught them with melon seeds, or watermelon or also to play with sticks.*)

SOFÍA: Yo con los juguetes. De más chico, le decía, "Agarra los carros, tienes tres, quítale dos. ¿Cuántos tienes?" Con los juguetes mismos. (*I did it with toys. When he was*

*younger, I would say, "Take the cars, you have three, take away two. How many do you
have?")*
GABRIELA: Si hay muchas cosas comunes. (*Yes, there are many common things.*)

Excerpt from a focus group with African American mothers

INTERVIEWER: What things do you have in your home that help your child learn about
   math?
DONNA: Actually, my daughter just got a job as a waitress. So, what she has been doing is
   leaving out some of her tips for my son to play with and put different combinations
   together for him to learn money. So he has been saving. He has his own little jar
   where he has been saving, and what have you. And she'll have him trying to learn
   that way. Trying to count.
INTERVIEWER: Does he buy things at the store, or not? Candy or anything?
DONNA: He is very particular about what he purchases. And he'll hold the line up like,
   "No, wait a minute, maybe not."
INTERVIEWER: Oh, "But mama you can pay for it."
DONNA: No, he doesn't do that. He wants to make sure that that dollar is going as far as it
   can go. *[Group laughs]* And it holds up the line, so we haven't gotten that far yet.
THERESA: That's one thing that I have always taught my son, how to manage money.
   I work like crazy hours, so when they are at my mom's or their grandparents,
   they always go there. So, my son always says he has a job. He does stuff for his
   grandmother, so they pay him. So, when we go out to the store and he's wanting
   something, I'll always say make sure you have your money. So, yesterday, we went
   into the Dollar Tree. And I said, "If you want something, you can get something. But
   you need to count how much you get before we go in." So, we just sat out in the car
   and counted the money. I try to teach him how many quarters make a dollar, and you
   know, how many quarters make fifty cents, and two dimes and a nickel. So, I teach
   him stuff like that. When he goes in there, and they ask for the money, he knows. He
   asks me, "Do I got tax?" *[Group laughs]* You got to have tax. *[Crosstalk]*
DONNA: You always gotta have tax. *[Group agrees]*
THERESA: So, when he asks for the money, "He says he got tax, he got twenty-five cents."
   [Group laughs] So, you know, when it comes down to money, he does that pretty
   well. He manages his money. He knows, "If you got money you can get it, if not, my
   money don't grow on trees." I tell them that.

---

school claimed to have an open door policy, classroom visitations were re-
stricted to specific days and times. Teachers were reluctant to be observed,
claiming it would disrupt the school day. This created distrust between parents and teachers, with parents worried about how their children were being
treated and unclear as to why they could not visit without an appointment.
This lack of seeming "openness" of the school building created the unintended consequence of restricting parents' engagement in the school and partnership with teachers and school staff, further supporting the notion of the
uninvolved African American parent. Furthermore, parents were generally
called to the school and asked to speak with teachers only to address issues

like negative behavior, creating additional distrust and contention between parents and school personnel.

In one of our schools we had several discussions in the Family–School Team about the importance of teachers calling parents to report something positive about the child and asking about the child's life outside of school. The teachers indicated that because some parents did not speak English, they would have a difficult time communicating with the parents, especially on the phone. Teachers also reported that they only called parents when there was "a problem" with the child, and although they believed it would be beneficial to communicate with parents more often they did not have the time to call parents on a regular basis. After this discussion the school hired an interpreter to help teachers in these phone calls. Also, the principal asked teachers to call all the children's families at least once in each quarter. Teachers were reluctant at first, but then they realized the value of these calls. One 2nd-grade teacher describes her experience:

> I call 'em happy calls. "I'm just calling to give so-and-so a happy call tonight." "He did a great job with this today" or, you know, "He's off to a good start" or "He did some kindness for someone today" or whatever. If you get in the door and they understand, "I care about your child. I'm here to do what's best for them. I know you're my partner in this." And you know, if they hear me calling saying what your kid does wonderful . . . 'cause that's that old saying, "They don't care what you know until they know that you care." And as long as they know that I care about their child, they're going to listen to any of that other stuff I need to talk to them about.

We encourage administrators and teachers to examine their school structures and to review their priorities and goals. We point out the contradictions between their beliefs about home–school partnerships and their practices, and encourage them to reframe the structures that already exist in the school so that they are more aligned to their beliefs. As a university–school collaboration project, FirstSchool has the opportunity to collect data through the use of questionnaires, focus groups, and classroom observations. Although some schools might not have the capacity to use these forms of data, basic surveys that provide families the chance to share feedback can provide useful information for school personnel who want to know "How am I doing?"

One of the ways to build trust with families is to ask their opinion about the quality of the education their child is receiving in school (Kyle, McIntyre, Miller, & Moore, 2002). It requires courage, since teachers are poised to be subject to criticism, but at the same time it conveys the message to families that teachers are making a genuine effort to provide the best possible experience for their children and that the families' opinions are valued. To address the needs of non-English-speaking parents, teachers need to ensure that translated copies of the survey are available. Also, for those parents who might not be able to complete a written survey, it might be necessary to conduct an interview rather than ask them to fill out a survey on their own.

Step Four: Integrating Children's Knowledge Acquired Through Their Participation in the Sociocultural Practices in Their Homes and Communities into the Classroom

We have found that supporting teachers to integrate children's knowledge acquired outside of school is our most challenging task. Examples in the literature illustrate these challenges especially when trying to involve a whole school. The often-cited work of N. González, Moll, and Amanti (2005) on using funds of knowledge demonstrates the value of using the families' knowledge and skills for running their households and for ensuring the well-being of the family as a resource for children's learning in the classroom. Subsequent studies by other researchers who have put these ideas into practice have demonstrated that teachers change their perceptions of parents as they interact with children and their families in contexts outside of school.

For example, Kyle, McIntyre, Miller, and Moore (2002) looked at the reflections of two 2nd-grade teachers as they conducted visits to children's homes over a period of 2 to 3 years, with the goal of helping their students achieve academically. The data from the study revealed that the teachers obtained better knowledge of the child by hearing the parents' perspective. They discovered children's talents, interests, and needs that otherwise would have taken a long time to uncover. For example, one of the teachers learned that one of her students spent a considerable amount of time building things. The teacher incorporated this interest in a unit in neighborhoods by asking the child to build a three-dimensional model. Moreover, the teachers changed their perspectives on how the parents valued their children's education, and acknowledged parents' efforts to support their children in school. They also recognized the financial and emotional challenges and concerns of the families and identified how these had an influence on children's behavior in school. Finally, they recognized the families' funds of knowledge and incorporated them as much as possible in their curriculum and instruction.

In a "culture circles" approach to inservice teacher education, Souto-Manning (2010a) engaged two Head Start teachers in examining literacy practices in their classrooms and their relationships with children's home literacy experiences. During frequent home visits, the teachers discovered language and literacy use in the children's homes. Rather than asking parents to describe traditional literacy practices, they observed children and families as they engaged in everyday practices. These observations provided a starting point for designing experiences in the classroom that were attuned to children's home experiences. For example, they observed that language and literacy practices in the homes were embedded in social interactions. Many of the families sang hymns both at church and as they were conducting routine chores. The teachers used this practice as a way to negotiate children's meaning in ways that "syncretize" (Volk & de Acosta, 2003) the home and the more traditional practices in the classroom. They introduced one of the hymns as a read-aloud and shared reading text and allowed children to guide them in the way the hymn was used in their community.

Both examples illustrate how teachers can become interested in children's experiences at home and incorporate them as important aspects of the curriculum and instruction. This process can occur only if teachers develop positive

Using a Resource-Oriented Lens in Bus Tours

Currently, many educators do not live in the neighborhoods and communities where they teach. In an attempt to help teachers become familiar with the lives of their students, schools frequently organize bus tours to the surrounding communities. Although this experience can be eye opening for some teachers, it can also reaffirm their "deficit" views of the school's children and families. When exploring the neighborhoods in which students live, ask the following questions:

- Does the community gather in specific places and for what purposes?
- What opportunities do children have to play with their peers in the neighborhood?
- How do children participate in the community activities?
- What kind of signs and announcements can be seen in the community? Are there languages other than English used in the community?
- Is there a central place that many members of the community frequently visit (e.g., store, plaza, service, and so on)?
- What are the activities of daily living that children and families participate in within the community (e.g., buying groceries in the store, going to the laundromat, going to church, and so on)?
- What are the community funds of knowledge that could be related to the Common Core Standards and/or the district curriculum?

relationships with families. Families must be willing to open their homes and allow teachers to be participants of their everyday routines and practices. In addition, teachers must be able to identify potential practices to incorporate in the classroom. Therefore, we help teachers develop a "resource-oriented" lens for approaching families. We provide literature that exemplifies ways in which schools have used funds of knowledge to develop curriculum and instruction (see Chapter 4). Through this process, we encourage teachers to make explicit connections between children's background knowledge and new knowledge.

CONCLUSION

Educators agree that home–school partnerships are beneficial for children's learning and development. Though they share a common interest in the welfare of the children, parents and schools need support in working together. As we described in this chapter, historically rooted beliefs have drawn teachers and parents apart. These beliefs have created structures in schools that have kept teachers and parents from having meaningful relationships. We hope bringing them to light will help teachers and administrators identify the challenges inherent in establishing home–school partnerships and bring schools and parents together in the task of raising children.

Questions and Activities

1. Re-examine your original list of reasons why home–school partnerships are important for children's learning and development. Would you change anything now?
2. If you are a teacher, create a "How am I doing?" survey and send it to your students' homes. Summarize the results and discuss them with a colleague. What did you learn? What surprised you? How can you use what you learned to rethink your teaching and relationship with your students' families?
3. Visit the home of one of the AALLI children in your classroom. In your visit use a "resource-oriented lens"; that is, take notes and try to identify potential opportunities for learning in the family's activities. Once you finish your visit, analyze your notes and think about how these family activities could be integrated into your instruction.

Part III

THE FUTURE FOR AFRICAN AMERICAN, LATINO, AND LOW-INCOME CHILDREN

Looking Forward:
Program and Policy Considerations

Carolyn T. Cobb and Richard M. Clifford

The previous chapters have focused primarily on change at the local school and classroom levels. Often those of us working "in the trenches" miss the larger framework in which our work is taking place, due to day-to-day pressures. This chapter aims to set the work of improving school in the PreK–3rd grade span within the larger world of education history and policy, and include issues at the federal, state, and district levels. We believe it is important to understand the historical and current context for our educational structures and policies, as well as how each level of government links to others, in order to understand the potential for change and restructuring. While roles and responsibilities are not always clear-cut, examining the leverage points at different levels of education and government can help to make better decisions about our own roles in building strong PreK–3rd learning systems. By understanding who (i.e., which level of government) has the authority and leverage points, educators at every level can better gauge what can be accomplished in their own settings.

SYSTEMIC PROGRAM AND POLICY ISSUES

The Haphazard Development of Early Learning

PreK–3 as a "system" straddles the early learning programs that have a specialized focus on young children and the traditional elementary education system as we have known it. Kagan and Kauerz (2012) note various definitions used in the early learning field: early care and education systems (typically birth to age 5), early learning systems (birth to age 8), and early childhood systems (which include both of the previous systems, but extend their reach to encompass comprehensive services for young children). Programs intended to affect both birth to age 5 and school-age children impact how we look at PreK–3 and its development.

Birth-to-five early childhood and K–12 education systems each developed largely without a notion of a continuum for children. Head Start was created in 1965; and although there were efforts to link the program's principles to traditional education with the Follow Through project, Head Start developed largely independent of the national education agenda. Similarly, private child care, followed later by state PreK programs, all helped to cement a birth-to-five framework largely divorced from the K–12 education system. Research, education, and advocacy groups developed separately within the rarely converging lines of these two camps (Takanishi, 2011).

Early childhood saw the development of four major programs targeting low-income and at-risk children with separate administrative bodies and funding streams: (1) Head Start; (2) Child Care Development Block Grant; (3) Individuals with Disabilities Education Act (IDEA)—both preschool (ages 3 to 5, Part B) and early intervention (from birth to age 3, Part C)—and (4) Title I federal programs. These programs focused on somewhat different, although at times overlapping, target populations. Hustedt, Friedman, and Barnett (2012) outline the development of and investments in these four programs. They note that, other than Head Start, most federal initiatives intended to promote specific goals (e.g., providing child care for working families) are complemented by state or local initiatives that extend the federal goals. This has led to a multitude of early childhood programs that support early childhood care and education, which connect in sometimes disjointed ways to the formal schooling that begins in kindergarten.

The federal government invests approximately $13 billion annually in these four programs (Cooper & Costa, 2012). Adding the costs of child-care tax credits, the child-care food program, home visiting, and Department of Defense child care, Hustedt, Friedman, and Barnett (2012) estimate that total funds invested in various early childhood programs in 2010 was $19.6 billion. J. J. Gallagher, Clifford, and Maxwell (2004) emphasize the problems of coordinating and creating a seamless system across all of these early childhood programs. For example, they point out, among others, institutional barriers (e.g., different support systems, accountability or data systems, personnel preparation, and technical assistance programs), psychological barriers (e.g., different historical beginnings, beliefs, and philosophical bases for programs), and political barriers (e.g., affiliation with one party or another). A case can clearly be made for the need for even more funding to be allocated in support of these services. However, it is also true that existing funds could be better utilized if programs were coordinated in goals, services,

FirstSchool Brings Reform: Lansing School System

When Yvonne Caamal Canul accepted the position of interim superintendent for the Lansing School District in Michigan, she found budget deficits, declining enrollment, underutilized facility capacity, the need to raise student achievement, and general inertia in the school system. After much preparation, she presented her school board with a restructuring plan that reflected research-based child development support for specific grades housed in each school. Other restructuring principles included the following:

- Focusing on long-term instructional vision
- Creating learning environments that meet the needs of a 21st-century learner
- Maximizing facility capacity
- Incorporating elements of previous proposals and community feedback

In addition, she obtained the buy-in of the executive team, board officers and members, unions, and the media. The message was "bold changes = smarter schools." Key factors included the restructuring of the grade spans to begin the necessary work to enhance all students' learning and strategic allocation of resources.

- Districtwide focus on early learning: PreK–3rd grade schools
- Emphasis on the middle years transition: 4th–6th grade schools
- Early career and college preparation: 7th–12th grade schools

The surprising early outcomes included observations of a "domino effect," where focusing on PreK–3 as a core impacted all the other grade configurations that followed. There was internal support; teachers and administrators "got it." The media (newspaper, TV, radio) reported "good news" in education, beginning to move beyond the institutional inertia that had existed. Reconfiguration led to changes in school leadership, a clear and coherent plan for professional learning using Title II funds (Preparing, Training, and Recruiting High Quality Teachers and Principals), and student data aligned to school performance. And not least of all is the overall momentum seen in the system that included expansion of themes, new initiatives, and a shift in ethos.

My experience in the implementation phase of the Kellogg Foundation-supported FirstSchool effort in Michigan brought home to me the central role of PreK–3 in setting the stage for a new way of looking at school and district reform.

—Yvonne Caamal Canul, superintendent

infrastructure, and outcomes from the federal to the local level. But, is this feasible in the federal, state, and local bureaucracies, given the way these programs have developed?

Incremental Change

Charles Lindblom (1959, 1979) offered the term "disjointed incremental-ism" to describe the way social policy was, and arguably should be, made. He contended that complex problems cannot be completely analyzed and thus we require strategies for "skillful incompleteness" (1979). Yet there comes a point in social systems' development and functioning when strategies cease to work smoothly and discontinuities lead to a paradigm shift (Kuhn, 1962)—or at least major rethinking. Thinking along these lines leads K. H. Scott (2012) to call for *conjoint incrementalism*, an approach that adopts sustained and purposeful strategies to remedy the disconnectedness of existing policies and programs.

So the question becomes, how do we take the constantly changing system and entrenched bureaucracies to develop new program structures, as well as coordinated goals and resources? J. J. Gallagher, Clifford, and Maxwell (2004) suggest that we could look at the infrastructure, or common support system elements, within early childhood services as one way to begin to coordinate these programs. Rather than expecting our country's early childhood programs to merge service delivery, a first step may be to blend their support systems into a single system of coordination and oversight that could back all four major programs referenced in the prior section. State PreK programs could be included in this approach as well. These authors suggest that the elements that could be included in a single support system include personnel preparation, technical assistance, evaluation, data systems, communication, planning, and standards.

MOMENT OF OPPORTUNITY? INCREASING CALLS FOR A MORE INTEGRATED PREK–3RD GRADE APPROACH

Given the fragmented development of systems for early childhood care and education that often prevents seamless learning and instruction in the early years of schooling, is there a moment of opportunity at this juncture of persistent gaps in achievement and demands for higher standards of learning (e.g., Common Core State Standards)? We think there is. The widely accepted view that we need to improve student outcomes has created a national conversation around the importance of a strong PreK–3 component as part of a P–16 or P–20 learning system, and numerous initiatives have begun to help focus this change—FirstSchool is one key example.

For the last few years national foundations, advocacy groups, and professional organizations have had a lead role in bringing attention to PreK–3rd grade as a fundamental component of our educational system. Among the leaders in these efforts are the W.K. Kellogg Foundation and the Foundation for Child Development, both of which have provided funding for FirstSchool. In 2001 Kellogg launched the Supporting Partnerships to Assure Ready Kids (SPARK) initiative in eight sites (seven states and the District of Columbia), designed to smooth the transition to school and to align early learning and elementary school systems for children from ages 3 to 6 who were vulnerable to poor achievement (W.K. Kellogg Foundation, 2003). Additional Kellogg funding following the SPARK initiative focused on "ready schools" (Ready kids + Ready school = Successful Learning), seeking to increase the quality of early learning experiences necessary for a child's later success in school.

The Foundation for Child Development has focused on policy research and program issues in many publications through its PreK–3rd grade initiative. Their publications and briefs are extensive and cover the rationale and research base for PreK–3 financing, implementation, teacher preparation, leadership, and policy at all levels (federal, state, and local).

An innovative initiative in Minnesota showed that private funders can produce important leverage in shaping the policy agenda (Hage, 2012). After a decade of budget cuts and setbacks to early childhood learning, a coalition of funders came together to provide the support to move a PreK–3 initiative forward. These funders developed a common agenda, enhanced legislative advocacy, and provided the ability to quickly use smaller amounts of money to conduct studies and write reports. Their work led to the establishment of a Deputy Commission in Education to oversee early learning and link to Health and Human Services, a design for the new governor to use in establishing an Early Learning Advisory Council and support for three successful federal grant submissions. This example serves to remind us that we must look broadly at coalitions and collaboration for unity in pursuing important policy and program goals. Local school district and individual schools can seek outside funding in the same way, particularly since we have, in recent years, seen a proliferation of community-based foundations.

National professional associations are also contributing to the vision for PreK–3 and related policy and systems development discussions. Educational associations have joined the early childhood world in calling for a more concentrated and cohesive focus on quality learning during the PreK through grade 3 years, paying attention to our most vulnerable children, and developing a coherent vision and system (Council of Chief State School Officers, 2009;

National Association of Elementary School Principals Foundation Task Force on Early Learning, 2010; National School Boards Association, 2008). The Council of Chief State School Officers (2009) recognized that serious action was needed to reduce the achievement gap and ensure that all children enter school ready for sustained success. They called for building coherent state early childhood systems, defining and demanding quality in all early childhood settings, fully aligning early childhood systems with elementary schools and crafting a new state–federal partnership that supports high-quality early childhood opportunities for all, especially our most vulnerable children, such as the African American, Latino, and low-income (AALLI) populations. The National Association for the Education of Young Children (NAEYC) has worked diligently to bring together early childhood and early elementary school personnel to discuss bridging the gap and bringing constructs of quality to elementary education, while the American Education Research Association (AERA) has worked to strengthen research in this area.

In 2010 the PreK–3rd Grade National Work Group was organized to promote high-quality learning experiences for children from PreK through 3rd grade (ages 3 to 8) by focusing on knowledge and understanding of effective PreK–3rd grade policy and practice, with an emphasis on instruction and engagement in learning. Members recognize that this requires an aligned system across early childhood and elementary education. A series of webinars titled *Reducing Achievement Gaps by 4th Grade: The PreK–3rd Approach in Action* was instituted in 2012 to focus on the PreK–3rd grade approach in action (PreK–3rd Grade National Work Group, 2013). Members include representatives of research, practice, policy, and professional organizations.

WHO'S IN CHARGE ANYWAY? ROLES AND RESPONSIBILITIES FOR PREK–3 POLICY AND PROGRAM REFORM

After nearly 25 years of effort to improve the early care and education system, we still have not clearly defined roles for the federal, state, and local governments as they seek to target resources. The vertical spread of responsibility over the three levels of government is further complicated by the horizontal spread across various agencies within each of these levels of government, especially across education, health, and human service bureaucracies. At all levels of government, we lack structures that span the birth–8 years whether it is in governance, funding, institutional organization, or personnel preparation.

Other nations have tackled this problem directly. Sweden chose to bring all of education, from birth to death under one national education agency, with a strong role for the national government but implementation largely left to local entities. Finland provides another example of a united focus toward educational excellence. While we should not expect to duplicate any other country's model, we can learn from others and use their experiences to help develop our own solutions to this complex issue.

Many state education agencies (SEAs) are ill equipped to deal with the shift to younger children entering school. Very few resources are directed toward enabling SEAs to establish a strong role in assisting local districts and schools to tailor their programs to meet the needs of younger children coming into the schools. States are in need of strong federal assistance to create the ability of the SEAs to provide substantive assistance to local districts and schools on a consistent basis. Here the federal role can be modest but still have a significant impact. Many states have now at least one person in their education agency focusing on early childhood, but the major move for optimizing the experience for children under the traditional age of entry to kindergarten requires considerably more state-level support to ensure that schools are able to truly meet the needs of these younger children, make PreK an integral part of schooling, and link the new PreK initiatives with the primary grades.

In the following sections, we attempt to further parse the historical, emerging, and potential roles across the levels of government.

PROMISING DIRECTIONS FOR LEADING PREK–3RD GRADE TRANSFORMATION

Federal Level Today

A critical role of the federal government—other than funding for targeted groups of at-risk children—can be to promote an agenda for early education. As part of the Improving Head Start for School Readiness Act (2007), governors were required to create or designate an existing entity for improving the coordination and quality of programs and services for children from birth to school entry. While these councils may go by other names, they generally are referred to as Early Childhood Advisory Councils (ECACs). Although authorized through the Head Start legislation, these councils are to include representatives from health, child care, education, Head Start, and IDEA–Part C and focus on the comprehensive needs of young children. They are also supposed to look for both barriers to and opportunities for collaboration across federal and state early childhood programs. These councils have begun to address coordination across agencies but have yet to work across age spans. Critics believe it is just another effort at Head Start "coordinating" the rest of the

Lessons from Finland: Another Way

Why do Finland, Canada, and Korea demonstrate consistently high learning results regardless of socioeconomic status while the United States cannot seem to move beyond decades of below average scores and wide performance variation? Clearly, the United States has put a lot of effort and money into improving education, yet we continue to fail our African American, Latino, and low-income children. While Finland is clearly different from the United States politically, economically, and demographically, lessons learned about how they went about educational reform are still appropriate to consider.

First, they believed in the value of time and research. For more than 30 years Finland has used research-based findings to make choices about effective practices. They do not group by ability, they have decreased the use of retention, and they pay systematic attention to special needs. They test less frequently, focus on formative assessment, and test only 10% of each age-level cohort on the national assessment. Finland's teachers teach less than other countries, although students learn more—approximately 600 hours annually compared to the US average of 1060 hours.

Although all these factors are important to their success, it is their teachers that seem to provide the "Finnish advantage." Teaching and instruction is at the core of schooling. Instead of focusing on teacher evaluation and accountability, they emphasized building a professional teaching force. The teaching profession is highly regarded, the field is competitive, and teachers' salaries are slightly above the national average.

Once in the classroom, teachers are respected for their knowledge, education, and personal attributes. Teachers have the opportunity to engage in school improvement, curriculum planning, and personal profession development during the school day. Collaboration, reflection, personalized learning and creative teaching are prioritized and teachers rely less on formal teaching time and homework as drivers of student learning.

In the 1980s *A Nation at Risk* declared the U.S. education system "mediocre" and created an enduring national conversation focused on greater equity for higher achievement among all students. Finland has made choices that have served their students well in order to accomplish similar objectives. It does not escape our notice that much of what has worked for them is also important to the FirstSchool approach. Let us use their successes and those of others to help us reconsider the drivers of educational reform and achievement. Perhaps there is another way.

Note. This summary of Finland's educational approach was taken from *Finnish Lessons: What Can the World Learn from Educational Change in Finland?*, by P. Sahlberg, 2011, New York: Teachers College Press.

system. Optimally, these councils *could* serve as a key coordinating body for PreK through grade 12 education.

In 2009 Arne Duncan, the U.S. Secretary of Education, addressed the National Association for the Education of Young Children and urged that we must better link early learning programs to K–12 education to create a P–16/20 continuum in order to prepare all children to succeed in the 21st century (Duncan, 2009). He appointed an advisor for Early Learning and in 2010 established the Office for Early Learning to address PreK to grade 3 priorities and to coordinate with the Department of Health and Human Services (DHHS). This office is now headed by a deputy assistant secretary. It is the principal office charged with supporting the Department of Education's Early Learning Initiative, with the goal of improving the health, social–emotional, and cognitive outcomes for children from birth through 3rd grade so that all children, particularly those with high needs, are on track for graduating from high school college- and career-ready.

In May 2011 the secretaries of Education and Health and Human Services jointly announced a $500 million state-level Race to the Top— Early Learning Challenge Grant (see www2.ed.gov/programs/racetothetop -earlylearningchallenge/index.html). The grant competition was intended to help states raise the quality of early learning programs by building bold, comprehensive early learning programs and services around a tiered quality rating and improvement system. A related goal is to provide a boost for states to advance high-quality, comprehensive, early childhood systems and services. While this grant focuses on birth to age 5, it is seen as a parallel to Race to the Top for kindergarten through 12th grade and must at least coordinate with the goals of that initiative. Importantly, there was an invitational priority for states to address plans for extending learning into the early grades of public schooling. This invitation offered states the opportunity to address a PreK–3rd continuum as part of their systems building. However, this priority was not required and did not include additional funding. So even in current, related grants issued by the federal government, alignment still remains an untapped opportunity.

In 2010 the U.S. Department of Education issued *A Blueprint for Reform: The Reauthorization of the Elementary and Secondary Education Act*. The priorities in this blueprint include raising standards for all students and building better aligned assessments, focusing on strengthening teacher and leader preparation and recruitment with an emphasis on improving teachers and leaders in high-need schools, ensuring equity and opportunity for all students, and promoting innovation and continuous improvement.

These priorities mirror those promoted by the American Recovery and Reinvestment Act of 2009 (ARRA), better known as the "Stimulus Bill." States applying for ARRA grants had to promise to make progress in four areas: (1)

rigorous standards and aligned assessments, (2) longitudinal data systems to track students' progress, (3) teacher effectiveness and equitable distribution of qualified teachers, and (4) interventions to turn around the lowest-performing schools (Kober & Rentner, 2011). While these may be important and ambitious goals, there is no mention of PreK–3 early learning as a key component in either the blueprint or ARRA.

Fullan (2011) critiques the traditional drivers of change that include standards, assessments, data systems, and teacher evaluation, saying they do not provide a solid foundation. The four drivers that he suggests as the anchors of whole-system reform are *capacity building, group work, pedagogy, and "systemness."* Fullan explains further: "Focusing on standards and assessments does not highlight adequately the *instructional improvements* that are the core driver in the equation. Put slightly differently, it is the learning–instruction–assessment link that is at the heart of driving student achievement" (p. 8). His emphasis on capacity building relies on collaborative practices, coaching, technical skills building, and the like. He asserts that no nation has improved education by emphasizing individual teacher quality. They instead developed the entire teaching profession—raising the bar for all.

As the administration moves forward with its educational proposals and priorities, they may want to reassess how they help states and schools prioritize the time and resources to build deep cultures of collaboration, trust, and group work. Regardless of the worthiness of the proposed federal blueprint and some beginning fanfare for PreK–3, holistic solutions have yet to emerge. At the very least, movement can and must be made to create and allow greater coordination among existing sources of funding that will allow states and districts to better align elements of the PreK–3rd grade years.

It is likely that with the move toward greater flexibility, and with targeted funds from the Race to the Top and the Early Learning Challenge grants, states already have the potential to provide greater coordination and coherence and to focus on PreK–3. In the PreK–3rd grade arena the Early Learning Challenge grants provide the most promising opportunities. The big question is whether they have the capacity, the priorities, and the will to make the most of these opportunities.

State Level Issues and Examples

Regardless of the federal role, states have the primary responsibility to frame and lead educational reform, interpreting the federal incentives and creating their own goals and directions. They can do so by setting policy, addressing governance that provides more coherence for a continuum between early childhood and education, addressing the requirements for credentialing of early childhood and education staff, establishing coordinated accountability and data systems, and providing essential professional development that addresses key knowledge and skills to implement PreK–3rd reforms for early learning teachers and leaders. While they may be somewhat limited by federal requirements and incentives to focus on Fullan's proposed "right" drivers of reform, they can look for ways to allow the time for collaborative structures, promote appropriate instruction, and develop effective instructional assessments.

Because of the essential need for leadership by states, Usdan and Sheekey (May 2012) examined the capacity of State Education Agencies (SEAs) to guide reform. They cite several think tank reports (Brown, Hess, Lautzenheiser, & Owen, 2011; Kober & Rentner, 2011; Murphy & Rainey, 2012) that concur on states' limited capacity to lead change. States have not to date been funded adequately or structured in ways that allow them to transform their bureaucracies. In addition, the "new normal" is to do more with less; yet using more limited funding strategically is not a skill most states have mastered. Despite the report from the Center on Education Policy (Kober & Rentner, 2011) that noted that most states reported they did not need federal funding or legislative changes to implement many reforms, federal government incentives will likely remain a driving impetus for some time, and as such, federal legislation should include incentives to strengthen the capacity of SEAs (Usdan & Sheekey, 2012).

A key federal effort to support states' capacity to assist districts and schools in meeting student achievement goals lies with the Comprehensive Centers Program. This consists of 5-year grants to 22 Comprehensive Centers—both Regional Centers and Content Centers—that provide a national network of technical assistance focused on building the capacity of State Education Agencies to implement, support, scale up, and sustain initiatives statewide and to lead and support their Local Education Agencies (LEAs) and schools in improving student outcomes (U.S. Department of Education, 2012). Regional centers, which have a long history in the federal-to-state connection, are embedded in their geographic regions and are intended to help states implement federal programs and help increase the capacity of states to assist their districts and schools. Seven content centers are designed to cover the spectrum of school improvement and technical assistance areas (U.S. Department of Education, 2011a). These content centers, including one for Enhancing Early Learning Outcomes, provide in-depth knowledge, expertise, and analyses in their respective areas to regional centers and states. How these centers will be implemented and used by states will unfold over time. It is hoped that this work will move beyond their predecessors, who showed only limited ability to help states with major reform efforts.

Despite limited federal support and leadership, a number of states have moved forward with a PreK–3rd grade agenda. A number of states have worked to establish offices of early learning that focus on birth to five separate from health and human services and education agencies, and a few have really attempted the linkage of PreK to the early grades in K–12.

New Jersey. The *Abbott v. Burke* school finance case (1988) initiated efforts for high-quality PreK for disadvantaged children. The timeline and course of early childhood PreK reform that became the cornerstone of a larger PreK–3rd agenda, joining high-quality PreK, full-day kindergarten, and data- and literacy-focused reforms in the early grades is reviewed by Mead (2009). This initiative required districts to establish a coherent, districtwide approach to early grades reading and benchmark assessments.

In 2007 the New Jersey Commissioner of Education established a new Division of Early Childhood Education, which had programmatic responsibility for preschool through 3rd grade programs—the first such state-level education office in the country (Mead, 2009). Although a promising development, its effectiveness has been limited by a lack of resources and a lack of authority over many programs related to PreK–3rd (e.g., bilingual education).

In response to the critical need to support district administrators who had no background in early childhood education, a leadership training series was developed in 2009. Although this series helped school leadership focus on appropriate PreK–3rd student assessment systems, Rice and Lesaux (2012) recommend that the state still needs to (1) strengthen state guidelines to support the development of PreK–3rd early learning assessment systems, (2) engage state administrator associations and departments of education in strengthening professional development for these efforts, (3) engage higher education in the assessment conversation, and (4) identify a cadre of school districts that are implementing best practices and circulate their successes.

Washington. The state of Washington pursued a different strategy that began to bring coherence and alignment to PreK–3, namely, a comprehensive set of early learning standards (Froelicher, 2012). The standards—Washington State Early Learning and Development Benchmarks—were established in 2005 (Kagan, Britto, Kauerz, & Tarrant, 2005) and are intended to (1) establish a common set of standards that support children's early learning and development by promoting reasonable expectations and suggesting practical strategies for parent and others who care for or teach young children, (2) align with the state's K–3 Standards and Grade Level Expectations, and (3) contribute to a unified vision for Washington State's early learning system. In addition to other efforts, an outreach plan is being created to inform parents and other caregivers about the benchmarks, along with tools and materials; and the benchmarks are being used by personnel in higher education, as well the professional development workforce, to provide early childhood teachers with stronger and more specific knowledge of children's learning and development. The ultimate goal is for a continuum of learning and development that aligns early learning and K–3 standards.

Pennsylvania. Pennsylvania illustrates yet another approach, which utilizes top-down governance and policy directives to bring greater coherence to a PreK–3rd continuum of learning (Dichter, 2012). In 2004 Governor Rendell established the Office of Childhood Development (OCD) at the Department of Public Welfare to manage all child-care initiatives, home-visiting programs, and infant–toddler early intervention services. In 2007 the governor followed with the creation of the Office of Child Development and Early Learning (OCDEL), a consolidated Office and staff to integrate the work of the OCD with early learning at the Department of Education. OCDEL reports to both the Secretaries of Public Welfare and of Education. This innovative governance structure has initiated a number of efforts:

- Alignment of learning standards for early childhood from infant–toddler through 3rd grade
- Cross-systems technical assistance, with core competencies for all technical assistance initiatives
- A new component for mandated professional development for school system instructional leaders that brings leaders from both K–12 and early childhood systems together to build mutual understanding and strengthen alignment
- Replacement of the K–6 teaching certificate with P–4th and 4th–8th grade certificates
- A focus on early and basic education transition strategies involving Title I elementary schools and the Community Engagement Groups
- Development of a system of accountability, including program and fiscal monitoring, across all programs

The OCDEL experience in Pennsylvania demonstrates the value added by a "consolidated, innovative governance effort" (Dichter, 2012, p. 251). Yet it seems that this innovative governance structure put in place by a governor without legislative mandate could be easily upended as leadership changes. As discussed earlier, the Early Childhood Advisory Councils have often provided a forum for examining opportunities for collaboration across early childhood programs, including the early grades in elementary school.

The promise of the Early Learning Challenge. The Early Learning Challenge (ELC) initiative addresses transformation and system redesign for birth to 5 in fairly specific ways (Dichter & Wat, 2012)—for example, state systems that show an ambitious early learning and development reform agenda, early learning data systems, promotion of early learning and development outcomes for children, a high-quality early childhood education workforce, and measurement of outcomes and progress. But these program components do not directly address the split in decision making across agencies and levels of government. Existing bureaucracies can still protect turf and money.

The invitational priority of ELC related to sustaining program effects in the early elementary grades focuses specifically on the PreK–3rd continuum by addressing the linkage and alignment of reform activities at the early childhood level with those at the early elementary grades. Nine ELC applications were originally funded, with six of the funded states (Delaware, Maryland, Massachusetts, North Carolina, Ohio, and Washington) including the priority of sustaining effects into the early elementary grades (U.S. Department of Education, 2011b). These states may hold the greatest promise of demonstrating ways to align early education with early learning in primary grades.

However, are states really committed to PreK–3 reform? The Education Commission of the States held a "State of the State" conference in March 2012. The priority of early learning (specifically PreK–3) was mentioned by six states plus the District of Columbia—not exactly an overwhelming majority (Workman, 2012). Advocates, early childhood professionals, educators, and the private sector will all need to coalesce around the PreK–3rd continuum as a priority to create a compelling need for change for policymakers at the state level.

District-Level Initiatives

Although many of the policy levers reside at the federal and state levels of governance, local school districts can still move forward within the current policy and funding frameworks. Three examples illustrate very different approaches with the same goal—to build a solid foundation for learning at the earliest ages and grades to ensure future success for *all* children.

Montgomery County, MD. The journey for the 140,000 plus students of Montgomery County Public Schools (MCPS) started in 1999 as the new superintendent, Jerry Weast, discovered that he had essentially two separate systems: one that was large, urban, high-poverty, and high-minority (Latino and African American), which he called the "Red Zone"; and one that was suburban, predominantly White, and well-to-do, which he called the "Green Zone."

An ambitious 15-year target that 100% of students would graduate and 80% would be college-ready by 2014 was established. Early reform efforts included the following: early success (focus on early learning), standards-based curriculum, a quality workforce, a system of shared accountability, data-driven decision making, and family and community partnerships (Bacquie, 2004). In a detailed report, which examined the then decade-long reform effort and its results, Geoff Marietta (2010b) framed his findings as five key lessons:

1. Establish a clear and compelling district-wide goal that maps back to early learning.
2. Craft integrated district-wide early-learning strategies to meet the clear and compelling goal.
3. Align early learning programs and services with the integrated K–12 strategies.
4. Balance teacher support and accountability to ensure effective and consistent implementation.
5. Innovate and monitor for continuous improvement. (p. 2)

Critical to their success was a clear commitment to high-quality early learning for everyone. The Early Success Performance Plan was established to provide access to PreK programs for the most impoverished children by attendance zones using blended resources of Head Start programs (which the district coordinated), Title I funds, and state funds and programs. Full-day kindergarten was implemented, beginning with Red Zone schools and gradually expanding to all schools. Over time, other features including more time for learning through extended learning opportunities (i.e., after-school and summer programs) were developed. Keeping children in the same school throughout their early learning years was found to be important. Broad-based collaboration efforts with community members and child care were emphasized.

Other components of MCPS's initiative included translating state standards into grade-level indicators and linking PreK to K–12 within the K–12 curriculum framework, diagnostic assessments linked to curriculum benchmarks at each grade level, and a focus on standards-based activities in reading, writing, math, and language development (Bacquie, 2004; Marietta, 2010b). While these efforts may sound academic, Weast maintained that they did not ignore balance or the social–emotional development of the young child and moved beyond the traditional debate between academic and developmentally appropriate instruction.

All of the changes required extensive new development of PreK–2 teachers. While the district developed formal training in curriculum and assessment, they also instituted a Professional Growth System that utilized consulting teachers, staff development teachers, job-embedded professional development, and peer assistance and review for new and struggling teachers. Weast likes to say that they balanced accountability for student learning with support for learning. Vertical teams composed of PreK through 4th-grade teachers met monthly to discuss curriculum, assessment data, instructional strategies, and individual students. One principal noted a sense of shared accountability: "We look at data, and we talk about our kids and have a focus. . . . We talk about what it looks like in preschool and what should it look like by 3rd grade. The philosophy here is it doesn't matter what grade you teach, we're all responsible for the kids" (Marietta, 2010b, p. 16).

Setting high goals, developing integrated strategies, building teacher competencies and power through vertical teams, among other things, has clearly led to success in raising overall student achievement and closing achievement gaps. For example, within the district, African American 3rd-graders proficient in Reading on the Maryland State Assessment rose from 48% in 2003 to 83% in 2009. The gap with White students fell from 35% to 12%. Proficiency in Math for 5th-grade African American students rose from 58% to 88%. The gap was reduced from 31% to 10%. The number of 8th-graders passing algebra (students who had started out in the early learning efforts) doubled. Weast describes what has happened as a "bubble going through a hose"; expectations and standards had to be continually raised as children met the higher expectations (New America Foundation, 2009).

Bremerton, WA. Bremerton is a very different school system. While urban in its proximity to Seattle, it has 5,000 students and 14 schools. It is 70% White and 60% low-income. The district began PreK–3rd grade reform slowly, starting with a top-down/bottom-up strategy by meeting with several elementary school teachers, a central office administrator, and staff from preschools in the districts over a year's time. This core group committed to early learning provided a foundation of trust for next steps (Marietta, 2010a). Key to their success was the superintendent who saw the value in elevating the attention given to the early years and who forged collaborative relationships across the community, teachers union, administration, parents, and staff. These relationships are maintained through ongoing communication, which includes the sharing of results and challenges and oversight by a PreK–3 Leadership Group comprised of school district staff and representatives of community preschools.

Intensive professional development for teachers focuses on research-based instructional practices and, additionally, is made available to all local early learning facilities, including center- and family-based providers. Teachers exchange data and instructional strategies and participate in the ongoing oversight of the PreK–3rd grade effort.

Throughout the system there is a strong link between data and instruction. At the school and district level, student performance in math and reading is assessed three times each year in K–5th grade and two times in PreK. The district also examines attendance and behavior data at the school and district level. Early release one day a week allows teachers and principals to consider grade-level and content-data and modify instruction accordingly. Teachers bring shared assessment data in reading and math to collaboratively plan instruction. The 5-year graduation rate in Bremerton increased from 59% in 2005–2006 to 87% in 2009–2010. Bremerton saw similar success in middle and high school achievement scores. Much attention is devoted to the "untested" years of PreK to grade 2 through data reports. Children's performance on the Dynamic Indicators of Basic Early Literacy Skills (DIBELS) has shown gradual improvement over these same 4 years, emphasizing the district's focus on improving the early years.

Lansing, MI. With a similar goal in mind, Lansing School District took yet another approach to prioritizing PreK–3rd education. Some of the story is told earlier in this chapter.

The first critical step toward reform was to literally restructure the schools so that 15 schools, previously configured according to the more traditional K–5 model, became PreK–3 schools. This allowed for the critical focus on young children and opened the door to reconceptualizing the elementary grades as 4th through 6th, and the later years as 7th through 12th. The second feature was to implement a comprehensive approach to improved instruction, built on the belief that research and data should guide practice and that classroom observation measures helped teachers and leaders think about instruction differently than they had previously. To accomplish this, the superintendent chose to utilize several components of the FirstSchool approach. She had been a leader in the FirstSchool work prior to becoming the Lansing superintendent and had become convinced of the efficacy of the data-driven work.

The process of building capacity for this new approach included full support from the central office and the board. Early on, a professional development day with district and school leadership was devoted to talking about the district vision, and the meaning, method, and purpose of collaborative inquiry. Additionally, the data process was made transparent and every principal and teacher had the opportunity to learn about the observation tools, and how the observation and feedback process would work.

The district used Title II funds to conduct a comprehensive, organized, and efficient data collection process. The FirstSchool Snapshot (which we have introduced in earlier chapters in this volume) was conducted in all PreK–3 classrooms and the CLASS (which we have also described earlier in Chapter

3) in all 4th- through 6th-grade classrooms. Graphs were developed for easy interpretation of the data and feedback was provided at the grade and school level. Still to come will be working with schools using the data to inform and improve instruction. The district has earmarked professional development funding from Title II (Preparing, Training, and Recruiting High Quality Teachers and Principals) and will ask schools to make proposals to address their needs based on the data they received.

WIELDING POLICY AND PROGRAM LEVERS WHEREVER YOU ARE

Perhaps the most powerful policy levers for PreK–3rd grade rest at the federal and state levels. These levers or "engines of change" (J. J. Gallagher et al., 2004) include legislation, court decisions, rulemaking, as well as professional advocacy and initiatives. The federal government is critical to moving toward greater integration of funding that targets at-risk students. This may require Congress to pass legislation that allows greater flexibility at the state level in specific programs than currently exists (e.g., greater role of states in Head Start). This hope, especially given the partisan gridlock of recent years and continued interest group resistance, may not be soon fulfilled. Nevertheless, the cabinet level offices of Education and Health and Human Services could work collaboratively toward greater coordination of program regulations across ESEA/Title I, Head Start, IDEA, and the Child Care Development Block Grant that provide for common infrastructure supports across programs, as advocated by J. J. Gallagher, Clifford, and Maxwell (2004) and Cooper and Costa (2012). This work has already begun under the current administration and shows some promise of removing barriers at the state level.

States and advocates at every level must work to sway the federal government to include more fundamental drivers of change (Fullan, 2011) that will build a strong PreK–3 component of the P–16/20 education system. Short of that, states still have considerable flexibility to make their own policies around program components such as building a strong teaching profession, teacher accountability combined with support, curriculum standards that align from PreK–grade 12, assessment that informs teaching and learning, and sustained technical assistance to districts and schools. And of course, states have the ability to realign state agencies and programs to better facilitate comprehensive and coordinated efforts on their own.

In addition, it is clear from the three school district examples shared in this chapter that school districts, even without new policy changes at the state and federal levels, can make dramatic movement toward a more seamless, coherent, and appropriate continuum of learning from PreK into the elementary grades. Leadership by superintendents, central office staff, and principals is critical to the success of these efforts. Thus leaders must arm themselves with knowledge of early learning, look creatively at all sources of funding, seek support of and collaborate with local community and funding organizations, and establish a powerful vision and compelling need for change. Further, these leaders must share the decision making with the teachers who daily make the ground-level decisions that directly affect student progress. The leaders must find ways to provide time and structures for teachers to work together to creatively find ways to meet the learning needs of all children, but in particular for those most in need of school support. This book has presented the features of a powerful PreK–3rd grade continuum of teaching and learning. Combining that knowledge with the levers for change can lead to success for African American, Latino, low-income, and other children, help close the achievement gaps, and renew enthusiasm for teaching and learning.

CONCLUSION

This chapter was intended to help educators develop an understanding of the larger program and policy contexts that influence their practice. The linkages among federal, state, district, and school programs are not always clear or linear. The development of early learning, especially for at-risk children, has been haphazard and incremental over several decades. As programs were added and amended, self-protecting bureaucracies became established. Additionally, who is in charge is sometimes confusing both vertically (federal, state, district) and horizontally (across agencies).

Nevertheless, the authors see an opportunity for more integration and development for PreK–3 programs and policies through calls by national organizations and coalitions, as well as federal initiatives that encourage states and districts to expand early learning and PreK–3 in more deliberative ways. While traditional drivers of change center around variables like standards, accountability, teacher evaluation, and data systems—and those factors appear to be emphasized in continuing federal programs—more consideration should be given to capacity building, pedagogy, group work, and coherent systems. These drivers are more consistent with FirstSchool's approach to PreK–3.

States are seen as key players in future change and emphasis must be given to enhancing their capacity for change and leading PreK–3 improvement. Districts can, however, also make great strides in PreK–3 improvement even without change at the federal and/or state levels. Several examples of state and district leadership were offered. Finally, while federal and state policy leadership offer the most dramatic opportunity for changing and strengthening PreK–3, policy and program levers can be wielded at any level with careful thought and planning.

CHAPTER 8

Directions for the Future

Sharon Ritchie

Throughout this volume we have made the case for well-articulated school transformation focused on changing the school experience for all children while shining a spotlight on the needs of African American, Latino, and low-income (AALLI) children who have been persistently underserved by our educational system. We posited that the reconceptualization of early education must include changes in how we support our educators, by making the case for increasing professionalism, using data as a tool for inquiry rather than evaluation; enriching curriculum to reflect AALLI children; focusing on instructional practices that insure caring, competence, and excellence; and making positive changes in the ways in which we relate with families. Additionally, we have discussed the support required at the federal, state, and local levels in order to achieve these goals.

We know that change is hard. While we have promoted a notion of continuous improvement and the willingness to operate under the assumption that there are no simple answers to hard questions, we have seen that even incremental shifts in practice take time to become rooted in school norms. Because the reforms that we propose require such sustained commitment, the results of years of implementation through intensive partnerships with schools are in many ways just beginning to feel established. At the end of a long journey, we realize that our work is surely not done. Thus this book represents both lessons learned and reflection on what we can continue to do better. In this chapter we find promise in the field and work to build on and take hope from the success we see.

Our years of doing this work have affected us deeply in both personal and professional ways. We, along with so many others, have dedicated ourselves to 2 decades of research projects, work in schools, teacher education, and policy development—and yet after all of this effort, we still fear for our next generations. FirstSchool was in large part prompted by alarming statistics, disappointing research results, and news reports that have led to a general consensus that our schools have failed to serve all children well. What we saw in classrooms was often just as disheartening, and it would be disingenuous to suggest that our reform efforts have made all of these challenges disappear. While visiting a 2nd-grade classroom, an African American girl asked me why I was there. I told her I just wanted to see what kids did in her classroom. She put her hand on her hip and said to me, "You are going to be *bored*!" The reality for a child who sees endless days stretching in front of her with little hope of interest or engagement is unacceptable; however, the responsibility for making her days more meaningful falls on the shoulders of a system that does not always prepare nor support educators for the task at hand.

Like us, you too may be overwhelmed by these inadequacies. Issues of inequity and poverty are persistent, pervasive, and daunting, and their effect on the daily lives of children in schools are not easily mitigated. As educators, way too much has been placed on your shoulders for solving the ills of the world. Yet the need for change is so pressing that we hope that you, like so many of the teachers and leaders we have worked with, are still thinking about what you want to do and change, and asking yourself questions like, "How can I begin? What is possible and hopeful? What can I do to ensure successful and equitable school experiences for AALLI children?"

Our data shows us that change is possible, but at times only achieved through many tiny, yet daily adjustments that add up to significant gains over the course of a school year. The big picture shows us that across the seven schools with which we have partnered, there are several examples of progress that we can point to as evidence of positive shifts in instructional strategies and improved experiences for students. We hope that these changes will become the "new normal" and, as a result, ultimately benefit the AALLI children under our partner teachers' care. For instance, in looking at overall data from the seven participating schools, we see these changes:

- At Timepoint 1, children were interacting with a teacher 50% of the time; at Timepoint 2, that had increased to 70%. This results in an average of 240 more hours of instructional/interactional time each year in each classroom.
- The amount of time students spent in transitions (e.g., waiting in line) decreased, on average, from 22% to 18%. Whereas this might sound like a small change, it results in an average of 48 hours of time gained each year, in each classroom—time which can be used for learning and instruction.

Changes for individual teachers were sometimes even more pronounced. In Figure 8.1, you can see that one teacher increased instruction in the following areas:

- Oral Language Development went up by 8%, which meant that 96 additional hours per year were devoted to meaningful conversations between herself and her students.
- Vocabulary Development increased by 3%, which meant that 34 additional hours per year were spent exposing children to new vocabulary.
- Compose (time spent writing) increased by 6%, which meant that an additional 72 hours was made available to children to hone their writing skills.

These changes were linked to research practices highlighted in our Cultures Framework (see Chapter 5), and are particularly important to the success of AALLI children. For example, we know that it is important for children to develop oral language skills at an early age. Oral language development influences vocabularies in young children and research shows vocabulary

Figure 8.1. Percentage of Time Spent on Classroom-Level Literacy Components at Two Timepoints

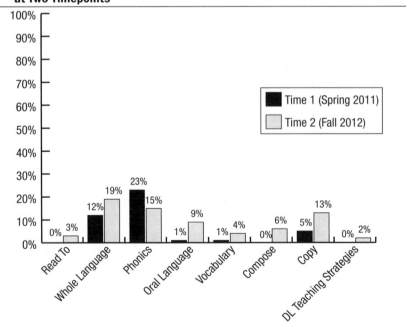

differences in prekindergarten children are relatively stable over time (Snow, Porche, Tabors, & Harris, 2007) suggesting discrepancies in young children's vocabularies in prekindergarten may remain throughout their schooling. Additionally, vocabulary proficiency is a predictor of academic achievement beginning as early as the 3rd grade (Storch & Whitehurst, 2002).

Another teacher dramatically changed her way of teaching and reduced whole-group instruction by 20%, and used 9% of that time for small-group instruction. The use of small-group settings for instruction helps promote peer interaction, prioritizes communication and has the potential to build higher-order thinking as interactions that encourage children to communicate and use language tend to occur when teachers interact individually or with small groups of students (Burchinal et al., 2008).

Teachers were reflective and pleased about how they were able to adjust their practice:

- "We are always so hard on ourselves . . . this really shows how much we do."
- "Thinking about the data is so much more complex than what is good and what is bad."
- "Change is possible . . . we see that we can do it . . . if you have a goal you can achieve it."
- "The information helps us know what direction to go to make *more* change . . . without it, how would you know?"

We know that teachers and leaders who are informed by data and research and given opportunities to work together can better articulate their practice, gain the respect of their colleagues and mentors, feel empowered to make changes, and become inclined to make more. While we saw lots of individual growth, we want to see those changes become more comprehensive and more reflective of an entire school culture. Our ongoing task, which includes all of you who are engaged in this work, is to recognize individual or small-scale change and work to make it the norm.

MOVING FROM RANDOM ACTS OF EQUITY AND POCKETS OF EXCELLENCE TO WIDE-RANGING REFORM

The results of the 2012 presidential election made it quite clear that our world has changed, that business as usual will no longer suffice, and that indeed we are experiencing an unprecedented demographic transformation. As a result of this changing landscape, it is increasingly critical that schools master the art of effectively educating an increasingly diverse generation of school-age children (Boykin, 2000; Wendler et al., 2010). The December 2012 Census Report tells us that the United States is projected to become a majority-minority nation for the first time in 2043. While the non-Hispanic White population will remain the largest single group, no group will make up a majority. All in all, minorities, now 37% of the U.S. population, are projected to comprise 57% of the population in 2060. (Minorities consist of all but the single-race, non-Hispanic White population.)

Given this reality, we see our task as increasing efficacy in addressing AALLI children and focusing on the development of teachers and leaders who are interested and capable of ensuring positive outcomes for these children. It is not useful to blame schools who are not meeting the needs of AALLI children without taking the responsibility to advocate for change, look for political and financial support, and provide real and manageable ways to change. While statistics make it easy to talk about the achievement gap and bring to light inequities in our schooling system, as we have done repeatedly in this volume, if we truly want to improve the school experiences of our AALLI children, then we must look at curriculum (see Chapter 4) and instruction (see Chapter 5) and use these ideas to promote understanding of the strengths that AALLI children bring to the classroom and change what we do to optimize them. Like Glenn Singleton, who has been working at the ground level to achieve racial equity in schools for more than 20 years, our quest is on behalf of children who deserve "qualified and skilled teachers who love [them] instead of fear [them], . . . who understand, value, and affirm their colorful African American, Latino, Asian, and other cultures . . . [and] who will be skilled in drawing out their innate brilliance, curiosity, and creativity" (Singleton & Linton, 2005, p. xiii).

A careful scanning of the literature that, despite the fact that it is far too scant, does provide insight into ways to truly value and affirm AALLI children, can help make school a place where their worlds of home and school are in concert and the task for students to negotiate them not too great. Scholars have challenged us to reshape schools in ways that are responsive, rather than counter to the strengths of the children who attend. This means giving far more than token nods to culture and language. We must do all we can to consistently contribute to knowledge of the strengths and values of diverse children and integrate them into curriculum and instructional approaches. We have addressed a strengths-based perspective in previous chapters and continue to do so here.

Many African Americans maintain a strong oral tradition, a term that refers to the stories, songs, proverbs, testimonies, and other cultural and historical mores that are not written down, but rather transmitted orally from one

Table 8.1. Salient Features of Individualism and Collectivism

Individualism (Representative of prevailing U.S. culture)	Collectivism (Representative of many immigrant cultures)
Fostering independence and individual achievement	Fostering interdependence and group success
Promoting self-expression, individual thinking, personal choice	Promoting adherence to norms, respect for authority, group consensus
Associated with egalitarian relationships and flexibility in roles	Associated with stable, hierarchical roles

Adapted from *Bridging Cultures in Our Schools: New Approaches That Work* by E. Trumbull, C. Rothstein-Fisch, & P. M. Greenfield, 2000, San Francisco, CA: WestEd.

generation to another. A preference for the spoken word is an enduring and distinctive cultural characteristic (Smitherman, 1977, 2000). Gardner-Neblett, Pungello, and Iruka (2011) review current research that shows that African American children are apt at creating complex stories characterized by vivid imagery and rich and rhythmic language—features reflective of African American oral discourse (Curenton, 2011; Reese, Leyva, Sparks, & Grolnick, 2010; Vernon-Feagans, Hammer, Miccio, & Manlove, 2001). These recent findings present promising opportunities for improving reading development and instruction among young African American readers (Feagans & Farran, 1994; Griffin, Hemphill, Camp, & Wolf, 2004; Hester, 2010; Klecan-Aker & Caraway, 1997).

Trumbull, Rothstein-Fisch, and Greenfield (2000) offer a framework of individualism and collectivism that helps teachers understand values that conflict with or are in concert with classroom expectations (see Table 8.1). Awareness of the values that children bring with them to school gives educators the opportunity to make wise decisions about how best to design their classroom environment and instructional approaches on behalf of the children whom they serve.

Fifteen years ago Rumberger and Larson (1998) found that bilingualism had positive outcomes on a number of achievement variables—that bilingual students attained better grades and had lower dropout rates than did monolingual students. Bilingual students benefit from the cultural advantage of Spanish proficiency, while their English proficiency provides an academic advantage. Still and all, being bilingual seems to have the reputation of being a deficit rather than a strength. Surely the ability to navigate two languages and their underlying cultures must be admired and nurtured, especially in our interrelated economic and social world.

From Research to Practice

Beyond the research literature, we look for and find hope in the places where promising practices do exist and leaders at all levels are making school a place where AALLI children can and do thrive. Even under challenging circumstances, this is happening throughout the United States. As a result, while I have spent many days observing classrooms and feeling disheartened (and yes, bored!), there have also been many days where I have had the good fortune to see evidence of schools that work.

During an inspiring visit to North Kenwood/Oakland (NKO) PreK–5th grade charter school on the Southside of Chicago, I saw many of the First-School principles in action. Part of what makes this school exemplary is its comprehensive structure and a strong, positive, professional working environment. The school is open from 7 A.M. to 6 P.M. and provides meals and before- and after-school care. Leadership and staff have chosen their curriculum to promote higher-order thinking skills, collaboration, and attention to balanced literacy and math as well as a focus on science and social studies. Brain breaks, yoga, and gross motor activities are prevalent throughout the day. Teachers have 160 minutes a week to meet in teams, and professional development is provided for 2 hours each week. Laptop carts ensure the availability of good, working computers to every student. There is a common language across the school to promote and help internalize values.

As I observed throughout the school day, it was clear that classroom curriculum and instruction was responsive to the race and culture of the children who are in the school. Second-graders were working on responding to an American Girl book, that told the story of Addy, a young slave girl. They were writing essays on why Addy's face showed no emotion as she served her master. First-graders were exploring African American inventors and their contributions to the growth of America. Children worked together, were encouraged to collaborate, clearly had the skill to moderate their own behavior and be productive, and were quick to engage with adults, eager to explain what they were working on. Positive relationships between these students and their teachers were evident in the confidence that children displayed, and in the lack of any apparent need for external discipline. One of the most consistent and robust findings is that teachers working in high-poverty schools who exhibit warmth and hold high expectations for all students in their classroom have students who are more academically successful (Werner, 1996). In this school that winning combination has led to 79.9% meeting or exceeding in reading expectations, 91.9% in math, and 92% in science. However, creating an environment for success is not just up to individual NKO teachers, since the entire learning community reflects a unified focus on serving children's needs, reflecting their culture, and encouraging their future endeavors. The classroom environments, resources, materials, and curriculum at NKO are representative of the students and families they serve. Murals in the hallways depict well-known Black leaders (Martin Luther King, Rosa Parks, Barack Obama) as well as past and current students reading. Over the doorway to each classroom is a quote chosen by the teacher to convey his or her feelings about reading. After-school staff serve as substitutes, former after-school staff have become teachers, the custodian works in the after-school program. These efforts to create continuity in an affirming school culture require consistent and intentional action by teachers and leaders who must counteract the negative stereotypes and subsequent lack of diverse role models that often characterize media representations of minority cultures. This school provides daily doses of positive racial and ethnic identity development that make it a place where children can have a vision to be whatever they want to be while offering resilience to an identity that is continually under assault. It is powerful to see that this can be done.

Supporting the day-to-day work is the mindset of continuous improvement. Leaders and teachers in this school are not satisfied by their successes, but rather are always seeking to be better. They are engaged in cross-school PLCs, which give them the opportunity to explore such topics as literacy, math, assessment, family engagement and social–emotional development with educators who work with children from infancy through 3rd grade. They have embarked on multiple journeys, and they are using their school data to carefully think about the trajectory of children who continue to struggle to achieve. Currently, they are examining a hypothesis that children who have a hard time remaining attentive and engaged at the PreK level are the ones who wrestle with success throughout their school career, and they are considering methodical and systematic responses. They are viewing videos of themselves and using a collaborative process to examine ways in which they support the development of higher-order thinking. They are considering some of the things they have learned by interacting with FirstSchool and are thinking more carefully about being responsive to boys and using time in effective ways. The staff turnover in this school is negligible—it is a place people want to be.

Other promising work is found in two major efforts in the United States to focus on poor and minority children, the 90/90/90 Schools and the Harlem Children's Zone. The 90/90/90 Schools (Reeves, 2000) describe schools where 90% or more of the students are eligible for free or reduced lunch, 90% or more come from ethnic-minority backgrounds, and 90% or more are proficient in reading or another academic area as indicated by district or state academic standards. In this noteworthy research, Reeves (2000) demonstrated that poverty and ethnic-minority status are not invariably linked to low student achievement. In fact, his data revealed striking numbers of poor and minority students who were academically proficient in various subject areas. Through site visits and categorical analysis of instructional practices, Reeves (2003) identified five common characteristics among these 90/90/90 Schools: (1) a focus on academic achievement, (2) clear curriculum choices, (3) frequent assessment of student progress and multiple opportunities for improvement, (4) an emphasis on non-fiction writing, and (5) collaborative scoring of student work.

The Harlem Children's Zone is a comprehensive and positive response to a community beset by poverty. Their premise is that "for children to do well, their families have to do well, and for families to do well, their community must do well." The two fundamental principles of The Zone Project are to (1) help children in a sustained way by starting early in their lives, and (2) create a critical mass of adults around them who understand what it takes to help children succeed. Work begins at the Baby College—a series of workshops for parents of children ages 0–3—and continues through children's school careers in order to include best-practice programs through college. Their approach includes in-school, after-school, social-service, health, and community-building programs. Children in the Zone either go through one of the three Promise Academy charter schools or are supported in their public schools during the school day with in-class assistants, and with after-school programs. The Promise Academy charter schools were created to ensure safe, enriching, learning environments where children know they are cared for and that people have high expectations for them. The children have an extended school day and year, which gives them the time to emphasize both basic skills as well as the arts and sciences. The students receive healthy, freshly made meals and participate in daily physical activity. In the after-school program, children get academic help and can choose from a variety of interest classes that include chess, music, photography, and web design. There is also a Saturday Academy for children who need additional help with their English and math skills. Results have been encouraging. At Promise Academy II, 100% of the 3rd-graders were at or above grade level on the 2008 statewide math test. At Promise Academy I, 97% of the 3rd-graders were at or above grade level in math (Harlem Children's Zone, 2013).

Broadening Our Perspectives

We also recognize that education is just part of an ecosystem of supports needed to fully address the challenging circumstances that typify the lives of low-income, minority children. Our FirstSchool Advisory Board and colleagues in our PreK–3rd Grade National Work Group are engaged in similar pursuits at a variety of levels and are addressing a variety of audiences throughout the United States. Each of their perspectives adds to our thinking and vision. We share three of their perspectives on AALLI children here.

Perspectives from the Field

First is the perspective of Karen W. Ponder, who is a member of the FirstSchool Advisory Board. She is an early childhood consultant whose work focuses on assisting states in developing comprehensive early childhood systems with state and local components. She is also the former president of Smart Start, which she helped create and implemented for almost 15 years.

> The best way to assure an equitable system for AALLI children, including children with special needs, is to ensure that they each have access to a high-quality early learning environment that is accessible to their families and meets their individual developmental needs and learning styles. In addition, their teachers must be educated, nurtured, and supported; and viewed as a true partner with the administration and families to best understand and respond to the uniqueness and particular needs of every child.

Next, we hear from Jonathan Kotch, also a member of the FirstSchool Advisory Board. He is a professor in the Department of Maternal and Child Health in the School of Public Health at the University of North Carolina at Chapel Hill.

> It is true, although not universally acknowledged, that good health is the foundation of good school performance. AALLI children have enough to deal with without entering school with a health disadvantage, and future directions for FirstSchool could be a model for strengthening the health component of early childhood education nationwide. There are many conditions that can be identified and resolved or improved in early childhood. AALLI children must have the advantage of up-to-date immunizations before starting kindergarten. In addition, they should be screened for the most common conditions that can directly affect school performance, such as anemia, early childhood caries, developmental and speech/language difficulties, chronic illnesses such as asthma and allergies, and vision or hearing impairment. In addition, determining eligibility for public or private health insurance, and referral to a medical care home, are opportunities in preschool to help the whole family.

Lastly, we hear from Tom Schultz, a member of the PreK-3rd Grade National Work Group. He is Project Director for Early Childhood Initiatives for the Council of Chief State School Officers.

When I think about what outcomes and opportunities matter the most to us, I recall advice that Larry Myatt, principal of Fenway High School in Boston, Massachusetts, gives to each class of new freshmen on how to succeed in his school: "Work hard, be yourself, and do the right thing." Working hard means that children develop the ability to focus attention and effort on a task or question, ignore distractions, and persist to complete the assignment, even when the work is challenging—as learning is for all of us at times. It also means learning to work with other students in collaborative projects, and learning how to meet the expectations of different teachers each year (just as we learn to "manage our bosses" in our careers).

To support young children in developing capabilities, teachers need to have high expectations for children to work hard every day, and be skillful in motivating children's hard work by providing meaningful, engaging learning experiences. We want them to see adults who work hard to meet high standards they set for themselves and their students and colleagues, and are willing to put in the long hours to prepare high-quality lessons and offer timely, relevant and helpful feedback on student work.

Supporting students to be themselves means that teachers strive to know each child as an individual and create classroom communities where there is space for individuals to express their differences and develop not only academic skills but as whole children. We want educators who put their unique personalities and talents and family and cultural heritage forward as they build relationships with students.

Helping children learn to do the right thing means holding high expectations, helping children become more able to treat each other how they would like to be treated, being skillful and sensitive in managing challenging behavior. And we want educators to treat all students fairly, and tell them the truth and act with integrity—whether someone else is watching or when no one else will ever know.

POWERFUL BEGINNINGS FOR TEACHERS AND LEADERS

Although FirstSchool dedicates most of its efforts to support teachers and leaders who are already working in schools, it is essential that we also contribute to the conversation about needed reform at the early career level. Becoming a teacher or a school leader and pursuing mastery is an intellectual, political, and personal endeavor. We have spoken throughout this volume of the importance of inquiry—of examining data, policy, and instructional practice in an individual and collective search for improvement. These elements need to be evident from the very start of a teacher's journey. It is also essential to add the word *critical* to the notion of inquiry, as doing so adds a political dimension—of power. Critical inquiry looks first to the knowledge, routines, and values that exist in the school community and asks what new knowledge is needed and what alternative values might be explored.

There is little argument that teachers and leaders coming into the field need to be better prepared to support the success of the children whom they serve. Part of more effective preparation comes through better partnership. A professional development model characterized by a social process in which novice and expert education professionals across the schools, community, and university collaborate to solve common problems and challenges within schools (Rogoff, 1990; Tharp & Gallimore, 1988) is the mindset we need to promote and achieve. This is truly engaged scholarship which requires clear and shared goals, a knowledge base for effective work in diverse communities, and long-term support and interaction.

Preparation of Teachers

We turn again to those who have put real time and attention to working in this area. UCLA Center X at the Graduate School of Education has, for the past 2 decades, been dedicated to dramatically changing schooling for the underserved students of Los Angeles (UCLA Center X, 2013). The 1992 Rodney King riots spurred Jeannie Oakes to make real changes in teacher education by focusing on preparing teachers to effectively work in inner-city Los Angeles. The program has taken seriously the need for race, social class, and culture to be central to conversations about effective teacher preparation. This is achieved through a social justice agenda that takes action to counter conditions where racial-minority children and children in poverty are more likely to attend programs with teachers who lack subject content knowledge, have lower academic achievement and are inexperienced (Peske & Haycock, 2006).

UCLA's Teacher Education Program (TEP) prepares aspiring teachers to become social justice educators who have the opportunity to

- Energize their passion for access, equity, and justice in schools
- Engage in coursework that attends to race, culture, class, and language
- Collaborate within a small community-based cohort of social justice educators
- Build powerful professional learning relationships
- Engage in critical inquiry and dialogue about the impact of race and poverty on themselves and others

To optimize the school–university connection, they have established partnerships with districts to engage in long-term plans for change through collaboration with teachers, site and district administrators, and parents. The focus of the partnership work is to strengthen curriculum, deepen teachers' content knowledge, improve instructional strategies, and understand student learning. Teacher educators, master teachers, and new teachers work together in the same way that teachers work with their students. They develop individual relationships, hold high expectations, respond to unique needs, and engage in activities that foster information gathering, hypothesis building, dialogue, and experimentation. All participants are experts in one way or another and are seen as sources of vital information and insight. Reflection is an indispensable part of the process. It compels an evolving approach to the classroom, leads to connections with other disciplines, and helps find balance between pedagogical theory and practice.

As teachers move into the partnership schools for their first year of teaching, they continue to be supported by Center X, return weekly for seminars, are supported in completing their master's degree projects, and continue as alumni to have access to collaborative inquiry groups. Collaborative inquiry is central to teacher education students' experience, and they become practiced in the art. They also find it to be the intellectual food on which they thrive. Working with partnership schools means that UCLA serves a limited number of schools and thus, over time, UCLA teachers begin to form a critical mass in schools that enables them to bring the practice of critical inquiry into the school culture.

Preparation of Leaders

Beyond efforts to forge partnerships between universities and schools to support early career development, there is little alignment between what happens in university preparation, and what happens to develop professionals once they are full-time workers. The experience of immersing oneself in learning over periods of weeks, months, or years on specific topics, the opportunity to demonstrate knowledge and learning in a variety of ways, and the

Perspectives from the Field

My philosophy of education plays a crucial role in how I perceive a challenge. I have a background in political science, so I had been exposed to Paulo Freire's theories on pedagogy in my undergraduate work, but I also studied him in my coursework at Center X, as well as bell hooks and Michael Apple. Their works influenced the development of my own educational philosophy and gave me an approach for working with students on a daily basis. In my view, I'm not in charge of "educating" these students and imparting my knowledge to them as passive recipients; but rather, it's a collaborative process in which my students bring a wealth of knowledge and experiences to the classroom and I serve as a facilitator who brings my own education from Center X to the classroom as part of the process. Classroom education is only one part of my students' developmental process, and I feel it's my responsibility to inspire them to learn more from their environment and the experiences life brings to them, while equipping them with the tools (such as language and ideas) that will help them navigate through, and ultimately surpass, the challenges they will face as they grow. My classes and professors at Center X helped me understand the dynamics of an urban setting and the challenges that may arise as a result. In addition, I was able to develop something more valuable than lesson plans—I developed this educational philosophy.

—Carmen Padilla, a graduate of Center X.

prioritization of dialogue are all too quickly exchanged for expediency at all levels—characterized by the seeking of simple solutions, the rush to get things done, and the lack of genuine feedback. In keeping with our belief that leadership is the key driver to change, we hope to find leaders who can use their role to inspire and support a love for learning and a thirst for knowledge in their hardworking staff. This has not yet been made easy for leaders. To date, despite research that points to the vital nature of good starts for children in the early years of their schooling, few principal preparation and professional development programs provide learning experiences on early childhood standards, early childhood brain research and learning theories, or funding and school laws and policies related to early childhood care and education programs and services (Hood, Hunt, & Okezie-Philips, 2009). We add to this the dearth of programs focused on developing leaders who are responsive to the educational and developmental needs of African American, Latino, and low-income students.

In their meta-analysis of research examining the effects of leadership on student achievement over the last 30 years, Waters, Marzano, and McNulty (2003) found that an increase in leadership ability leads to an increase in student achievement and that specific leadership characteristics have the most leverage to create effective school environments. In fact, the magnitude of that change is impressive: an increase of one standard deviation in leadership ability leads to a 10% increase in student achievement on standardized test measures. Conversely they found that a one standard deviation decrease in leadership ability leads to a 19% decrease in student achievement. They identified the following characteristics of leadership essential to improving student academic achievement, and we have added a description of these attributes from a FirstSchool perspective:

1. *Knowledge of curriculum, instruction, and assessment.* From a PreK–3 perspective with a social justice agenda, this means supporting leaders to become effective at examining curriculum for bias, alignment across the grades, relevance to students' lives, and support for development across multiple domains. It means helping teachers develop their ability to use research-based practices that are linked to success for AALLI children and to choose assessment that is developmentally appropriate for young children, formative in nature, addressing the presence of bias, and used wisely to make decisions on behalf of children's progress.

2. *Being an optimizer—encouragement and support of a "can do" attitude.* From a FirstSchool perspective, this means moving toward a mastery orientation where continuous improvement is the mindset. It means that opportunities for educators to talk about their work, share and demonstrate their expertise, generate interest in new topics, and articulate their practice are prioritized and seen by leaders as a way of recognizing and supporting professionalism.

3. *Providing intellectual stimulation.* FirstSchool teachers again and again have thanked us for providing them with the research that validates what they are already doing, provokes them to further their efforts, and arms them to be effective advocates for their students. Stimulating good conversation means changing the conversations. From our point of view, this means, for example, thinking about instruction from a different point of view: how practices impact children differentially based on race, culture, language, class, and gender; how lessons from developmental science could help them better understand the importance of relationships with and between their students; the value of teaching children self-regulation; the importance of cognitive flexibility for both academic and social success.

4. *Being a change agent.* This entire volume is about change, the need for it, and some ways to approach or achieve it. It is up to leadership to work on behalf of young children to demonstrate for their staff that part of everyone's job is to question policy and practice that does not recognize the needs of young learners or improve the school experiences and outcomes for AALLI children.

5. *Monitoring and evaluating.* The guiding light for FirstSchool is the effective use of data. This provides the greatest potential for real change. Data-literate leaders are able to determine the questions that need to be answered, thoughtfully choose data that provides insight and opportunity for interpretation, and couple this with an environment that clearly says, "We use data to inquire into our practice, and guide and monitor our change efforts. We do not use data to punish or coerce."

6. *Flexibility.* At FirstSchool this means that leaders are able to be reflective about their leadership style, to be responsive to people and circumstances, to keep the needs of children central to their decisions, and to recognize that being fair means giving people what they need, not giving everyone the same thing. Moreover, it means taking a broad view of leadership. There are leaders in every corner of the school. They need to be mentored, honored, and supported as they use their own expertise to help others and broaden perspectives.

7. *Consistent ideals and beliefs.* Leaders have to know themselves. They have to decide what they believe in and make sure their actions remain in concert. Leaders provide the vision for the people whom they guide, and they need to set the pathways for achieving them.

CONCLUSION

We have no shortage of lofty goals and we know that it takes intense and purposeful work to achieve them. We also believe that it is possible, that people who engage in this kind of work feel better about themselves and their jobs, and most of all that it is essential to our society that education is reformed on behalf of young AALLI children and their families. We cannot afford for our children to be "*bored,*" marginalized, neglected, or harmed physically or psychologically as they make their way. As we reach the end of this chapter and this book, it would logically be time to conclude. That is hard for us. We are ever formative in our work and are constantly evolving. The mindset of continuous improvement is surely ours. The pursuit of excellence on behalf of young children, boys, African American, Latino, and low-income students and their families is a constant in our lives. We thrive on spending our time with hardworking teachers and leaders; we push ourselves to be ever more succinct and real about what we are doing; we strive to use the time of the professionals around us in excellent ways; we reach for larger and larger audiences; and we look for experts to help us improve. We wish for you the same vital lives we have designed for ourselves and hope that some of our words have inspired you to be ever better at who you are and what you do.

References

Abbott v. Burke (V), 153 N.J. 480, 710 A.2d 450 C.F.R. (1998).

Aaronson, D., Barrow, L., & Sander, W. (2007). Teachers and student achievement in the Chicago public high schools. *Journal of Labor Economics, 25*(1), 95–135.

Adams, M., & Bertram, B. (1980). *Background knowledge and reading comprehension* (Reading Education Report No. 13). Urbana, IL: University of Illinois, Center for the Study of Reading.

Adamson, F., & Darling-Hammond, L. (2011). *Speaking of salaries: What it will take to get qualified, effective teachers in all communities.* Washington, DC: Center for American Progress. Retrieved from http://www.americanprogress.org/wp-content/uploads/issues/2011/05/pdf/teacher_salary.pdf

Agnello, M. F. (2007). Public understanding to political voice: Action research and generative curricular practices in issues and reform. *The Social Studies, 98*(5), 217–222.

Alabama Math, Science, and Technology Initiative (AMSTI). (2004). *Summary of AMSTI external evaluation: Student achievement data.* Retrieved from http://amsti.org/About/Evaluations/tabid/133/Default.aspx

Alexander, K. L., Entwisle, D. R., & Dauber, S. L. (1993). First grade classroom behavior: Its short- and long-term consequences for school performance. *Child Development, 64*, 801–814.

American Freedmen's Inquiry Commission. (1863). *Preliminary report touching the condition and management of emancipated refugees.* New York, NY: John F. Trow.

Anderson, J. (1988). *The education of Blacks in the South, 1860–1935.* Chapel Hill, NC: University of North Carolina Press.

Association for Supervision and Curriculum Development (ASCD). (2013). *Whole child initiative.* Retrieved from http://www.ascd.org/whole-child.aspx

Au, W. (2007). High-stakes testing and curricular control: A qualitative metasynthesis. *Educational Researcher, 36*(5), 258–267.

Aud, S., Fox, M. A., & KewalRamani, A. (2010). *Status and trends in the education of racial and ethnic groups* (NCES 2010-015). Washington, DC: U.S. Government Printing Office.

Ayres, A. J. (2005). *Sensory integration and the child (25th anniv. ed.).* Los Angeles, CA: Western Psychological Services.

Bacquie, J. (2004, October 7). *Early success: Closing the opportunity gap for our youngest learners.* Paper presented at the annual forum of the Foundation for Child Development, New York, NY.

Bagwell, C. S. (2012). *Home-school partnerships: A case study of teachers and African American families.* Ann Arbor, MI: ProQuest.

Baker, E. L., Barton, P. E., Darling-Hammond, L., Haertel, E., Ladd, H. F., Linn, R. L., . . . Shepard, L. (2010). *Problems with the use of student test scores to evaluate teachers* (Briefing

Paper No. 278). Washington, DC: Economic Policy Institute. Retrieved from http://www.epi.org/page/-/pdf/bp278.pdf

Balfanz, R., Bridgeland, J., Bruce, M., & Fox, J. (2013). *Building a grad nation: Progress and challenge in ending the high school dropout epidemic—2013 annual update.* Washington, DC: Civic Enterprises, The Everyone Graduates Center at Johns Hopkins University School of Education, America's Promise Alliance, and the Alliance for Excellent Education. Retrieved from http://www.americaspromise.org/Our-Work/Grad-Nation/Building-a-Grad-Nation.aspx

Ball, J., & Pence, A. (2001). A "generative curriculum model" for supporting child care and development programs in First Nations communities. *Journal of Speech–Language Pathology and Audiology, 25*(2), 114–124.

Bambino, D. (2002). Critical friends. *Educational Leadership, 59*(6), 25–27.

Bandura, A. (1977). Self-Efficacy: Toward a unifying theory of behavioral change. *Psychological Review, 84*(2), 191–215.

Bandura, A. (1994). Self-efficacy. In V. S. Ramachaudran (Ed.), *Encyclopedia of human behavior* (Vol. 4, pp. 71–81). New York, NY: Academic Press.

Bandura, A. (1995). Exercise of personal and collective efficacy in changing societies. In A. Bandura (Ed.), *Self-efficacy in changing societies* (pp. 1–45). Cambridge, England: Cambridge University Press.

Barbarin, O. A., Early, D., Clifford, R. M., Bryant, D., Frome, P., Burchinal, M., . . . Pianta, R. (2008). Parental conceptions of school readiness: Relation to ethnicity, socioeconomic status, and children's skills. *Early Education and Development, 19*(5), 671–701.

Barbarin, O. A., McCandies, T., Early, D., Clifford, R. M., Bryant, D., Burchinal, M., . . . Pianta, R. (2006). Quality of prekindergarten: What families are looking for in public sponsored programs. *Early Education and Development, 17*(4), 619–642.

Barber, T. (2002). A special duty of care: Exploring the narration and incidence of teacher caring. *British Journal of Sociology of Education, 23*(3), 383–395.

Barnes, C. J. (2006). Preparing preservice teachers to teach in a culturally responsive way. *The Negro Educational Review, 57*(1–2), 85–100.

Barnett, W. S., Carolan, N. E., Fitzgerald, J., & Squires, J. H. (2011). *The state of preschool 2011.* New Brunswick, NJ: National Institute of Early Education Research, Rutgers, The State University of New Jersey. Retrieved from http://nieer.org/yearbook

Beck, I. L., McKeown, M. G., & Kucan, L. (2013). *Bringing words to life: Bringing robust vocabulary instruction* (2nd ed.). New York, NY: Guilford Press.

Beecher, M., & Sweeny, S. (2008). Closing the achievement gap with curriculum enrichment and differentiation: One school's story. *Journal of Advanced Academics, 19*(3), 502–530.

Beijaard, D., Verloop, N., & Vermunt, J. D. (2000). Teachers' perceptions of professional identity: An exploratory study from a personal knowledge perspective. *Teaching and Teacher Education, 16*(7), 749–764.

Berlin, I., Glymph, T., Miller, S. F., Reidy, J. P., Rowland, L. S., & Saville, J. (Eds.). (1990). *The wartime genesis of free labor: The Lower South. Freedom: A Documentary History of Emancipation, 1861–1867, Series 1,Vol. 3.* Cambridge, England: Cambridge University Press.

Berlin, I., Miller, S. F., Reidy, J. P., & Rowland, L. S. (Eds.). (1993). *Freedom: A documentary history of emancipation, 1861–1867, Series I,Vol. II-The wartime genesis of free labor: The upper south.* Cambridge, England: Cambridge University Press.

Bernard, B. (1991). The case for peers. *Peer Facilitator Quarterly, 8*, 20–27.

Berretta, S., & Privette, G. (1990). Influence of play on creative thinking. *Perceptual and Motor Skills, 71*(2), 659–666.

Berry, B., Smylie, M., & Fuller, E. (2008). *Understanding teacher working conditions: A review and look to the future.* Hillsborough, NC: Center for Teaching Quality. Retrieved from http://www.teachingquality.org/content/understanding-teacher-working-conditions -review-and-look-future

Bielick, S. (2008, December). *1.5 million homeschooled students in the United States in 2007* (Issue Brief). Washington, DC: U.S. Department of Education, National Center for Education Statistics. Retrieved from http://nces.ed.gov/pubs2009/2009030.pdf

Blair, C., & Diamond, A. (2008). Biological processes in prevention and intervention: The promotion of self-regulation as a means of preventing school failure. *Development and Psychopathology, 20*, 899–911.

Bodrova, E., & Leong, D. J. (2007). *Tools of the mind: The Vygotskian approach to early childhood education* (2nd ed.). Upper Saddle River, NJ: Pearson Education.

Boggiano, A. K., Barrett, M., Weiher, A. W., McClelland, G. H., & Lusk, C. M. (1987). Use of the maximal-operant principle to motivate children's intrinsic interest. *Journal of Personality and Social Psychology, 53*, 866–879.

Bondy, E., & Ross, D. D. (1998). Confronting myths about teaching Black children: A challenge to teacher educators. *Teacher Education and Special Education, 21*(4), 241–254.

Bowman, B., Donovan, S., & Burns, S. (2001). *Eager to learn: Educating our preschoolers.* Washington, DC: National Academy Press.

Boyd-Dimock, V., & McGree, K. M. (1994). *Leading change from the classroom: Teachers as leaders.* Austin, TX: Southwest Educational Development Laboratory.

Boykin, A. W. (2000). The talent development model of schooling: Placing students at promise for academic success. *Journal of Education for Students Placed At Risk, 5*(1/2), 3–25.

Brock, B., & Grady, M. (2000). *Rekindling the flame: Principals combating teacher burnout.* Thousand Oaks, CA: Corwin Press.

Bronfenbrenner, U. (2005). *Making human beings human.* Thousand Oaks, CA: Sage.

Brown v. Board of Education of Topeka, 347 U.S. 483 (1954).

Brown, C., Hess, F. M., Lautzenheiser, D. K., & Owen, I. (2011, July 27). *State education agencies as agents of change: What it will take for states to step up on education reform.* Washington, DC: Center for American Progress. Retrieved from http://www. americanprogress.org

Bullock, H. A. (1967). *A history of Negro education in the South: From 1619 to the present.* Cambridge, MA: Harvard University Press.

Burchinal, M., Howes, C., Pianta, R., Bryant, D., Early, D. M., Clifford, R., & Barbarin, O. (2008). Predicting child outcomes at the end of kindergarten from the quality of pre-kindergarten teacher-child interactions and instruction. *Applied Developmental Sciences, 12*(3), 140–153.

Burns, S. M., & Brainerd, C. J. (1979). Effects of constructive and dramatic play on perspective taking in very young children. *Developmental Psychology, 15*(5), 512–521.

Camburn, E. M., & Han, S. W. (2011). Two decades of generalizable evidence on U.S. instruction from national surveys. *Teachers College Record, 113*(3), 561–610.

Campbell, F. A., & Ramey, C. T. (1995). Cognitive and school outcomes for high-risk African-American students at middle adolescence: Positive effects of early intervention. *American Educational Research Journal, 32*(4), 743–772.

Campbell, R. (2011, May). The power of the listening ear. *English Journal, 100*(5), 66–70.

Carnes, M. C., & Garraty, J. A. (2006). *The American nation: A history of the United States since 1865* (12th ed., Vol. 2). New York, NY: Longman.

Castelli, D. M., Hillman, C. H., Buck, S. M., & Erwin, H. E. (2007). Physical fitness and academic achievement in third- and fifth-grade students. *Journal of Sport and Exercise Psychology, 29*, 239–252.

Chall, J. S., & Snow, C. E. (1988). School influences on the reading development of low-income children. *Harvard Educational Newsletter, 4*(1), 1–4.

Chang, F., Crawford, G., Early D., Bryant D., Howes, C., Burchinal, M., . . . Pianta, R. (2007). Spanish-speaking children's social and language development in pre-kindergarten class-rooms. *Early Education and Development, 18*(2), 243–269.

Clifford, R. M., Barbarin, O., Chang, F., Early, D. M., Bryant, D., Howes, C., . . . Pianta, R. (2005). What is pre-kindergarten? Characteristics of public pre-kindergarten programs. *Applied Developmental Science, 9*(3), 126–143.

Clifford, R. M., Early, D. M., & Hills, T. W. (1999). Almost a million children in school before kindergarten: Who is responsible for early childhood services? (Public Policy Report). *Young Children, 54*(5), 48–51.

Clotfelter, C. T., Ladd, H. F., & Vigdor, J. L. (2007). Teacher credentials and student achievement: Longitudinal analysis with student fixed effects. *Economics of Education Review, 26*(6), 673–682.

Cobb, P., & Jackson, K. (2011). Assessing the quality of the common core standards for mathematics. *Educational Researcher, 40*(4), 183–185.

Coleman, R., & Goldenberg, C. (2012, February). The Common Core challenge for English language learners. *Principal Leadership, 12*, 46–51.

Connor, C. M., Morrison, F. J., & Katch, E. L. (2004). Beyond the reading wars: The effect of classroom instruction by child interactions on early reading. *Scientific Studies of Reading, 8*(4), 305–336.

Cooper, D., & Costa, K. (2012, June). *Increasing the effectiveness and efficiency of existing public investments in early childhood education: Recommendations to boost program outcomes and efficiency.* Washington, DC: Center for American Progress.

Cordiero, P., & Fisher, B. (Eds.). (1994). *Generating curriculum: Primary voices.* Urbana, IL: National Council of Teachers of English.

Corno, L., & Mandinach, E. B. (1983). The role of cognitive engagement in classroom learning and motivation. *Educational Psychologist, 18*(2), 88–108.

Council of Chief State School Officers. (2009, November). *A quiet crisis: The urgent need to build early childhood systems and quality programs for children birth to age five* (A Policy Statement of the Council of Chief State School Officers). Washington, DC: Council of Chief State School Officers. Retrieved from http://www.ccsso.org/Documents/2009/Policy_Statement_A_Quiet_Crisis_2009.pdf

Council of the Great City Schools. (2010, March). *Beating the odds: Individual district profiles (Results from the 2008–09 school year).* Washington, DC: Retrieved from http://www.cgcs.org/cms/lib/DC00001581/Centricity/Domain/35/BTO_analysis.pdf

Cowan, R. J., Swearer, S. M., & Sheridan, S. M. (2004). Home-school collaboration. *Encyclopedia of Applied Psychology, 2*, 201–208.

Crawford, G., Clifford, R., Early, D., & Reszka, S. (2009a). Early education in the United States: Converging systems, diverse perspectives. In R. Clifford & G. Crawford (Eds.),

Beginning school: US policies in international perspective (pp. 1–12). New York, NY: Teachers College Press.

Crawford, G., Clifford, R., Early, D., & Reszka, S. (2009b). Education for children three to eight years old in the United States. In R. Clifford & G. Crawford (Eds.), *Beginning school: U.S. policies in international perspective* (pp. 13–31). New York, NY: Teachers College Press.

Crocco, M. S., & Costigan, A. T. (2007). The narrowing of curriculum and pedagogy in the age of accountability: Urban educators speak out. *Urban Education, 42*(6), 512–534.

Cromwell, J. W. (1904). *The early Negro convention movement.* Washington, DC: American Negro Academy.

Crouch, R. (2012). *The United States of education: The changing demographics of the United States and their schools.* Alexandria, VA: Center for Public Education. Retrieved from www.centerforpubliceducation.org/Main-Menu/Staffingstudents/Changing-Demographics-At-a-glance/The-United-States-of-education-The-changing-demographics-of-the-United-States-and-their-schools.html

Cunningham, A. E., & Stanovich, K. E. (1997). Early reading acquisition and its relation to reading experience and ability 10 years later. *Developmental Psychology, 33*(6), 934–945.

Curenton, S. (2011). Understanding the landscapes of stories: The association between preschoolers' narrative comprehension and production skills and cognitive abilities. *Early Child Development and Care, 181*(6), 791–808.

Daley, G., & Kim, L. (2010). *A teacher evaluation system that works.* (Working Paper). Santa Monica, CA: National Institute for Excellence in Teaching. Retrieved from http://www.tapsystem.org/publications/wp_eval.pdf

Danielson, C. (2010). Evaluations that help teachers learn. *Educational Leadership, 68*(4), 35–39.

Darling-Hammond, L. (2000). Reforming teacher preparation and licensing: Debating the evidence. *Teachers College Record, 102*(1), 28–56.

Darling-Hammond, L. (2012, March 5). Value-added evaluation hurts teaching. *Education Week.* Retrieved from http://www.edweek.org/ew/articles/2012/03/05/24darlinghammond_ep.h31.html

Davis, B. M. (2012). *How to teach students who don't look like you: Culturally relevant teaching strategies* (2nd ed.). Thousand Oaks, CA: Corwin.

DeBaun, B. (2012). *Inseparable imperatives: Equity in education and the future of the American economy.* Washington, DC: Alliance for Excellent Education.

Deci, E. L., & Ryan, R. M. (2000). The "what" and "why" of goal pursuits: Human needs and the self-determination of behavior. *Psychological Inquiry, 11*, 227–268.

Delpit, L. (1995). *Other people's children: Cultural conflict in the classroom.* New York, NY: New Press.

Delpit, L. (2006). *Other people's children: Cultural conflict in the classroom* (2nd ed.). New York, NY: New Press.

Deming, D., & Dynarski, S. (2008). *The lengthening of childhood.* (Working Paper No. 14124). Cambridge, MA: National Bureau of Economic Research. Retrieved from http://www.nber.org/papers/w14124

DeVries, R., & Zan, B. (1995). Creating a constructivist classroom atmosphere. *Young Children, 51*(1), 4–13.

Dichter, H. (2012). Governance in early childhood systems: The view from Pennsylvania. In S. L. Kagan & K. Kauerz (Eds.), *Early Childhood Systems: Transforming Early Learning* (pp. 245–251). New York, NY: Teachers College Press.

Dichter, H., & Wat, A. (2012). Analysis of Race to the Top: Early Learning Challenge application section on "Sustaining effects into the early elementary grades." Chicago, IL: Ounce
of Prevention Fund. Retrieved from http://www.ounceofprevention.org/national-policy/
Sustaining-Effects-6-10-12.pdf

Dickinson, D., & Porche, M. V. (2011). Teachers' language practices and academic outcomes
of pre-school children. *Science, 333*, 964–967.

Doucet, F. (2011). Parent involvement as ritualized practice. *Anthropology and Education
Quarterly, 42*(4), 404–421.

Dubois, W.E.B. (1935). *Black reconstruction in America.* New York, NY: Harcourt, Brace.

Duncan, A. (2009, November 19). *The early learning challenge: Raising the bar.* Paper presented at the annual conference of the National Association for the Education of Young
Children, Washington, DC.

Dupree, D., Spencer, M. B., & Bell, S. (1977). African-American children. In G. Johnson-
Powell & J. Yamamotoa (Eds.), *Transcultural child development: Psychological assessment
and treatment* (pp. 237–268). New York, NY: Wiley.

Early, D. M., Iruka, I. U., Ritchie, S., Barbarin, O. A., Winn, D.-M. C., Crawford, G. M. . . .
Pianta, R. C. (2010). How do pre-kindergarteners spend their time? Gender, ethnicity
and income as predictors of experiences in pre-kindergarten classrooms. *Early Childhood
Research Quarterly, 25*, 177–193.

Early, D. M., Maxwell, K. L., Burchinal, M., Alva, S., Bender, R. H., Bryant, D. . . . Zill, N.
(2007). Teachers' education, classroom quality, and young children's academic skills:
Results from seven studies of preschool programs. *Child Development, 78*(2), 558–580.

Eccles, J. S., & Wigfield, A. (2002). Motivational beliefs, values, and goals. *Annual Review of
Psychology, 53*, 109–132.

Elmore, R. F. (1995). Teaching, learning, and school organization: Principles of practice and
the regularities of schooling. *Educational Administration Quarterly, 31*(3), 355–374.

Ensign, F. C. (1921). *Compulsory school attendance and child labor.* Iowa City, IA: Athens Press.

Epstein, J. L. (1990). School and family connections: Theory, research, and implications for integrating sociologies of education and family. *Marriage and Family Review, 15*(1/2), 99–126.

Epstein, J. L., Coates, L., Salinas, K. C., Sanders, M. G., & Simon, B. S. (1997). *School, family,
and community partnerships: Your handbook for action.* Thousand Oaks, CA: Corwin
Press.

Epstein, J. L., & Dauber, S. L. (1991). School programs and teacher practices of parent involvement in inner-city elementary and middle schools. *Elementary School Journal,
91*(3), 289–305.

Epstein, J. L., & Sanders, M. G. (2006). Prospects for change: Preparing educators for school,
family, and community partnerships. *Peabody Journal of Education, 81*(2), 81–120.

Erikson, E. H. (1950). *Childhood and society.* New York, NY: Norton.

Evans, A., Banerjee, M., Meyer, R., Aldana, A., Foust, M., & Rowley, S. (2012). Racial socialization as a mechanism for positive development among African American youth.
Child Development Perspectives, 6(3), 251–257.

Fantuzzo, J. W., Davis, G. Y., & Ginsburg, M. D. (1995). Effects of parent involvement in
isolation or in combination with peer tutoring on student self-concept and mathematics
achievement. *Journal of Educational Psychology, 87*(2), 272–281.

Fawcett, L. M., & Garton, A. F. (2005). The effect of peer collaboration on children's
problem-solving ability. *British Journal of Educational Psychology, 75*, 157–169.

Feagans, L. V., & Farran, D. C. (1994). The effects of daycare intervention in the preschool years on the narrative skills of poverty children in kindergarten. *International Journal of Behavioral Development, 17*(3), 503–523.

Feitelson, D., & Ross, G. S. (1973). Neglected factor—play. *Human Development, 16*(3), 202–223.

Fink, R. S. (1976). Role of imaginative play in children's cognitive development. *Psychological Reports, 39*, 895–906.

Firestone, W. A. (1993). Why "professionalizing" teaching is not enough. *Educational Leadership, 50*(6), 6–7.

Foner, P. S., & Walker, G. E. (Eds.). (1980). *Proceedings of the Black state conventions, 1840–1865* (Vol. 1–2). Philadelphia, PA: Temple University Press.

Fordham, A. E., & Anderson, W. W. (1992). Play, risk-taking and the emergence of literacy. In V. J. Dimidjian (Ed.), *Play's place in public education for young children* (pp. 105–114). Washington, DC: NEA.

Frede, E., Jung, K., Barnett, W. S., & Figuera, A. (2009, June). *The APPLES blossom: Abbott Preschool Program Longitudinal Effects Study (APPLES) preliminary results through 2nd grade*. New Brunswick, NJ: National Institute of Early Education Research; Rutgers, The State University of New Jersey. Retrieved from http://nieer.org/pdf/apples_second_grade_results.pdf

Fredricks, J. A., Blumenfeld, P. C., & Paris, A. H. (2004). School engagement: Potential of the concept, state of the evidence. *Review of Educational Research, 74*, 59–109.

Froelicher, S. (2012). Washington State's early learning and development benchmarks: A foundation for an aligned system. In S. L. Kagan & K. Kauerz (Eds.), *Early childhood systems: Transforming early learning* (pp. 226–231). New York, NY: Teachers College Press.

Fullan, M. (1996). Professional culture and educational change. *School Psychology Review, 25*(4), 496.

Fullan, M. (2011, April). *Choosing the wrong drivers for whole system reform* (CSE Seminar Series Paper No. 204). East Melbourne, Australia: Centre for Strategic Education.

Fullan, M., & Hargreaves, A. (1996). *What's worth fighting for in your school?* New York, NY: Teachers College Press.

Gallagher, H. A. (2004). Vaughn Elementary's innovative teacher evaluation system: Are teacher evaluation scores related to growth in student achievement? *Peabody Journal of Education, 74*(4), 79–107.

Gallagher, J. J., Clifford, R. M., & Maxwell, K. (2004). Getting from here to there: To an ideal early preschool system. *Early Childhood Research & Practice, 6*(1).

Garcia, E. E. (2010). Developing and learning in more than one language: The challenges and opportunities for transitions in early education settings. In S. L. Kagan & K. Tarrant (Eds.), *Transitions for young children: Creating connections across early childhood systems* (pp. 93–106). Baltimore, MD: Brookes.

García Coll, C. T., & Magnuson, K. (2000). Cultural differences as sources of developmental vulnerabilities and resources. In J. P. Shonkoff & S. Meisels (Eds.), *Handbook of early childhood interventions* (pp. 94–114). New York, NY: Cambridge University Press.

Gardner-Neblett, N., Pungello, E., & Iruka, I. (2011). Oral narrative skills: Implications for the reading development of African American children. *Child Development Perspectives, 6*(3), 218–224.

Garner, B. K. (2008). When students seem stalled. *Educational Leadership, 65*(6), 32.

Gartrell, D. (1995). Misbehavior or mistaken behavior? *Young Children, 1*, 27–34.

Gee, J. P. (2000). Identity as an analytic lens for research in education. *Review of Research in Education, 25,* 99–125.

Gillanders, C., McKinney, M., & Ritchie, S. (2012). What kind of school would you like for your children? Exploring minority mothers' beliefs to promote home–school partnerships. *Early Childhood Education Journal, 40*(5), 285–294.

Gonzalez, J. M. (1993). School meanings and cultural bias. *School and Urban Society, 5,* 254–269.

González, N., Moll, L. C., & Amanti, C. (Eds.). (2005). *Funds of knowledge: Theorizing practices in households, communities and classrooms.* Mahwah, NJ: Erlbaum.

Gordon, R., Kane, T. J., & Staiger, D. O. (2006, April). *Identifying effective teachers using performance on the job* (The Hamilton Project, Discussion Paper 2006-01). Washington, DC: Brookings Institution. Retrieved from http://www3.brookings.edu/views/papers/200604hamilton_1.pdf

Graue, E. (2011). Are we paving paradise? *Educational Leadership, 68*(7), 12–17.

Graue, E., & Brown, C. P. (2003). Preservice teachers' notions of families and schooling. *Teaching and Teacher Education, 19*(7), 719–735.

Griffin, T. M., Hemphill, L., Camp, L., & Wolf, D. P. (2004). Oral discourse in the preschool years and later literacy skills. *First Language, 24,* 123–147.

Grusec, J. E. (2011). Socialization processes in the family: Social and emotional development. *Annual Review of Psychology, 62,* 243–269.

Guernsey, L., & Mead, S. (2010, March). *A next social contract for the primary years of education.* Washington, DC: New America Foundation. Retrieved from http://newamerica.net/sites/newamerica.net/files/policydocs/The%20Next%20Social%20Contract%20for%20Education.pdf

Gutiérrez, K. D., Morales, P. Z., & Martinez, D. C. (2009). Re-mediating literacy: Culture, difference, and learning for students from nondominant communities. *Review of Research in Education, 33,* 213–245.

Gutiérrez, K. D., & Rogoff, B. (2003). Cultural ways of learning: Individual traits or repertoires of practice. *Educational Researcher, 32*(5), 19–25.

Gutman, H. (Ed.). (1987). *The post-emancipation origins of Afro-American Education in Power and culture: Essays on the American working class.* New York, NY: The New Press.

Hage, D. (2012, September). *Into the fray: How a funders coalition restored momentum to early learning in Minnesota.* Washington, DC: Foundation for Child Development. Retrieved from http://fcd-us.org/sites/default/files/FCDCaseStdyMinnesota.pdf

Halpern, D. F. (1998). Teaching critical thinking for transfer across domains: Dispositions, skills, structure training, and metacognitive monitoring. *American Psychologist, 53,* 449–455.

Hamre, B. K., & Pianta, R. C. (2001). Early teacher–child relationships and the trajectory of children's school outcomes through eighth grade. *Child Development, 72*(2), 625–638.

Haniford, L. C. (2009). Tracing one teacher candidate's discursive identity work. *Teaching and Teacher Education, 26,* 987–996.

Hannaford, C. (1995). *Smart moves: Why learning is not all in your head.* Alexander, NC: Great Ocean.

Hargreaves, A. (1991). Contrived collegiality: The micropolitics of teacher collaboration. In J. Blase (Ed.), *The politics of life in schools* (pp. 46–72). New York, NY: Sage.

Harlem Children's Zone. (2013). The HCZ project. Retrieved from http://www.hcz.org/about-us/the-hcz-project

Hartford Institute of Religious Research. (2011, August). *A decade of change in American congregations: 2000 to 2010*. Retrieved from http://faithcommunitiestoday.org/sites/faithcommunitiestoday.org/files/Decade of Change Final_0.pdf

Harwell, S. H. (2003). *Teacher professional development: It's not an event, it's a process*. Waco, TX: CORD.

Hauser-Cram, P., Sirin, S. R., & Stipek, D. (2003). When teachers' and parents' values differ: Teachers' ratings of academic competence in children from low-income families. *Journal of Educational Psychology, 95*(4), 813–820.

Haycock, K. (1998). *Good teaching matters: How well-qualified teachers can close the gap*. Washington, DC: Education Trust. Retrieved from http://www.edtrust.org/sites/edtrust.org/files/publications/files/k16_summer98.pdf

Head Start Resource Center. (2011). *The Head Start parent, family, and community engagement framework: Promoting family engagement and school readiness from prenatal to age eight*. Arlington, VA: Office of Head Start, Administration for Children and Families, U.S. Department of Health and Human Services.

Hedrick, A. M., San Souci, P., Haden, C. A., & Ornstein, P. A. (2009). Mother–child joint conversational exchanges during events: Linkages to children's memory reports over time. *Journal of Cognition and Development, 10*, 143–161.

Henderson, A. T., Mapp, K. L., Johnson, V., & Davies, D. (2007). *Beyond the bake sale: The essential guide to family/school partnerships*. New York, NY: The New Press.

Henderson, A. T., & Mapp, K. L. (2002). *A new wave of evidence: The impact of school, family, and community connections on student achievement*. Austin, TX: Southwest Educational Development Laboratory.

Henderson, N., & Milstein, M. M. (2003). *Resiliency in the schools: Making it happen for students and educators*. Thousand Oaks, CA: Corwin Press.

Hendrick, J. (1996). *The whole child: Developmental education for the early years*. Englewood Cliffs, NJ: Merrill/Prentice Hall.

Hester, E. (2010). Narrative correlates of reading comprehension in African American children. *Contemporary Issues in Communication Sciences and Disorders, 37*, 73–85.

Hiatt-Michael, D. B. (1994). Parent involvement in American public schools: An historical perspective 1642–1994. *School Community Journal, 4*, 247–258.

Hiatt-Michael, D. B. (2008). *Teaching, curriculum and the community*. Charlotte, NC: Information Age.

HighScope Educational Research Foundation. (2006). Ready School Assessment. Ypsilanti, MI: HighScope Press. Retrieved from http://www.readyschoolassessment.org

Hill, H. C. (2009). Fixing teacher professional development. *Phi Delta Kappan, 90*(7), 470–477.

Hill, J., & Flynn, K. (2006). *Classroom instruction that works for English language learners*. Alexandria, VA: ASCD.

Holbrook, H. T. (1983). Oral language: A neglected language art? *Language Arts, 60*(2), 255–258.

Hood, L., Hunt, E., & Okezie-Philips, E. (2009, April). *Building a seamless learning continuum: Looking at the role of leadership to bridge the gap between Pre-K and K–12 care and education systems*. Paper presented at the annual meeting of the American Educational Research Association, San Diego, CA.

Hoover-Dempsey, K. V., Bassler, O. C., & Brissie, J. S. (1987). Parent involvement: Contributions of teacher efficacy, school socioeconomic-status, and other school characteristics. *American Educational Research Journal, 24*(3), 417–435.

Hornby, G., & Lafaele, R. (2011). Barriers to parental involvement in education: An explanatory model. *Educational Review, 63*, 37–52.

Howard, T. C., & Denning del Rosario, C. (2000). Talking race in teacher education: The need for racial dialogue in teacher education programs. *Action in Teacher Education, 21*, 127–137.

Howes, C., & Ritchie, S. (2002). *A matter of trust: Connecting teachers and learners in the early childhood classroom.* New York, NY: Teachers College Press.

Hughes, J., & Kwok, O. (2007). Influence of student–teacher and parent–teacher relationships on lower achieving readers' engagement and achievement in the primary grades. *Journal of Educational Psychology, 99*, 39–51.

Hustedt, J. T., Friedman, A. H., & Barnett, W. S. (2012). Investment in early education. In R. C. Pianta (Ed.), *Handbook of early childhood education* (pp. 48–72). New York, NY: Guilford Press.

Ingersoll, R. M. (2001). Teacher turnover and teacher shortages: An organizational analysis. *American Educational Research Journal, 38*(3), 499–534.

Ingersoll, R. M., & Smith, T. M. (2003). The wrong solution to the teacher shortage. *Educational Leadership, 60*(8), 30–33.

Iruka, I. U., Winn, D.-M. C., Kingsley, S. J., & Orthodoxou, Y. J. (2011). Links between parent–teacher relationships and kindergartners' social skills: Do child ethnicity and family income matter? *Elementary School Journal, 111*(3), 387–408.

Jacob, B. A., Lefgren, L., & Sims, D. P. (2008). *The persistence of teacher-induced learning gains* (NBER Working Paper No. 14065). Cambridge, MA: National Bureau of Economic Research.

Jennings, J. (2012). *Reflections on a half-century of school reform: Why have we fallen short and where do we go from here?* Washington, DC: Center on Education Policy.

Jensen, E. (1998). *Teaching with the brain in mind.* Alexandria, VA: ASCD.

Jensen, E. (2000). Moving with the brain in mind. *Educational Leadership, 5*(3), 34–38.

Jeynes, W. H. (2010). The salience of the subtle aspects of parental involvement and encouraging that involvement: Implications for school-based programs. *Teachers College Record, 112*(3), 747–774.

Johnson, A. S., Baker, A., & Breuer, L. (2007). Interdependence, garbage dumping, and feral dogs: Three lifeworld resources of young children in a rural school. *Early Childhood Education Journal, 34*(6), 371–377.

Johnson, C. S. (1954). Some significant social and educational implications of the U.S. Supreme Court's decision. *Journal of Negro Education, 23*(3), 364–371.

Johnson, D. W. (1981). Student–student interaction: The neglected variable in education. *Educational Researcher, 10*(1), 5–10.

Johnson, F., Zhou, L., & Nakamoto, N. (2011). *Revenues and expenditures for public elementary and secondary education: School Year 2008–09 (Fiscal Year 2009)* (NCES 2011-329). Washington, DC: National Center for Education Statistics. Retrieved from http://nces.ed.gov/pubsearch

Johnson, R. T., & Johnson, D. W. (2013). Research matters—to the science teacher: Encouraging student/student interaction. Retrieved from http://www.narst.org/publications/research/encourage2.cfm

Johnson, S. M. (2006). *The workplace matters: Teacher quality, retention and effectiveness* (NEA Research Working Paper). Washington, DC: National Education Association. Retrieved from http://www.nea.org/assets/docs/HE/mf_wcreport.pdf

Jones, J. (1980). *Soldiers of light and love: Northern teachers and Georgia Blacks, 1865–1873.* Chapel Hill: University of North Carolina Press.

Justice, L. M., Mashburn, A. J., Hamre, B. K., & Pianta, R. C. (2008). Quality of language and literacy instruction in preschool classrooms serving at-risk pupils. *Early Childhood Research Quarterly, 23,* 51–68.

Kagan, S. L., Britto, P. R., Kauerz, K., & Tarrant, K. (2005). *Washington early learning and development benchmarks: A guide to young children's learning and development from birth to kindergarten entry.* Olympia, WA: State of Washington.

Kagan, S. L., & Kauerz, K. (2012). Early childhood systems: Looking deep, wide and far. In S. L. Kagan & K. Kauerz (Eds.), *Early childhood systems: Transforming early learning* (pp. 3–17). New York, NY: Teachers College Press.

Kane, T. J., & Staiger, D. O. (2008). *Estimating teacher impacts on student achievement: An experimental evaluation* (NBER Working Paper No. 14607). Cambridge, MA: National Bureau of Economic Research.

Kaplan, A., Middleton, M. J., Urdan, T., & Midgley, C. (2002). Achievement goals and goal structures. In C. Midgley (Ed.), *Goals, goal structures, and patterns of adaptive learning* (pp. 21–54). Mahwah, NJ: Erlbaum.

Kelly, A. V. (2009). *The curriculum: Theory and practice* (6th ed.). London: Sage.

Kempermann, G., Kuhn, H. G., & Gage, F. H. (1997). More hippocampal neurons in adult mice living in an enriched environment. *Nature, 386,* 493–495.

Klecan-Aker, J. S., & Caraway, T. H. (1997). A study of the relationship of storytelling ability and reading comprehension in fourth and sixth grade African-American children. *European Journal of Disorders of Communication, 32,* 109–125.

Kliebard, H. M. (2004). *The struggle for the American curriculum, 1893–1958* (3rd ed.). New York, NY: RoutledgeFalmer.

Knapp, M. S., & Associates. (1995). *Teaching for meaning in high-poverty classrooms.* New York, NY: Teachers College Press.

Knopf, H., & Swick, K. (2007). How parents feel about their child's teacher/school: Implications for early childhood professionals. *Early Childhood Education Journal, 34*(4), 291–296.

Kober, N., & Rentner, D. S. (2011). *More to do, but less capacity to do it: States' progress in implementing the Recovery Act education reforms.* Washington, DC: Center on Education Policy.

Kornfeld, J., & Goodman, J. (1998). Melting the glaze: Exploring student responses to liberatory social studies. *Theory into Practice, 37*(4), 306–313.

Kubesch, S., Walk, L., Spitzer, M., Kammer, T., Lainburg, A., & Heim, R. (2009). A 30-minute physical education program improves students' executive attention. *Mind, Brain, and Education, 3*(4), 235–242.

Kuhn, T. S. (1962). *The structure of scientific revolutions.* Chicago, IL: University of Chicago Press.

Kyle, D. M., McIntyre, E., Miller, K. B., & Moore, G. H. (2002). *Reaching out: A K–8 resource for connecting families and schools.* Thousand Oaks, CA: Corwin Press.

Lachat, M. A., Williams, M., & Smith, S. C. (2006). Making sense of all your data. *Principal Leadership, 7*(2), 16–21.

Ladd, H. (2009). *Teachers' perceptions of their working conditions: How predictive of policy outcomes?* (CALDER Working Paper No. 33). Washington, DC: CALDER,Urban Institute. Retrieved from http://www.urban.org/uploadedpdf/1001440-Teachers-perceptions.pdf

Ladson-Billings, G. (1995). Toward a theory of culturally relevant pedagogy. *American Educational Research Journal, 32,* 465–491.

Lankford, H., Loeb, S., & Wyckoff, J. (2002). Teacher sorting and the plight of urban schools: A descriptive analysis. *Educational Evaluation and Policy Analysis, 24,* 37–62.

Lasky, S. (2005). A sociocultural approach to understanding teacher identity, agency and professional vulnerability in a context of secondary school reform. *Teaching and Teacher Education, 21*(8), 899–916. doi: DOI 10.1016/j.tate.2005.06.003

Lau v. Nichols, 414 U.S. 563 (1974).

Lawson, M. A. (2003). School–family relationships in context: Parent and teacher perceptions of parent involvement. *Urban Education, 38,* 77–133.

Lawson, M. A., & Alameda-Lawson, T. (2012). A case study of school-linked, collective parent engagement. *American Educational Research Journal, 49*(4), 651–684.

Leandro v. State of North Carolina, 488 S.E.2d 249 (N.C. 1997).

Lee, J. S., & Ginsburg, H. P. (2007). Preschool teachers' beliefs about appropriate early literacy and mathematics education for low- and middle-SES children. *Early Education & Development, 18*(1), 111–143.

Lesch, J. (2000, August). *Insider/outsider relationships: Reconsidering outsider staff development through the prism of race, class, and culture.* Paper presented at the annual meeting of the American Educational Research Association, New Orleans, LA.

Levy, A. K., Wolfgang, C. H., & Koorland, M. A. (1992). Sociodramatic play as a method for enhancing the language performance of kindergarten age students. *Early Childhood Research Quarterly, 7*(2), 245–262.

Lindblom, C. (1959). The science of "muddling through." *Public Administration Review, 19*(2), 79–88.

Lindblom, C. (1979). Still muddling, not yet through. *Public Administration Review, 39*(6), 517–526.

Loeb, S., Darling-Hammond, L., & Luczak, J. (2005). How teaching conditions predict teacher turnover in California schools. *Peabody Journal of Education, 80*(3), 44–70.

Lord, B. (1994). Teachers' professional development: Critical colleagueship and the role of professional communities. In N. Cobb (Ed.), *The future of education: Perspectives on national standards in America* (pp. 178–194). New York, NY: College Entrance Examination Board.

Madison, J. (1788, January 26). The alleged danger from the powers of the Union to the State governments considered. *The Independent Journal,* p. 1. Retrieved from thomas.loc.gov/home/histdox/fed_45.html

Marietta, G. (2010a, September). *PreK–3rd: How superintendents lead change* (FCD PreK–3rd Policy to Action Brief No. 5). New York, NY: Foundation for Child Development.

Marietta, G. (2010b, December). *Lessons for PreK–3rd from Montgomery County Public Schools: An FCD case study.* New York, NY: Foundation for Child Development. Retrieved from fcd-us.org/sites/default/files/FINAL%20MC%20Case%20Study.pdf

Marshall, E., & Toohey, K. (2010). Representing family: Community funds of knowledge, bilingualism, and multimodality. *Harvard Educational Review, 80*(2), 221–242.

Mason, P. A., & Galloway, E. P. (2012, February/March). What children living in poverty do bring to school: Strong oral skills. *Reading Today, 29*(4), 29–30.

Maxim, G. W. (1997). *The very young: Guiding children from infancy through the early years* (5th ed.). Upper Saddle River, NJ: Merrill.

McKinsey & Company. (2009). *The economic impact of the achievement gap in America's schools: Summary of findings.* Retrieved from cdm16064.contentdm.oclc.org/cdm/ref/collection/p266901coll4/id/2923

McMurrer, J. (2008). *Instructional time in elementary schools: A closer look at changes for specific subjects.* Washington, DC: Center on Education Policy.

McWayne, C., Hampton, V., Fantuzzo, J., Cohen, H. L., & Sekino, Y. (2004). A multivariate examination of parent involvement and the social and academic competencies of urban kindergarten children. *Psychology in the Schools, 41*(3), 363–377.

Mead, S. (2009). *Education reform starts early: Lessons from New Jersey's PreK–3rd reform efforts.* Washington, DC: New America Foundation.

Meece, J. L., Anderman, E. M., & Anderman, L. H. (2006). Classroom goal structures, student motivation, and academic achievement. *Annual Review of Psychology, 57*, 487–503.

Mendez v. Westminster School District, et al, 64 F. Supp. 544 (S.D. Cal. 1946).

Merseth, J., Sommer, J., & Dickstein, S. (2008, Summer). Bridging worlds: Changes in personal and professional identities of pre-service urban teachers. *Teacher Education Quarterly,* 89–108.

Meyers, M., & Jordan, L. P. (2006). Choice and accommodation in parental child care decisions. *Journal of the Community Development Society, 37*(2), 53–70.

Miedel, W. T., & Reynolds, A. J. (1999). Parent involvement in early intervention for disadvantaged children: Does it matter? *Journal of School Psychology, 37*(4), 379–402.

Milanowski, A. (2004). The relationship between teacher performance evaluation scores and student achievement: Evidence from Cincinnati. *Peabody Journal of Education, 79*(4), 33–53.

Miller, E., & Almon, J. (2009). *Crisis in the kindergarten: Why children need to play in school.* College Park, MD: Alliance for Childhood. Retrieved from www.allianceforchildhood. org/sites/allianceforchildhood.org/files/file/kindergarten_report.pdf

Milosovic, S. (2007). Building a case against scripted reading programs: A look at the NCLB's Reading First initiative's impact on curriculum choice. *The Education Digest, 73*, 27–30.

Minke, K. M., & Anderson, K. J. (2005). Family–school collaboration and positive behavior support. *Journal of Positive Behavior Interventions, 7*(3), 181–185.

Miri, B., David, B., & Uri, Z. (2007). Purposely teaching for the promotion of higher-order thinking skills: A case of critical thinking. *Research in Science Education, 37*(4), 353–369.

Moll, L. C., Amanti, C., Neff, D., & González, N. (1992). Funds of knowledge for teaching: Using a qualitative approach to connect homes and classrooms. *Theory into Practice, 31*(2), 132–141.

Moore, A. (2000). *Teaching and learning: Pedagogy, curriculum and culture.* New York, NY: Routledge.

Morrison, G. S. (1997). *Fundamentals of early childhood education.* Upper Saddle River, NJ: Merrill/Prentice Hall.

Morton, B. Q., & Dalton, B. (2007). *Changes in instructional hours in four subjects by public school teachers of grades 1 through 4.* Washington, DC: U.S. Department of Education, National Center for Education Statistics. Retrieved from nces.ed.gov/pubs2007/2007305. pdf

Murphy, P. J., & Rainey, L. (2012, September). *Modernizing the state education agency: Different paths toward performance management.* Seattle: Center on Reinventing Public Education, University of Washington. Retrieved from www.crpe.org/sites/default/files/ pub_states_ModernizingSEAs_sept12.pdf

Murrell, P. C., Jr. (2002). *African-centered pedagogy: Developing schools of achievement for African American children.* Albany: State University of New York, NY Press.

National Association of Elementary School Principals Foundation Task Force on Early Learning. (2010). *Building and supporting an aligned system: A vision for transforming education*

across the Pre-K–grade three years. Alexandria, VA: National Association of Elementary School Principals Foundation. Retrieved from www.naesp.org/transforming-early
-childhood-education-pre-k-grade-3

National Center for Children in Poverty (NCCP). (2007). *Who are America's poor children? The official story.* New York, NY: Columbia University, Mailman School of Public Health.

National Center for Education Research. (2008). *Effects of preschool curriculum programs on school readiness: Report from the preschool curriculum evaluation research initiative.* Retrieved from ies.ed.gov/ncer/pubs/20082009/

National Center for Education Statistics (NCES). (2001). *Education achievement and Black-White inequality* (NCES 2001–061). Washington, DC: U.S. Government Printing Office. Retrieved from nces.ed.gov/pubs2001/2001061.PDF

National Center for Education Statistics (NCES). (2009). *Reading 2009: The National Assessment of Educational Progress at Grades 4 and 8.* (NCES 2010–458). Washington, DC: Institute of Educational Sciences, U.S. Department of Education. Retrieved from nces.ed.gov/nationsreportcard/pdf/main2009/2010458.pdf

National Commission on Excellence in Education. (1983). *A nation at risk: The imperative for education reform.* Washington, DC: U.S. Government Printing Office. Retrieved from www.ed.gov/pubs/NatatRisk/risk.html

National Governors Association Center for Best Practices & Council of Chief State School Officers. (2010). *Common Core State Standards.* Washington, DC: Author. Retrieved from www.corestandards.org/the-standards

National School Boards Association. (2008, June 24). Pre-K coalition letter to the House Committee on Education and Labor. Retrieved from www.nsba.org/Advocacy/Key
-Issues/EarlyEducation/ReProvidingResourcesEarlyforKidsActPreKActHR3289.html

Ndura, E. (2004). ESL and cultural bias: An analysis of elementary through high school textbooks in the western United States of America. *Language, Culture, and Curriculum, 17*(2), 143–153.

Neuman, S. B., & Roskos, K. (1993). Access to print for children of poverty: Differential effects of adult mediation and literacy-enriched play settings on environmental and functional print tasks. *American Educational Research Journal, 30*(1), 95–122.

New America Foundation (Producer). (2009, June 2). Fighting fade-out through PreK–3rd. [Video]. Retrieved from newamerica.net/pressroom/2009/new_america_releases_video
_effective_school_reform_features_montgomery_county_schools

Newport, F. (2010). *Americans' church attendance inches up in 2010: Increase accompanies rise in economic confidence.* Retrieved from the Gallup website: http://www.gallup.com/
poll/141044/Americans-Church-Attendance-Inches-2010.aspx#1

Noblit, G. W., Malloy, W. W., & Malloy, C. E. (Eds.). (2001). *The kids got smarter: Case studies of successful Comer schools.* Cresskill, NJ: Hampton.

Noddings, N. (1992). *The challenge to care in schools: An alternative approach to education.* New York, NY: Teachers College Press.

North Carolina Board of Education. (2007). *The Power of K: North Carolina Position Statement on Kindergartens of the 21st Century.* Retrieved from www.eclearnnc.sharpschool.com/
cms/One.aspx?portalId=4501308&pageId=4833216

North Carolina Ready Schools Collaboration Team. (2011). *Ready Schools toolkit part 1: Pathways to success for young children pre-kindergarten through third grade* (1st ed.). Raleigh, NC: North Carolina Partnership for Children (NCPC). Retrieved from hugh.ncsmartstart.
org/wp-content/uploads/2011/05/Upfront-Materials-Cover-Sec-1-4.pdf

North Carolina Teacher Working Conditions Initiative. (2010). *North Carolina teaching working conditions survey: Analyses of current trends* (Research Brief). Santa Cruz, CA: New Teacher Center. Retrieved from www.ncteachingconditions.org/research2010

Nye, B., Konstantopoulos, S., & Hedges, L. V. (2004). How large are teacher effects? *Educational Evaluation and Policy Analysis, 26*(3), 237–257.

Owen, M. T., Klasli, J. F., Mata-Otero, A., & Caughy, M. O. (2008). Relationship-focused child care practices: Quality of care and child outcomes for children in poverty. *Early Education and Development, 19*, 302–329.

Paris, D. (2012). Culturally sustaining pedagogy: A needed change in stance, terminology, and practice. *Educational Researcher, 41*, 93–97.

Parker, F. L., Boak, A. Y., Griffin, K. W., Ripple, C., & Peay, L. (1999). Parent–child relationship, home learning environment, and school readiness. *School Psychology Review, 28*(3), 413–425.

Paus, T., Zijdenbos, A., Worsley, K., Collins, D. L., Blumenthal, J., Giedd, J. N., . . . Evans, A. C. (1999). Structural maturation of neural pathways in children and adolescents: In vivo study. *Science Education, 283*, 1908–1911.

Peck, S., & Serrano, A. (2002, April). *Open Court and English language learners: Questions and strategies.* Paper presented at the annual meeting of the American Association for Applied Linguistics, Salt Lake City, UT.

Peisner-Feinberg, E. S., Burchinal, M. R., Clifford, R. M., Culkin, M. L., Howes, C., Kagan, S. L., . . . Zelazo, J. (2000). *The children of the cost, quality, and outcomes study go to school* (Technical Report). Chapel Hill: University of North Carolina at Chapel Hill, FPG Child Development Institute.

Pellegrini, A. D., & Galda, L. (1982). The effects of thematic-fantasy play training on the development of children's story comprehension. *American Educational Research Journal, 19*, 443–452.

Peske, H. G., & Haycock, K. (2006). *Teaching inequality: How poor and minority students are shortchanged on teacher quality: A report and recommendations by the Education Trust.* Washington, DC: The Education Trust.

Pew Forum on Religion & Public Life. (2008, February). *U.S. religious landscape survey.* Retrieved from religions.pewforum.org/pdf/report-religious-landscape-study-full.pdf

Phillips Smith, E., Gorman-Smith, D., Quinn, W. H., Rabiner, D. L., Tolan, P. H., & Winn, D.-M. (2004). Community-based multiple family groups to prevent and reduce violent and aggressive behavior: The GREAT families program. *American Journal of Preventive Medicine, 26*(1, Suppl. 1), 39–47.

Pianta, R. C. (2001). *The Student–Teacher Relationship Scale.* Lutz, FL: Psychological Assessment Resources.

Pianta, R. C., Belsky, J., Vandergrift, N., Houts, R., & Morrison, F. (2008). Classroom effects on children's achievement trajectories in elementary school. *American Educational Research Journal, 45*(2), 365–397.

Pianta, R. C., La Paro, K., & Hamre, B. K. (2008). *Classroom assessment scoring system.* Baltimore: Paul H. Brookes.

Pianta, R. C., & Stuhlman, M. W. (2004). Teacher-child relationships and children's success in the first years of school. *School Psychology Review, 33*, 444–458.

Pickett, J. P. (Ed.). (2001). *The American heritage dictionary* (4th ed.). New York, NY: Dell.

Pintrich, P. R., & Schunk, D. H. (2002). *Motivation in education: Theory, research, and applications* (2nd ed.). Columbus, OH: Merrill-Prentice Hall.

Porter, A., McMaken, J., Hwang, J., & Yang, R. (2011). Common Core Standards: The new U.S. intended curriculum. *Educational Researcher, 40,* 103–116.

PreK–3rd Grade National Work Group. (2013). *Reducing achievement gaps by 4th grade: The PreK–3rd Approach in Action.* Retrieved from www.prek-3rdgradenationalworkgroup. org/events

Ratey, J. (2008). *Spark: The revolutionary new science of exercise and the brain.* New York, NY: Little Brown.

Rawick, G. P. (Ed.). (1977). *The American slave: A composite autobiography, Volume 2.* Westport, CT: Greenwood Press.

Ray, A., Aytch, L., & Ritchie, S. (2007, May 15). *Kids like Malik, Carlos, and Kiana: Culturally responsive practice in culturally and racially diverse schools.* Paper presented at the First School Symposium: Early School Success: Equity and Access for Diverse Learners, Chapel Hill, NC.

Ray, A., Bowman, B., & Robbins, J. (2006). *Preparing early childhood teachers to successfully educate all children: The contribution of four-year undergraduate teacher preparation programs.* New York, NY: Foundation for Child Development.

Reardon, S. F. (2011). The widening academic achievement gap between the rich and the poor: New evidence and possible explanations. In R. Murnane & G. Duncan (Eds.), *Whither opportunity: Rising inequality and the uncertain life changes of low-income students* (pp. 91–115). New York, NY: Russell Sage Foundation Press.

Reese, E., Leyva, D., Sparks, A., & Grolnick, W. (2010). Maternal elaborative reminiscing increases low-income children's narrative skills relative to dialogic reading. *Early Education and Development, 21*(3), 318–342.

Reeve, J. (2009). *Understanding motivation and emotion* (5th ed.). Hoboken, NJ: Wiley.

Reeves, D. (2000). *Accountability in action: A blueprint for learning organizations.* Denver, CO: Advanced Learning Centers.

Reeves, D. (2003). *High performance in high poverty schools: 90/90/90 and beyond.* Denver, CO: Center for Performance Assessment.

Reynolds, A. J. (2003). *The added value of continuing early interventions into the primary grades: Early childhood programs for a new century.* Washington, DC: Children's Welfare League of America Press.

Reynolds, A. J., Magnuson, K., & Ou, S.-R. (2006). *PK–3 education: Programs and practices that work in children's first decade.* New York, NY: Foundation for Child Development.

Reynolds, A. J., & Temple, J. A. (2008). Cost-effective early childhood development programs from preschool to third grade. *Annual Review of Clinical Psychology, 4,* 109–139.

Rice, C. C., & Lesaux, N. (2012, October). *Early learning instructional leaders and strong PreK–3rd student assessment systems: The New Jersey story.* Newark, NJ: Advocates for Children of New Jersey. Retrieved from www.acnj.org/admin.asp?uri=2081&action =15&di=2302&ext=pdf&view=yes

Riegle-Crumb, C. (2006). The path through math: Course sequences and academic performance at the intersection of race-ethnicity and gender. *American Journal of Education, 113*(1), 101–122.

Riojas-Cortez, M. (2008). Trying to fit in a different world: Acculturation of Latino families with young children in the United States. *International Journal of Early Childhood, 40*(1), 97–100.

Ritchie, S., Clifford, R. M., Malloy, W. W., Cobb, C., & Crawford, G. M. (2010). Ready or not? Schools' readiness for young children. In S. L. Kagan & K. Tarrant (Eds.), *Transitions in the early years: Creating a system of continuity* (pp. 161–173). Baltimore, MD: Paul H. Brookes.

Ritchie, S., & Crawford, G. (2009). *Issues in PreK–3rd education: Time is of the essence*. Chapel Hill: University of North Carolina at Chapel Hill, FPG Child Development Institute, FirstSchool.

Ritchie, S., Weiser, B., Kraft-Sayre, M., & Howes, C. (2007). *FirstSchool Snapshot*. Chapel Hill: University of North Carolina at Chapel Hill.

Ritchie, S., Weiser, B., Mason, E., Holland, A., & Howes, C. (2010). *FirstSchool Snapshot*. Chapel Hill: University of North Carolina at Chapel Hill.

Rivkin, S. G., Hanushek, E. A., & Kain, J. F. (2005). Teachers, schools, and academic achievement. *Econometrica, 73*(2), 417–458.

Roberts v. City of Boston, 59 Mass (5 Cush) 198 (1850).

Robinson, E. L., & Fine, M. J. (1994). Developing collaborative home–school relationships. *Preventing School Failure, 39*(1), 9–15.

Rockoff, J. E. (2004). The impact of individual teachers on student achievement: Evidence from panel data. *American Economic Review, 94*(2), 247–252.

Rockoff, J. E., & Speroni, C. (2010). Subjective and objective evaluations of teacher effectiveness. *American Economic Review, 100*(2), 261–266.

Rogoff, B. (1990). *Apprenticeship in thinking: Cognitive development in social context*. New York, NY: Oxford University Press.

Rothstein, J. (2010). Teacher quality in educational production: Tracking, decay, and student achievement. *Quarterly Journal of Economics, 125*(1), 175–214.

Rothstein, R. (2008, April 7). "A nation at risk" twenty-five years later. *Cato Unbound*. Retrieved from www.cato-unbound.org/2008/04/07/richard-rothstein/a-nation-at-risk-twenty-five -years-later/

Rothstein, R. (2010). *How to fix our schools: It's more complicated, and more work, than the Klein-Rhee "Manifesto" wants you to believe* (Issue Brief No. 286). Washington, DC: Economic Policy Institute. Retrieved from www.epi.org/page/-/pdf/ib286.pdf

Rowley, S. J., Helaire, L., & Banerjee, M. (2010). Reflecting upon racism: School involvement as a function of remembered discrimination in African American mothers. *Journal of Applied Developmental Psychology, 31*(1), 83–93.

Rumberger, R. W., & Larson, K. A. (1998). Toward explaining differences in educational achievement among Mexican-American language minority students. *Sociology of Education, 71*, 69–93.

Rumelhart, D. E. (1980). Schemata: The building blocks of cognition. In R. J. Spiro, B. C. Bruce, & W. F. Brewer (Eds.), *Theoretical issues in reading comprehension* (pp. 33–58). Hillsdale, NJ: Erlbaum.

Ryan, R. M., & Deci, E. L. (2002). An overview of self-determination theory. In E. L. Deci & R. M. Ryan (Eds.), *Handbook of self-determination research* (pp. 3–33). Rochester, NY: University of Rochester Press.

Saft, E. W., & Pianta, R. C. (2001). Teachers' perceptions of their relationships with students: Effects of child age, gender, and ethnicity of teachers and children. *School Psychology Quarterly, 16*(2), 125–141.

Sahlberg, P. (2011). *Finnish lessons: What can the world learn from educational change in Finland?* New York, NY: Teachers College Press.

Saltz, E., & Johnson, J. (1974). Training for thematic-fantasy play in culturally disadvantaged children: Preliminary results. *Journal of Educational Psychology, 66*, 623–630.

Salzman, J., Smith, D. L., & West, C. (Eds.). (1996). *Encyclopedia of African American culture and history*. New York, NY: MacMillan Library Reference.

Sandoval-Taylor, P. (2005). Home is where the heart is: Planning a funds of knowledge based curriculum module. In N. González, L. Moll & C. Amanti (Eds.), *Funds of knowledge: Theorizing practice in households, communities, and classrooms* (pp. 153–165). Mahwah, NJ: Erlbaum.

Schweinhart, L. J., Montie, J., Xiang, A., Barnett, W. S., Gelfield, C. R., & Nores, M. (2005). *Lifetime effects: The HighScope Perry preschool study through age 40*. Ypsilanti, MI: High-Scope Educational Research Foundation.

Scott, J. A., Jamieson-Noel, D., & Asselin, M. (2003). Vocabulary instruction throughout the day in 23 Canadian upper-elementary classrooms. *Elementary School Journal, 103*, 268–269.

Scott, K. H. (2012). Perspectives on and visions of early childhood systems. In S. L. Kagan & K. Kauerz (Eds.), *Early childhood systems: Transforming early learning* (pp. 18–24). New York, NY: Teachers College Press.

Serrano v. Priest, 5 Cal.3d 584 (1971).

Shanahan, T. (2009). *Introduction to Report of the National Early Literacy Panel*. Washington, DC: National Center for Family Literacy. Retrieved from lincs.ed.gov/publications/pdf/NELPReport09.pdf

Sheldon, S. B. (2002). Parents' social networks and beliefs as predictors of parent involvement. *Elementary School Journal, 102*(4), 301–316.

Shonkoff, J. P., & Phillips, D. A. (Eds.). (2000). *From neurons to neighborhoods: The science of early childhood development*. Washington, DC: National Academy Press.

Shore, R. (2009). *The case for investing in PreK–3rd education: Challenging myths about school reform* (FCD PreK–3rd Policy to Action Brief No.1). New York, NY: Foundation for Child Development.

Singleton, G., & Linton, C. (2005). *Courageous conversations about race: A field guide for achieving equity in schools*. Thousand Oaks, CA: Corwin Press.

Slattery, P. (2006). *Curriculum development in the postmodern era* (2nd Ed.). New York, NY: Taylor & Francis.

Slavin, R. E. (1990). *Cooperative learning*. Englewood Cliffs, NJ: Prentice-Hall.

Sloan, K. (2006). Teacher identity and agency in school worlds: Beyond the all-good/all-bad discourse on accountability-explicit curriculum policies. *Curriculum Inquiry, 36*(2), 119–152.

Smith, P. K., & Syddall, S. (1978). Play and non-play tutoring in preschool children: Is it play or tutoring which matters? *British Journal of Educational Psychology, 48*, 315–325.

Smith, R., Moallem, M., & Sherrill, D. (1997). How preservice teachers think about cultural diversity: From self-analysis to self-reflection. *Educational Foundations, 11*(2), 41–62.

Smith, T., & Rowley, K. (2005). Enhancing commitment or tightening control: The function of teacher professional development in an era of accountability. *Educational Policy, 19*(1), 126–154.

Smitherman, G. (1977). *Talkin and testifyin: The language of Black America*. Detroit, MI: Wayne State University Press.

Smitherman, G. (2000). *Talkin that talk: Language, culture and education in African America*. London: Routledge.

Snow, C. E., Porche, M. V., Tabors, P. O., & Harris, S. R. (2007). *Is literacy enough?: Pathways to academic success for adolescents*. Baltimore, MD: Brookes.

Souto-Manning, M. (2010a). Challenging ethnocentric literacy practices: (Re)Positioning home literacies in a Head Start classroom. *Research in the Teaching of English, 45*(2), 150–178.

Souto-Manning, M. (2010b). Family involvement: Considering challenges, building on strengths. *Young Children, 65*(2), 82–88.

Sprenger, M. (1999). *Learning and memory: The brain in action.* Alexandria, VA: ASCD.

Squire, K., MaKinster, J., Barnett, M., Luehmann, A., & Barab, S. (2003). Designed curriculum and local culture: Acknowledging the primacy of classroom culture. *Science Education, 87*(4), 468–489.

Stabb, C. (1986). What happened to the sixth graders: Are elementary students losing their need to forecast and to reason? *Reading Psychology, 7*(4), 289–296.

Storch, S. A., & Whitehurst, G. J. (2002). Oral language and code-related precursors to reading: Evidence from a longitudinal structural model. *Developmental Psychology, 38*, 934–947.

Stroud, G. M. (1827). *Sketch of the laws relating to slavery in the several states of the United States of America.* Philadelphia, PA: Kimber & Sharpless.

Stuhlman, M. W., & Pianta, R. C. (2002). Teachers' narratives about their relationships with children: Associations with behavior in classrooms. *School Psychology Review, 31*(2), 148–163.

Stuhlman, M. W., & Pianta, R. C. (2009). Profiles of educational quality in 1st grade. *Elementary School Journal, 109*, 323–342.

Takanishi, R. (2011). Transforming America's primary education system for the 21st century. In E. Zigler, W. Gilliam, & W. S. Barnett (Eds.), *The Pre-K debates: Current controversies and issues* (pp. 181–183). Baltimore, MD: Brookes.

Task Force on Teacher Leadership. (2001). *Leadership for student learning: Redefining the teacher as leader.* Washington, DC: Institute for Educational Leadership.

Tatum, B. D. (1997). *"Why are all the Black kids sitting together in the cafeteria?" and other conversations about race.* New York, NY: Basic Books.

Taylor, E. V. (2009). The purchasing practice of low-income students: The relationship to mathematical development. *Journal of the Learning Sciences, 18*(3), 370–415.

Terry, P. M. (1997). The principal and instructional leadership. In L. Wildman (Ed.), *National Council of Professors of Educational Administration 1997 Yearbook* (pp. 220–229). Lancaster, PA: Technomic.

Tharp, R. G., & Gallimore, R. (1988). *Rousing minds to life: Teaching, learning, and schooling in social context.* Cambridge, UK: Cambridge University Press.

Theobald, N. D., & Malen, B. (Eds.). (2000). *Balancing local control and state responsibility for K-12 education* (American Education Finance Association Annual Yearbook, Vol. 21). Larchmont, NY: Eye on Education.

Tomporowski, P. D., Davis, C. L., Miller, P. H., & Naglieri, J. A. (2008). Exercise and children's intelligence, cognition, and academic achievement. *Educational Psychology Review, 20*(2), 111–131.

Tomporowski, P. D., Lambourne, K., & Okumura, M. S. (2011). Physical activity interventions and children's mental function: An introduction and overview. *Preventive Medicine, 52*, S3–S9.

Trent, S. C., & Artiles, A. J. (1995). Serving culturally diverse students with behavior disorders: Broadening current perspectives. In J. M. Kauffman, J. W. Lloyd, D. P. Hallahan, & T. A. Astuto (Eds.), *Issues in the educational placement of pupils with emotional or behavioral disorders* (pp. 215–249). Hillsdale, NJ: Erlbaum.

Trumbull, E., & Rothstein-Fisch, C., & Greenfield, P. M. (2000). *Bridging cultures in our schools: New approaches that work (Knowledge brief).* San Francisco, CA: WestEd.

Tsay, M., & Brady, M. (2010). A case study of cooperative learning and communication pedagogy; Does working in teams make a difference? *Journal of the Scholarship of Teaching and Learning, 10*(2), 78–89.

UCLA Center X. (2013). *Transforming Public Schools: UCLA Center X.* Retrieved from centerx.gseis.ucla.edu/

U.S. Const. amend. X

United States Work Projects Administration. (1936). *Born in slavery: Slave narratives from the Federal Writers' Project* (Vol. 4, Part 3). Washington, DC: Manuscript Division, Library of Congress.

Urdan, T. (2004). Using multiple methods to assess students' perceptions of classroom goal structures. *European Psychologist, 9*(4), 222–231.

U.S. Census Bureau. (2012a). Census Bureau releases estimates of undercount and overcount in the 2010 census [Press release]. Retrieved from http://2010.census.gov/news/releases/operations/cb12-95.html

U.S. Census Bureau. (2012b). US Census Bureau projections show a slower growing, older, more diverse nation a half century from now [Press release]. Retrieved from http://www.census.gov/newsroom/releases/archives/population/cb12-243.html

U.S. Department of Education. (2010, March). *A blueprint for reform: The reauthorization of the Elementary and Secondary Education Act.* Washington, DC: Education Publications Center. Retrieved from http://www2.ed.gov/policy/elsec/leg/blueprint/blueprint.pdf

U.S. Department of Education. (2011a). Comprehensive Centers Program. Retrieved from http://www2.ed.gov/programs/newccp/index.html

U.S. Department of Education. (2011b, December 16). We can't wait: Nine states awarded Race to the Top–Early Learning Challenge Grants Awards will help build statewide systems of high quality early education programs [Press release]. Retrieved from http://www.ed.gov/news/press-releases/we-cant-wait-nine-states-awarded-race-top-early-learning-challenge-grants-awards

U.S. Department of Education. (2012, September 28). Education department awards $52 million I grants to 22 Comprehensive Centers to advance reform goals and student achievement [Press release]. Retrieved from http://www.ed.gov/news/press-releases/education-department-awards-52-million-grants-23-comprehensive-centers-advance-r

Usdan, M. D., & Sheekey, A. D. (2012, May 14). States lack capacity for reform. *Education Week, 31*(31). Retrieved from http://www.edweek.org/ew/articles/2012/05/16/31usdan_ep.h31.html

Valadez, J., & Freve, Y. (2002). Teaching hands-on/minds-on science improves student achievement in reading: A Fresno study. *FOSS Newsletter, 20.*

Valdés, G. (1996). *Con respeto: Bridging distances between culturally diverse families and schools.* New York, NY: Teachers College Press.

Valencia, R. R. (2005). The Mexican American struggle for equal educational opportunity in Mendez v. Westminster: Helping to pave the way for Brown v. Board of Education. *Teachers College Record, 107*(3), 389–423.

Vernon-Feagans, L., Hammer, C. S., Miccio, A., & Manlove, E. (2001). Early language and literacy skills in low-income African American and Hispanic children. In S. Neuman & D. K. Dickinson (Eds.), *Handbook for research on early literacy* (pp. 192–210). New York, NY: Guilford Press.

Volk, D., & de Acosta, M. (2003). Reinventing texts and contexts: Syncretic literacy events in young Puerto Rican children's homes. *Research in the Teaching of English, 38*(1), 8–48.

Vygotsky, L .S. (1986). *Thought and language.* Cambridge, MA: MIT Press.

W.K. Kellogg Foundation. (2003, July 1). Kellogg Foundation awards five-year implementation grants. Retrieved from http://www.wkkf.org/news/articles/2003/07/kellogg-foundation-awards-five-year-implementation-grants.aspx

Wager, A. A. (2012). Incorporating out-of-school mathematics: From cultural context to embedded practice. *Journal of Mathematics Teacher Education, 15*(1), 9–23.

Wanat, C., & Zieglowsky, L. T. (2010). Social networks and structural holes: Parent-school relationships as loosely coupled systems. *Leadership and Policy in Schools, 9*(2), 131–160.

Wang, M. C., Oates, J., & Weishew, N. (1995). Effective school responses to student diversity in inner-city schools: A coordinated approach. *Education and Urban Society, 27*(4), 484–503.

Waters, J. T., Marzano, R. J., & McNulty, B. (2003). *Balanced leadership: What 30 years of research tells us about the effect of leadership on student achievement.* Aurora, CO: Mid-continent Research for Education and Learning. Retrieved from http://www.mcrel.org/PDF/LeadershipOrganizationDevelopment/5031RR_BalancedLeadership.pdf

Weiss, H. B., Lopez, M. E., & Rosenberg, H. (2010). *Beyond random acts: Family, school and community engagement as an integral part of education reform.* National Policy Forum for Family, School, and Community Engagement Cambridge, MA: Harvard Family Research Project.

Wendler, C., Bridgeman, B., Cline, F., Millett, C., Rock, J., Bell, N., & McAllister, P. (2010). *The path forward: The future of graduate education in the United States.* Princeton, NJ: Educational Testing Service.

Wenglinsky, H. (2002). The link between teacher classroom practices and student academic performance. *Education Policy Analysis Archives, 10*(12), 1–30.

Werner, E. (1996). How kids become resilient: Observations and cautions. *Resiliency in Action, 1*(1), 18–28.

Whitman, D. (2008). *Sweating the small stuff: Inner-city schools and the new paternalism.* Washington, DC: Thomas B. Fordham Institute Press.

Wiggins, G., & McTighe, J. (1998). *Understanding by design.* Alexandria, VA: Association of Supervision and Curriculum Development.

Wilcox, W. B., Cherlin, A. J., Uecker, J. E., & Messel, M. (2012). No money, no honey, no church: The deinstitutionalization of religious life among the White working class. *Research in the Sociology of Work, 23*, 227–250.

Wildhagen, T. (2012). How teachers and schools contribute to racial differences in the realization of academic potential. *Teachers College Record, 114*(7), 1–27.

Williams, H. A. (2005). *Self-taught: African American education in slavery and freedom.* Chapel Hill: University of North Carolina Press.

Workman, E. (2012, March). *2012 State of the State addresses: Governors' top education issues.* Denver, CO: Education Commission of the States. Retrieved from http://www.ecs.org/html/educationIssues/ECSStateNotes.asp?nIssueID=116

Wright, R. R., Jr. (1909). *Self-help in Negro education.* Cheyney, PA: Committee of twelve for the advancement of the interests of the Negro race.

Wright, W. E. (2002). The effects of high stakes testing in an inner-city elementary school: The curriculum, the teachers, and the English language learners. *Current Issues in Education, 5*(5).

Zull, J. (2002). *The art of changing the brain.* Sterling, VA: Stylus.

About the Editors and Contributors

Sharon Ritchie has participated in the field of education for over 35 years, making contributions as a teacher, program director, teacher educator, and researcher. She has taught all ages from 3-year-olds to graduate students and has worked in special, regular, and gifted education. She has played multiple roles in work with elementary schools, and public and private early childhood programs at local, state, and national levels. Ritchie was on the UCLA faculty preparing elementary educators for 11 years, coordinated the accreditation study for NAEYC, and cowrote the new Self-Study Materials. She played multiple roles in national studies examining children in early learning settings, including NCEDL and LAExCELS. She currently serves as the director of FirstSchool at the Frank Porter Graham Child Development Institute at the University of North Carolina at Chapel Hill.

Laura Gutmann is a doctoral student in the Culture, Curriculum and Change program at the School of Education at the University of North Carolina at Chapel Hill. Her research focuses on the effect of educational policy on teachers' professional identity development and classroom practice. She currently works as a research assistant for the FirstSchool project, but has prior experience in nonprofit management and early childhood education, including as a kindergarten teacher. She has an MSEd from Bank Street College and a BA in public policy studies from Duke University.

Cindy Bagwell, EdD, is the project manager for the North Carolina Department of Public Instruction's Race to the Top Early Learning Challenge Grant. She has a doctoral degree in curriculum and instruction and expertise in early childhood education, particularly curriculum, standards, assessment, and family engagement. With over 30 years of experience in education, Bagwell has directed a variety of early childhood programs and coordinated numerous statewide initiatives, including development and implementation of North Carolina's first early learning standards, as well as the creation of preschool demonstration classrooms and play-based assessment centers. She has contributed to numerous resource materials for early educators.

Richard M. Clifford, PhD, is a senior scientist emeritus at the Frank Porter Graham Child Development Institute at the University of North Carolina at Chapel Hill. He is the author and editor of numerous publications on early education including works on early learning environments, public finance, and public policies affecting young children and their families. His research has had far reaching impact on both policy and practice in the United States and other countries. He is a past president of the National Association for the Education of Young Children.

Carolyn T. Cobb has over 30 years of experience in education, early childhood, and psychology. She served as director of the Office of Early Learning in North Carolina, establishing the state's Pre-K program for at-risk children in 2001. Subsequently, she helped to initiate the statewide Ready Schools (PreK–3rd) Initiative and has worked as the state outreach consultant for FirstSchool. She received her BA (psychology) and MA (school psychology) degrees from the University of North Carolina at Chapel Hill and her PhD (psychology) from North Carolina State University.

Gisele M. Crawford, MAA, is a research specialist at the Frank Porter Graham Child Development Institute at the University of North Carolina at Chapel Hill. Early in her career she served as an assistant teacher in a classroom for 4-year-olds and a lead teacher for 2½–3-year-olds, as well as a teacher of English for children and adults in Taiwan. Since then she has worked on numerous studies of young children and their environments and experiences, including large-scale studies of public prekindergarten in the United States. Crawford is currently on the staff of FirstSchool, a prekindergarten through 3rd-grade initiative to improve the school experiences and outcomes of African American, Latino, and low-income children. She has published articles and book chapters relating to serving diverse populations of children in early education settings.

Diane M. Early is a scientist at the Frank Porter Graham Child Development Institute at the University of North Carolina at Chapel Hill specializing in prekindergarten quality and research methods. She has served as part of the evaluation team for FirstSchool.

Sandra C. García is a graduate student currently working toward her PhD in education at the University of North Carolina at Chapel Hill. She worked in early childhood education prior to developing an interest in research and has since then worked with Latino families and children in California and North Carolina. Her research interests include issues of school readiness and classroom quality for culturally and linguistically diverse children as well as literacy development of dual-language learners.

Cristina Gillanders, PhD, is a scientist at the Frank Porter Graham Child Development Institute at the University of North Carolina at Chapel Hill. She has been involved in the field of early childhood for more than 20 years as a bilingual early childhood teacher, director of an early childhood program, teacher educator, and researcher. Her research focuses on young Latino emergent literacy, bilingualism, early childhood teaching practices for Latino dual-language learners, and minority parents' beliefs and practices related to young children's learning and development. She currently serves as an investigator in FirstSchool, providing her expertise in working with home–school partnerships and Latino children.

Adam L. Holland, PhD, is an investigator at the Frank Porter Graham Child Development Institute at the University of North Carolina at Chapel Hill. He has taught in PreK, kindergarten, and 1st grade. His research concerns motivation in young children, as well as how classrooms function as unique environments to shape children's development. Currently a member of the FirstSchool team, Holland works with schools and educators around the country to improve the PreK to 3rd-grade experiences of young African American, Latino, and low-income children.

Iheoma U. Iruka, PhD, is a scientist and research assistant professor at Frank Porter Graham Child Development Institute at the University of North Carolina at Chapel Hill. Her research examines how early experiences impact low-income and ethnic minority children's development, including their school readiness, academic and social competence, and well-being, and the role of the family and education environments and systems in this process. In particular, she is focused on determining the interplay between race/ethnicity, poverty, risk factors, parenting, and early care and education in young children's development and later outcomes. Iruka is engaged in several projects and initiatives focused on how policies, systems, and practices in early education and elementary schools can support the optimal development, learning, and experiences of ethnic-minority children, as well as the connection with families and communities, including quality rating and improvement system. She has also published extensively on issues focused on the importance of examining the early experiences for children of color and children from low-income households.

Jenille Morgan, MA, is a social research assistant at the Frank Porter Graham Child Development Institute at the University of North Carolina at Chapel Hill. She specializes in research examining factors (i.e., historical, cultural, familial) that foster the academic success of African American children and children from high-risk/low-resource environments. She has extensive experience conducting longitudinal research in this area and has worked on numerous studies and interventions spanning prekindergarten to early college. She is particularly focused on identifying the unique and interactive ways in which race, ethnicity, and socioeconomic status impact parental involvement, the development of social capital, and the process through which family support promotes academic achievement.

Sam Oertwig, EdD, is currently the director of school implementation for FirstSchool. Before joining the FirstSchool project, she served 25 years in public education as an elementary teacher, principal, director of elementary programs, and director of professional development. She brings a wealth of experience and expertise pertaining to quality education from both the teacher and administrative perspective. For the past 10 years, her work has been focused on achieving educational equity for minority students by assisting teachers and schools to become more culturally proficient in practice and policy. Oertwig has also done extensive work in developing professional learning communities, high-quality professional learning opportunities for teachers and administrators, and resiliency. She has a BA in elementary education from the College of Santa Fe, and received both an MSA and an EdD from the University of North Carolina at Chapel Hill.

Index

90/90/90 Schools, 177–178
2009 Report Card on Reading (National Center for Education Statistics), 13

AALLI (African American, Latino, and low-income) students, 12, 13, 20–22, 24, 27, 30, 48–49. *See also* Underserved students
Aaronson, D., 30, 102
Abbot v. Burke, 162
A-BIRD framework. *See* FirstSchool curriculum framework—principles
Academic trajectories, 12
Achievement, 4, 13–14, 64–65, 89
Activism, 128–129
Activity settings, 10–11, 58–61, 75
Adams, M., 89
Adamson, F., 47
Administration. *See* Leadership role
AERA (American Education Research Association), 156
African American, Latino, and low-income (AALLI) students. *See* AALLI (African American, Latino, and low-income) students
African Americans, 128–129, 138–139, 144, 174–175
Agnello, M. F., 89
Alabama Math, Science, and Technology Initiative (AMSTI), 92
Alameda-Lawson, T., 131
Aldana, A., 98
Alexander, K. L., 12, 107
Almon, J., 37–38
Alva, S., 17
Amanti, C., 87, 135

American Education Research Association (AERA), 156
American Freedmen's Inquiry Commission, 128
American Recovery and Reinvestment Act (ARRA), 159–160
AMSTI (Alabama Math, Science, and Technology Initiative), 92
Anderman, E. M., 65, 119
Anderman, L. H., 65, 119
Anderson, J., 128, 129
Anderson, K. J., 126, 127
Anderson, W. W., 112
ARRA (American Recovery and Reinvestment Act), 159–160
Artiles, A. J., 129–130
Asselin, M., 116
Assessment. *See also* Classroom Assessment Scoring System (CLASS); HighScope Ready Schools Assessment
and data cycle, 68
and federal policy, 155–160, 161
Finland educational system, 158
informing practice, 69–71
state-level, 161, 162, 165–166, 167
student misconceptions, 118
Association for Supervision and Curriculum Development, 99
Attitude change. *See* Mindset change
Au, W., 92
Aud, S., 13
Audience for book, 5
Authors' home district, 17–18
Autonomy development, 112, 113
Ayres, A. J., 111
Aytch, I., 13

Baby College, 178
Background knowledge. *See* Funds of knowledge
"Backward mapping," 92
Bacquie, J., 165
Bagwell, C. S., 136, 138
Baker, A., 88
Baker, E. L., 36
Balanced curriculum, 92–95, 119
Balfanz, R., 4
Ball, J., 89
Bambino, D., 44
Bandura, Albert, 107, 108
Banerjee, M., 98, 136, 138
Barab, S., 85
Barbarin, O. A., 2, 16, 17, 173
Barber, T., 37
Barnes, C. J., 110
Barnett, M., 85
Barnett, W. S., 2, 15, 16, 152
Barrett, M., 106
Barrow, L., 30, 102
Barton, P. E., 36
Bassler, O. C., 127
Beck, I. L., 116
Beecher, M., 120
Beeson, Terrie, 124
Beijaard, D., 49
Bell, N., 173–174
Bell, S., 13
Belsky, J., 104
Bender, R. H., 17
Bender, S., 17
Berlin, I., 129
Bernard, B., 114
Berretta, S., 121
Berry, B., 41
Bertram, B., 89
Bielick, S., 5
Bilingual developmental education, 18, 20
Bilingualism, 175
Birth rates, 4
Blair, C., 113
Blueprint for Reform, A (U.S. Dept. of Education), 159
Blumenfeld, P. C., 106

Blumenthal, J., 95
Boak, A. Y., 125
Bodrova, E., 114
Boggiano, A. K., 106
Bogue Sound Elementary School (N.C.), 70
Bondy, E., 13
Book selection, 85–86
Bowman, B., 13, 35
Boyd-Dimock, V., 48
Boykin, A. W., 173–174
Boys' experience in the classroom, 10–11
Brady, M., 115
Brain development, 110–111
Brainerd, C. J., 121
Bremerton (Wash.), 166–167
Breuer, L., 88
Bridgeland, J., 4
Bridgeman, B., 173–174
Brissie, J. S., 127
Britto, P. R., 162
Brock, B., 37
Bronfenbrenner, U., 103
Brown, C. P., 132, 161
Brown v. Board of Education, 129
Bruce, M., 4
Bryant, D., 2, 16, 17, 173
Buck, S. M., 10
Bullock, H. A., 128
Burchinal, M., 17, 173
Burchinal, M. R., 15, 17
Burns, S., 13
Burns, S. M., 121
Bus tours, 147

Caamal Canul, Yvonne, 153
Camburn, E. M., 4
Camp, L., 175
Campbell, F. A., 15
Campbell, R., 121
Caraway, T. H., 175
Carnes, M. C., 127
Carolan, N. E., 2
Carolina Abecedarian Project, 15
Castelli, D. M., 10
Caughy, M. O., 132
Center on Education Policy, 161

Center X, 181, 182, 183
Chall, J. S., 13
Chang, F., 2, 16, 17
Cherlin, A. J., 131
Chicago Child Parent Centers (CPC), 15
Child Care Development Block Grant, 152, 168
Child-centered instructional approach, 112
CLASS (Classroom Assessment Scoring System), 72–73, 123
Classroom Assessment Scoring System (CLASS), 72–73, 123
Classroom culture
    caring overview, 27, 103–104
    competence, 27, 103–104, 111–116
    excellence overview, 103–104
    management, 105
    positive relationships, 104–107
    racial identity, 107, 109–110
    self-efficacy, 107–110
    student-adult interactions, 72
    whole-child development, 110–111
Classroom instruction
    approaches to, 117–119
    curriculum, 119–120
    and higher-order thinking, 120–121
    motivation, 119
    and play, 121–122
    project activities, 122–123
Clifford, R. M., 2, 3–4, 15, 16, 17, 152, 154, 168, 173
Cline, F., 173–174
Clotfelter, C. T., 30
Coates, L., 126
Cobb, C., 17
Cobb, P., 86
Coding instruction, 58
Cognitive development, 99, 110
Cohen, H. L., 125
Coleman, R., 97
Collaborative inquiry, 19, 21, 25, 26–27, 29, 61–68
    building school culture, 61–68
    as FirstSchool principle, 19, 21, 25, 26–27
    and professionalism, 29, 46, 51, 78

teacher preparation, 182
Collaborative professional development.
    See Professional Learning Communities
Collectivism, 175
Collins, D. L., 95
Common Core State Standards, 39, 83, 84–89, 115. *See also* Standards
Communication, 111, 115–116, 135
Communities of Practice, 42–43
"Competence period," 112
Comprehensive Centers Program, 161
Compulsory education, 127–128
Conforming culture, 10
Conjoint incrementalism, 154
Connor, C. M., 120
Continuous-improvement mindset, 22, 24, 25
Continuum of learning, 22, 73–74, 100, 152, 168–169. *See also* Seamless education
"Contrived collegiality," 43
Conversational shifts, 51–52
Cooper, D., 152, 168
Cordiero, P., 89
Core programs, 83–87
Cornerstones of FirstSchool initiative, 23, 26–28
Corno, L., 114
Costa, K., 152, 168
Costigan, A. T., 85
Council of Chief State School Officers, 86, 115, 155–156
Council of Great City Schools, 13
Cowan, R. J., 126, 127
CPC (Chicago Child Parent Centers), 15
Crawford, G. M., 3–4, 17, 67
"Critical friends," 44, 67
Critical inquiry, 181
Crocco, M. S., 85
Cromwell, J. W., 129
Crouch, R., 4
Crowe, Connie, 79
Culkin, M. L., 15
Cultural backgrounds of students, 87–88.
    See also Funds of knowledge

"Cultural deprivation," 87
"Culture circles," 146–147
Culture of change, 50–52
"Culture of poverty," 87
Cunningham, A. E., 116
Curenton, S., 175
Curriculum—general, 20, 81–82, 84.
    See also FirstSchool curriculum
    framework—levels; FirstSchool
    curriculum framework—principles
Customization of lessons, 84–86, 106–107

Daley, G., 35
Dalton, B., 92
Danielson, C., 35
Darling-Hammond, L., 30, 35, 36, 41, 47,
    102
Data. *See also* Data sources
    analysis, 78, 80
    application, 78–80
    collection, 69, 77–78
    defining issues for study, 68–69, 70
    dissemination, 79–80
    guiding change, 27, 33, 45, 57–58
    impact on teaching, 79
    literacy, 78
    from other schools, 59
    relevant data cycle, 68
    use, 10, 61–62
Data sources. *See also* Data
    classroom, 59, 63, 71–73
    families, 76–77
    FirstSchool Snapshot measure, 58–60,
        93, 94, 115, 123
    school, 73–76
    students, 69, 71
    student-teacher relationship scale, 71
Dauber, S. L., 12, 107, 125
David, B., 120
Davies, D., 140
Davis, B. M., 106, 110
Davis, C. L, 111
Davis, G. Y., 125
De Acosta, M., 146–147
DeBaun, B., 4
Deci, E. L., 104, 106, 107

Decisionmaking, 112
Deficit view, 87, 136
Delaware early learning reform, 164
Delpit, L., 110, 132
Deming, D., 2
Demographic landscape, 173–174
Demonstration of learning, 88–89
Denning del Rosario, C., 110
Desegregation, 129–130
Developmental curriculum, 99–101
Developmental domains, 100, 102–103
Developmental science and standards,
    37–38
DeVries, R., 112
DHHS (U.S. Dept. of Health and Human
    Services), 159, 168
Dialogue with students, 71–72
Diamond, A., 113
DIBELS (Dynamic Indicators of Basic
    Early Literacy Skills), 167
Dichter, H., 162, 164
Dickenson, D., 116
Dickstein, S., 49
Didactic teaching approach, 117, 118
Discipline, 43, 105
Discrimination, 139
"Disjointed incrementalism," 154
District-level early education reform,
    164–169
District of Columbia standards. *See*
    Common Core State Standards
Donovan, S., 13
Doucet, F., 136, 138
Drivers of change, 160
Dropout prevention, 18, 21
Dual-language programs, 18, 20
Dubois, W. E. B., 129
Duncan, Arne (U.S. secretary of
    education), 159
Dupree, D., 13
Dynamic Indicators of Basic Early Literacy
    Skills (DIBELS), 167
Dynarski, S., 2

Early, D. M., 2, 3–4, 16, 17, 173
Early Childhood Advisory Councils, 157, 163

Early childhood education—general. *See also* Education—general
  academic emphasis, 3, 37–38
  federal role, 157–160, 168, 169
  funding, 3
  PreK programs, 2, 3
  program development, 151–154
  quality of schooling, 16
  research, 14–17
  seamless transitions, 3
Early Childhood Longitudinal Study—Kindergarten (ECLS-K), 16
Early Learning Advisory Council (Minn.), 155
Early Learning Challenge, 160, 164
Early Learning Initiative, 159
Early Success Performance Plan, 165
Eccles, J. S., 65
Education Commission of the States, 164
Education—general. *See also* Early childhood education—general
  environment of, 70–73
  equity, 4, 174
  Eurocentric curriculum, 109
  legal battles, 129–130
  and mainstream standards, 87
  national budget, 1
  public school system, 1–2
  trends, 1–3, 47
  vision and policy integration, 40
Effective instructional approach, 102–104
Effective leaders, 184–185
Effective school culture, 44–47
Elementary and Secondary Education Act (ESEA)/Title I, 168
Elmore, R. F., 63
Emotional support of students, 72–73, 98–99
Enhancing Early Learning Outcomes, 161
Enriched curriculum, 27–28
Ensign, F. C., 128
Enthusiasm, 51–52
Entry age to school, 2–3
Entwisle, D. R., 12, 107
Epstein, J. L., 125, 126, 132
Erickson, E. H., 112

Erwin, H. E., 10
ESEA (Elementary and Secondary Education Act)/Title I, 168
Ethnicity issues, 110
Eurocentric curriculum, 109
Evans, A., 98
Evans, A. C., 95
Exemplars of FirstSchool principles, 109, 176–177

Factory model of schooling, 128
Fantuzzo, J. W., 125
Farran, D. C., 175
Fawcett, L. M., 115
Feagans, L. V., 175
Feitelson, D., 121
Figuera, A., 16
Fine, M. J., 126
Fink, R. S., 121
Finland education system, 157, 158
Firestone, W. A., 40
FirstSchool Advisory Board, 178, 179
FirstSchool basic principles, 23, 26–28, 176–177
FirstSchool curriculum framework—levels
  core programs, 83–87
  funds of knowledge, 83, 87–88
  generative, 83, 88–89
  overview, 82–83
FirstSchool curriculum framework—principles
  alignment, 90–92
  balance, 92–95
  developmental appropriateness, 99–101
  integration, 95–96, 97
  overview, 89–90, 101
  relevance, 96–99
FirstSchool Snapshot (Ritchie et al.), 10, 167
FirstSchool Snapshot measure, 10–11, 58–60, 93, 94, 115, 123
Fiscal challenges, 5
Fisher, B., 89
Fitzgerald, J., 2
Flynn, K., 121
Focus groups, 141–142
Follow Through, 152

Foner, P. S., 129
Fordham, A. E., 112
Foundation for Child Development, 9, 155
Foust, M., 98
Fox, J., 4
Fox, M. A., 13
Frede, E., 16
Fredricks, J. A., 106
Freve, Y., 92
Friedman, A. H., 152
Froelicher, S., 162
Frome, P., 17
From Neurons to Neighborhoods (Shonkoff
    & Phillips), 14
Fullan, Michael, 40, 102, 168
Fuller, E., 41
Funds of knowledge, 83, 87–88, 96–97, 146
Future prospects for reform
    challenge overview, 170–173
    leader preparation, 182–185
    new perspectives on AALLI students,
        178–180
    scope of change, 173–175
    teacher preparation, 181–182
    using research, 176–178

Gage, F. H., 111
Galda, L., 121
Gallagher, H. A., 35
Gallagher, J. J., 152, 154, 168
Gallimore, R., 181
Galloway, E. P., 116
Garcia, E. E., 13
García Coll, C. T., 13
Gardner-Neblett, N., 175
Garner, B. K., 89
Garraty, J. A., 127
Garton, A. F., 115
Gartrell, D., 112
Gee, J. P., 49
Gelfield, C. R., 15
Generalizations-based practice, 140
Generative curriculum, 83, 88–89
Giedd, J. N., 95
Gillanders, C., 134, 138
Ginsburg, H. P., 103

Ginsburg, M. D., 125
Glymph, T., 129
Goldenberg, C., 97
Gonzalez, J. M., 85
González, N., 87, 135, 146
Goodman, J., 89
Gordon, R., 47
Gorman-Smith, D., 127
Graded curriculum, 128
Graduation rates, 4
Grady, M., 37
Grau, E., 118, 132
Greenfield, P. M., 175
"Green Zone," 164
Griffin, K. W., 125
Griffin, T. M., 175
Grolnick, W., 175
Gross motor activities, 59
Grusec, J. E., 112
Guernsey, L., 14, 17
Gutiérrez, K. D., 135, 140
Gutman, H., 129

Haden, C. A., 117
Haertel, E., 36
Hage, D., 155
Halpern, D. F., 120
Hammer, C. S., 175
Hampton, V., 125
Hamre, B. K., 72, 84, 106, 107
Han, S. W., 4
Haniford, L. C., 49
Hannaford, C., 111
Hanushek, E. A., 30–31, 102
Hargreaves, Andy, 44, 102
Harlem Children's Zone, 177, 178
Harris, S. R., 172–173
Hartford Institute of Religious Research,
    131
Harwell, S. H., 42
Hauser-Cram, P., 126
Haycock, K., 34, 181
Head Start Parent, Family and Community
    Engagement Framework, 131
Head Start Parent program, 152
Head Start program, 131, 157, 168

Head Start Resource Center, 131
Hedges, L. V., 30–31, 102
Hedrick, A. M., 117
Heim, R., 111
Helaire, L., 136, 138
Hemphill, L., 175
Henderson, A. T., 125, 140
Henderson, N., 37
Hendrick, J., 112
Hess, F. M., 161
Hester, E., 175
Hiatt-Michael, D. B., 127, 128, 130
Higher-order thinking skills, 86, 120–121
HighScope Educational Research
      Foundation, 25, 74, 76
HighScope Perry Preschool, 15
HighScope Ready Schools Assessment, 25,
      74, 76
Hill, H. C., 40
Hill, J., 121
Hillman, C. H., 10
Hills, T. W., 2
History of U.S. schooling, 127
Holbrook, H., 115
Holland, A., 10, 58
Home–school partnerships. *See also under*
      Parent involvement
   barriers, 133–140
   cultural awareness and understanding,
      140
   data from families, 76–77
   FirstSchool beliefs, 28, 133–136
   and FirstSchool initiatives, 22, 25
   historical views, 126–130
   one-size-fits-all mentality, 137–138
   parent outreach, 162–163
   phone calls to parents, 144–145
   present-day views, 130–133
   reciprocal communication, 135
   reframing views, 141–142, 144–148
   research, 126–127
   shared vision, 133–135
   structural supports, 140–141
   time to interact, 137
Hood, L., 183
Hoover-Dempsey, K. W., 127

Hornby, G., 136
Houts, R., 104
Howard, T. C., 110
Howes, C., 2, 10, 15, 16, 17, 58, 71, 173
Hughes, J., 126
Human body research, 110, 111
Human psychology and learning, 108–109
Hunt, E., 183
Hustedt, J. T., 152
Hwang, J., 84, 86

IDEA (Individuals with Disabilities
      Education Act), 152, 168
Immigrant families, 131
Immigration trends, 4
Improving Head Start for School
      Readiness, 157
Incorporating sociocultural practices, 134
Independence, 111–113
Individualism, 175
Individuals with Disabilities Education Act
      (IDEA), 152, 168
Ingersoll, R. M., 40, 41
Instruction
   activity settings, 10–11, 173
   alignment with standards, 90–92
   approaches to, 117–118
   versus curriculum, 82
   developmentally appropriate, 39
   gaps in, 92–93
   honoring students, 98, 143–144, 183
   time devoted to, 58–59, 92–94
Instructional leaders. *See under* Leadership
      role
Intensive schoolwide consultation, 18, 22
Intentional application of data, 78–80
Intentional application of standards, 84–86
Interactive learning, 67
Iruka, I., 175
Iruka, I. U., 17, 126

Jackson, K., 86
Jacob, B. A., 30, 102
Jamieson-Noel, D., 116
Jennings, J., 34
Jensen, E., 10, 92, 111

Jeynes, W. H., 125
Johnson, A. S., 88
Johnson, C. S., 130
Johnson, D. W., 114
Johnson, F., 1
Johnson, J., 121
Johnson, R. T., 114
Johnson, S. M., 41
Johnson, V., 140
Jones, J., 128
Jordan, L. P., 131
Jung, K., 16
Justice, L. M., 84

Kagan, S. L., 15, 151, 162
Kain, J. F., 30–31, 102
Kammer, T., 111
Kane, T. J., 30, 47
Kaplan, A., 65
Katch, E. L., 120
Kauerz, K., 151, 162
Kelly, A. V., 81
Kempermann, G., 111
KewalRamani, A., 13
Kim, L., 35
Kingsley, S. J., 126
Klasli, J. F., 132
Klecan-Aker, J. S., 175
Kliebard, H. M., 127
Knapp, M. S., & Associates, 13
Knopf, H., 126
Kober, N., 161
Konstantopoulos, S., 30–31, 102
Koorland, M. A., 121
Kornfield, J., 89
Kotch, Jonathan, 179
Kraft-Sayre, M., 10, 58
Kubesch, S., 111
Kucan, L., 116
Kuhn, H. G., 111
Kuhn, T. S., 154
Kwok, O., 126
Kyle, D. M., 145, 146

Lachat, M. A., 78
Ladd, H. F., 30, 36, 41

Ladson-Billings, G., 35, 110
Lafaele, R., 136
Lainburg, A., 111
Lambourne, K., 111
Lankford, H., 47
Lansing (Mich.), 167–168
Lansing School District (Mich.), 153, 167
La Paro, K., 72
Larson, K. A., 175
Lasky, S., 49
Latino mothers, 143–144
Lautzenheiser, D. K., 161
Lau v. Nichols, 129–130
Lawson, M. A., 131
Layers of curriculum. *See* FirstSchool
    curriculum framework—levels
Leader preparation, 182–185
Leadership effects, 184
Leadership role
    bridge to community, 98–99
    as change agent, 183
    creating an enriched environment,
        123–124
    creating support structures, 36–37
    disseminating data, 79
    empowering teachers, 47, 53
    improving AALLI outcomes, 48–49, 53
    improving communities of practice,
        42–43, 53
    supporting teacher development, 49–50,
        92
    working within the system, 52–53
Leandro v. State of North Carolina, 129–130
Learning styles, 70
Lee, J. S., 103
Lefgren, L., 30, 102
Legal battles in education, 129–130
Leong, D. J., 114
Lesaux, N., 162
Lesch, J., 42
Levels of curriculum. *See* FirstSchool
    curriculum framework—levels
Levy, A. K., 121
Leyva, D., 175
Lindblom, C., 154
Linn, R. L., 36

Linton, C., 174
Literacy components data, 60, 172
Literacy instruction time, 93–94
Local authority, 2
Localized reform, 171–173
Loeb, S., 41, 47
Lopez, M. E., 137
Lord, B., 44, 67
Luczak, J., 41
Luehmann, A., 85
Lusk, C. M., 106

Madison, J., 2
Magnuson, K., 3, 13, 16
Majority-minority nation, 174
MaKinster, J., 85
Malen, B., 2
Malloy, C. E., 126
Malloy, W. W., 17, 126
Mandinach, E. B., 114
Manlove, E., 175
Mapp, K. L., 125, 140
Marietta, G., 165, 166
Marshall, E., 88
Martinez, D. C., 135
Maryland early learning reform, 164
Maryland State Assessment, 166
Marzano, R. J., 48, 184
Mashburn, A. J., 84
Mason, E., 10, 58
Mason, P. A., 116
Massachusetts early learning reform, 164
Mastery experiences, 108
Mastery orientation, 66, 119
Mata-Otero, A., 132
Math achievement, 13
Maxim, G. W., 112
Maxwell, K. L., 17, 152, 154, 168
McAllister, P., 173–174
McCandies, T., 17
McClelland, G. H., 106
McGree, K. M., 48
McIntyre, E., 145, 146
McKeown, M. G., 116
McKinney, M., 134, 138
McKinsey & Company, 13, 14

McMaken, J., 84, 86
McMurrer, J., 92
McNulty, B., 48, 184
MCPS (Montgomery County Public Schools [Md.]), 164–165
McTighe, J., 89
McWayne, C., 125
Mead, S., 14, 17, 162
Meece, J. L., 65, 119
Mendez v. Westminster, 129
Merseth, J., 49
Messel, M., 131
Metacognition, 118
Mexican American activism, 129
Meyer, R., 98
Meyers, M., 131
Miccio, A., 175
Middleton, M. J., 65
Midgely, C., 65
Miedel, W. T., 125
Milanowski, A., 35
Miller, E., 37–38
Miller, K. B., 145, 146
Miller, P. H., 111
Miller, S. F., 129
Millett, C., 173–174
Millspaugh, Erin, 57
Milosovic, S., 85
Milstein, M. M., 37
Mindset change, 51–52, 63, 64–66, 80
Minke, K. M., 126, 127
Minnesota Deputy Commission in Education, 155
Minnesota initiative, 155
Minority population, 174
Miri, B., 120
Moallem, M., 110
Moll, L. C., 87, 135, 146
Montgomery County (Md.), 164–166
Montgomery County Public Schools (Md.) (MCPS), 164–165
Montie, J., 15
Moore, A., 85
Moore, G. H., 145, 146
Morales, P. Z., 135
Morrison, F., 104

Morrison, F. J., 120
Morrison, G. S., 112
Morton, B. Q., 92
Mothers' ideas about learning at home, 142–144
Motivation, 119
Movement and learning, 111
Murphey, P. J., 161
Murrell Jr., P. C., 13

NAEYC (National Association for the Education of Young Children), 156, 159
Naglieri, J. A., 111
Nakamoto, N., 1
National Association for the Education of Young Children (NAEYC), 156, 159
National Association of Elementary School Principals Foundation, 155–156
National Center for Children in Poverty, 131
National Center for Early Development and Learning, 16
National Center for Education Research, 121
National Center for Education Statistics, 13
National Commission on Excellence in Education, 1, 13
National Governors Association Center for Best Practices, 86, 115
National Research Council Report, 14
National School Boards Association, 155–156
National standards. *See* Common Core State Standards
Nation at Risk, A (National Commission on Excellence in Education), 1, 13
NCLB (No Child Left Behind Act), 33–35
NCPC (North Carolina Partnership for Children), 25
Ndura, E., 85
Neff, D., 135
Neuman, S. B., 121
New America Foundation, 166
New Jersey Early Childhood Education, 162

New Jersey early learning reform, 162–163
Newport, F., 131
Noblit, G. W., 126
No Child Left Behind Act (NCLB), 33–35
Noddings, N., 37, 104
Non-English-speaking parents, 145
Nores, M., 15
North Carolina Board of Education, 23
North Carolina Dept. of Public Instruction, 25
North Carolina Dept. of Public Instruction Office of School Readiness, 18
North Carolina early learning reform, 164
North Carolina Partnership for Children (NCPC), 25
North Carolina Position Statement on Kindergartens of the 21st Century (North Carolina Board of Education), 23
North Carolina Ready Schools Collaboration Team, 25
North Carolina Teacher Working Conditions Initiative, 41, 42
North Kenwood/Oakland (NKO) school (Ill.), 176–177
Nye, B., 30–31, 102

Oakes, Jeannie, 181
Oates, J., 107
Observation schedule, 58
OCD (Pennsylvania Office of Childhood Development), 163
OC-DEL (Pennsylvania Office of Child Development and Early Learning), 163
Office for Early Learning, 159
Ohio early learning reform, 164
Okezie-Philips, E., 183
Okumura, M. S., 111
Open-ended questions, 118
Openness of school building, 142–143
Oral language development, 21, 116
Oral language tradition, 174–175
Organization of book, 5
Origins of FirstSchool, 9
Ornstein, P. A., 117

Orthodoxou, Y. J., 126
"Other-regulation," 113
Ou, S.-R., 3, 16
Out-of-school experiences, 132
Owen, I., 161
Owen, M. T., 132

Padilla, Carmen, 183
Parent involvement, 125, 131, 137–138, 143–144, 152. *See also under* Home-school partnerships
Paris, A. H., 106
Paris, D., 87, 130
Parker, F. L., 125
Paths of learning, 88–89
Paus, T., 95
Peay, L., 125
Peck, S., 85
Peer influence. *See* Students: peer influence
Peisner-Feinberg, E. S., 15
Pellegrini, A. D., 121
Pence, A., 89
Pennsylvania Dept. of Public Welfare, 163
Pennsylvania early learning reform, 163
Pennsylvania Office of Child Development and Early Learning (OC-DEL), 163
Pennsylvania Office of Childhood Development (OCD), 163
Performance expectations, 116–117
Performance orientation, 64–65, 119
Peske, H. G., 181
Pew Forum on Religion & Public Life, 131
Phillips, D. A., 14, 15
Phillips Smith, E., 127
Physical activity, 10, 111
Physical development, 110
Pianta, R. C., 2, 16, 17, 30, 71, 72, 84, 104, 106, 107, 173
Pickett, J. P., 133
Pintrich, P. R., 65
Planning time, 68
Play, 121–122
PLCs (professional learning communities), 41–42, 63
Ponder, Karen W., 179
Porche, M. V., 116, 172–173

Porter, A., 84, 86
Power of K, 23, 24
Praise, 105
Prejudice, 110
PreK–3rd Grade National Work Group, 156, 178, 179
PreK–K teacher institute, 19
Pressure on teachers, 32
Privette, G., 121
Process focus in learning, 118
Professional development, 29
Professionalism, 29–31, 39
Professional learning communities (PLCs), 41–42, 63
Professional organizations, 155–156
Professional relationships, 48–49
Project-based instruction, 122–123
Promise Academy schools, 178
Prospects for future, 170–171
Pungello, E., 175
Purpose of the book, 5–6

Quinn, W. H., 127

Rabiner, D. L., 127
Race, 109, 110, 139, 174
Race to the Top, 2, 159, 160
Race to the Top—Early Learning Challenge Grant, 159
Rainey, L., 161
Ramey, C. T., 15
Ratey, J., 111
Rawick, G. P., 128
Ray, A., 13, 35
Reading achievement, 13
Reading Report Card, 13
Ready Schools Assessment, 24, 74, 76
Ready Schools Initiative, 23, 25
Ready Schools Tool Kit, 25
Ready to Promote Academic Success for Boys of Color, 18, 21
Reardon, S. F., 4, 14
"Red shirting," 2–3
Reducing Achievement Gaps by 4th Grade (PreK–3rd Grade National Work Group), 156

"Red Zone," 164
Reese, E., 175
Reeve, J., 107
Reeves, D., 177, 178
Reflective teaching, 45, 64–68, 117–118,
    173
Reform beginnings, 171–173
Reidy, J. P., 129
Relatedness, 104–105
Remediation approach, 136
Rendell, Ed (governor of Pennsylvania),
    163
Rentner, D. S., 161
Research-guided practice, 17–23, 27
Reszka, S., 3–4, 17
Retention of knowledge, 118
Reynolds, A. J., 3, 15, 16, 125
Rice, C. C., 162
Riegle-Crumb, C., 13
Riojas-Cortez, M., 88
Ripple, C., 125
Ritchie, S., 10, 13, 17, 58, 67, 71, 134, 138
Rivkin, S. G., 30–31, 102
Robbins, J., 35
Roberts v. City of Boston, 129
Robinson, E. L., 126
Rock, J., 173–174
Rockoff, J. E., 30–31, 35, 102
Rogoff, B., 140, 181
Role models and identity, 109
Rosenberg, H., 137
Roskos, K., 121
Ross, D. D., 13
Ross, G. S., 121
Rothstein, J., 30–31, 102
Rothstein, R., 13, 30
Rothstein-Fisch, C., 175
Rowland, L. S., 129
Rowley, K., 44
Rowley, S. J., 98, 136, 138
Rumberger, R. W., 175
Rumelhart, D. E., 89
Ryan, R. M., 104, 106, 107

Saft, E. W., 30
Sahlberg, P., 158

Salinas, K. C., 126
Saltz, E., 121
Salzman, J., 128
Sander, W., 30, 102
Sanders, M. G., 126, 132
Sandoval-Taylor, P., 88
San Souci, P., 117
Saturday Academy, 178
Scaffolding instructional approach, 117
School–home partnerships. See Home-
    school partnerships
School–university partnerships, 76–77,
    182
Schoolwide integration of content learning,
    96
Schultz, Tom, 179
Schunk, D. H., 65
Schweinhart, L. J., 15
Scott, J. A., 116
Scott, K. H., 154
Seamless education, 3, 46, 74, 92, 159, 164.
    See also Continuum of learning
SEAs (state education agencies), 157,
    161–162
Segregated schooling, 129
Sekino, Y., 125
Self-concept, 114–115
Self-efficacy, 107–108
Self-Efficacy (Bandura), 107
Self-esteem, 114–115
Self-regulation, 107, 111, 113–114
Sensory motor integration, 111
Serrano, A., 85
Serrano v. Priest, 129–130
Shanahan, T., 15
Sheekey, A. D., 161
Sheldon, S. B., 131
Shepard, L., 36
Sheridan, S. M., 126, 127
Sherrill, D., 110
Shonkoff, J. P., 14, 15
Shore, R., 16
Simon, B. S., 126
Sims, D. P., 30, 102
Singleton, G., 174
Sirin, S. R., 126

Sirkin, Marsha, 108
Slattery, P., 27–28, 81–82
Slavin, R. E., 115
Sloan, K., 34
Smith, D. L., 128
Smith, P. K., 121
Smith, R., 110
Smith, S. C., 78
Smith, T. M., 40, 44
Smitherman, G., 175
Smylie, M., 41
Snow, C. E., 13, 172–173
Social development, 114–115
Social institutions, 131
Social modeling, 108
Social persuasion, 108
Sommer, J., 49
Souto-Manning, M., 88, 135, 146
SPARK (Supporting Partnerships to Assure
    Ready Kids), 155
Sparks, A., 175
Spencer, M. B., 13
Speroni, C., 35
Spitzer, M., 111
Sprenger, M., 95
Squire, K., 85
Squires, J. H., 2
Stabb, C., 115
Staff feedback, 46
Staff trust, 48
Staiger, D. O., 30–31, 47
Standards, 34, 39, 40, 90–92, 159–160,
    165. See also Common Core State
    Standards; Washington State
    Early Learning and Development
    Benchmarks
Stanovich, K. E., 116
"Starting School" unit, 96
State education agencies (SEAs), 157,
    161–162
State-level early education reform, 160–
    164, 168, 169
"Stimulus Bill," 159–160
Stipek, D., 126
Storch, S. A., 116, 173
Stroud, G. M., 128

Structural issues in education, 3–5
Structured learning centers, 122
Students
    activity settings, 58–60, 61–62, 74–75,
        173
    classroom management, 43, 106–107
    collaboration among, 114
    demographic, 4–5
    growth goals for, 43
    independence development, 111–113
    peer influence, 109, 111, 112, 114–115
    productivity, 113
    relationships with teachers, 71, 72
Student-Teacher Relationship Scale, 71
Stuhlman, M. W., 16, 17, 30, 106
Supporting Partnerships to Assure Ready
    Kids (SPARK), 155
Support structures for change, 36
Swearer, S. M., 126, 127
Sweden education policy, 156–157
Sweeny, S., 120
Swick, K., 126
Syddall, S., 121
Systematic education, 127
Systematic norms in education, 52–53

Tabors, P. O., 172–173
Takanishi, R., 152
Tarrant, K., 162
Task Force on Teacher Leadership, 48
Tatum, B. D., 110
Taylor, E. V., 127
"Teacher-proof" curricula, 84
Teachers
    and achievement orientation, 65–66
    agency, 33–34, 84
    collaboration among, 43–44
    empowerment of, 47–48
    evaluation of, 35–36
    influence on student success, 30
    job satisfaction, 41
    as learners, 65–66
    mindset of, 33
    preservice preparation, 24, 181–182
    professional development, 18, 19, 24,
        132, 165–167, 168

Teachers *(continued)*
  professionalism, 29–32, 39
  resistance, 32
  and student management, 43
  and the workplace, 30, 40–41
"Teacher talk," 115
Teacher Working Conditions survey, 41
Temple, J. A., 15
TEP (UCLA Teacher Education Program),
    181–182
Terry, P. M., 48
Tharp, R. G., 181
Theobald, N. D., 2
Time given to literacy components, 172
Title I federal programs, 152
Tolan, P. H., 127
Tomporowski, P. D., 111
Toohey, K., 88
Training for district leaders, 162
Transferability of learning, 98
Transitions between activities/classes, 59,
    60, 62–63, 66
Transitions in education level. *See*
    Continuum of learning; Seamless
    education
Trent, S. C., 129–130
Trumbull, E., 175
Tsay, M., 115
Two-way bilingual/immersion program,
    18, 20

UCLA Center X, 181, 182, 183
UCLA Graduate School of Education, 181
UCLA Teacher Education Program (TEP),
    181–182
Uecker, J. E., 131
Underserved students, 12, 16–17, 18, 138–
    139, 181. *See also* AALLI (African
    American, Latino, and low-income)
    students
University of North Carolina at Chapel
    Hill, 9
University–school partnerships, 76–77, 182
Urdan, T., 65
Uri, Z., 120
U.S. Census Bureau, 4

U.S. Constitution, 2
Usdan, M. D., 161
U.S. Dept. of Education, 159, 161, 164, 168
U.S. Dept. of Health and Human Services
    (DHHS), 159, 168
U.S. public school system, 1–2
U.S. Supreme Court, 129
U.S. Work Projects Administration, 128

Valadez, J., 92
Valdés, G., 130
Valencia, R. R., 129
Validity, 77
Vandergrift, N., 104
Verloop, N., 49
Vermunt, J. D., 49
Vernon-Feagans, L., 175
Vigdor, J. L., 30
Visits to families, 146
Vocabulary development, 116
Volk, D., 146–147
Vygotsky, L. S., 67

Wager, A. A., 88
Walk, L., 111
Walker, G. E., 129
Wanat, C., 131
Wang, M. C., 107
Washington State Early Learning and
    Development Benchmarks, 162–163
Washington State early learning reform,
    162–163, 164
Wat, A., 164
Waters, J. T., 48, 184
Weast, Jerry, 164, 165, 166
Weiher, A. W., 106
Weiser, B., 10, 58
Weishew, N., 107
Weiss, H. B., 137
Wendler, C., 173–174
Wenglinski, H., 36
Werner, E., 176
West, C., 128
What's Worth Fighting for in Your School?
    (Fullan & Hargreaves), 102
Whitehurst, G. J., 116, 173

Whitman, D., 87
Whole-child development, 110–111
Whole-child instruction, 37–38
Wigfield, A., 65
Wiggins, G., 89
Wilcox, W. B., 131
Wildhagen, T., 158
Williams, H. A., 128, 129
Williams, M., 78
Winn, D.-M. C., 17, 126, 127
W.K. Kellogg Foundation, 9, 155
Wolf, D. P., 175
Wolfgang, C. H., 121
Working within the system, 52–53
Workman, E., 164
Worsley, K., 95

Wright, W. E., 85
Wright Jr., R. R., 128
Wyckoff, J., 47

Xiang, A., 15

Yang, R., 84, 86

Zan, B., 112
Zelazo, J., 15
Zhou, L., 1
Zieglowsky, L. T., 131
Zijdenbos, A., 95
Zill, N., 17
Zone Project, 177, 178
Zull, J., 118